RAMÓN J. SENDER:
An Annotated Bibliography,
1928-1974

by

CHARLES L. KING

The Scarecrow Press, Inc.

Metuchen, N.J.   1976

Library of Congress Cataloging in Publication Data

King, Charles L.
　Ramon J. Sender : an annotated bibliography,
1928-1974.

　Includes indexes.
　1.　Sender, Ramón José, 1901-　　--Bibliography.
Z8807.8.K47　[PQ6635.E65]　　016.863'6'2
ISBN 0-8108-0933-8　　　　　　　　　76-9020

to

PROFESSOR DOROTHY E. McMAHON
who directed both my master's
and doctor's theses on Sender
I affectionately dedicate
this Bibliography

FOREWORD

Few contemporary Spanish novelists have a greater reputation today than Ramón Sender. Some consider him the greatest living Spanish novelist. Yet Sender is not only a novelist; he has written plays, short stories, critical studies, book reviews, poetry, and though it is not widely known he has contributed numerous articles to newspapers and magazines. His fiction has been translated into many languages. In short, Ramón Sender's versatility is a challenge to any bibliographer who desires to record faithfully what he has published and what has been written about him.

Charles King is one of the few individuals who could in a successful way meet this challenge. He has been a student of Sender's works for more than a quarter of a century; his Ph. D. dissertation was on Sender (no. 1340); in 1967, Hispania published his "Una bibliografía Senderiana española" (no. 1198), and in 1970 the American Book Collector his "A Senderian bibliography in English, 1950-1968, with an addendum" (no. 1199). In 1974 Twayne published his very well received Ramón Sender (no. 1140). Numerous articles and reviews of his concerning Sender have appeared in periodicals of the United States and Spain. In short he is a scholar completely immersed in the life and works of a man to whose works he has devoted a good part of his scholarly career.

This bibliography is to a great extent an extraordinarily thorough revision and an updating of the Hispania and American Book Collector bibliographies. He has visited Spanish libraries and secured the assistance of many individuals both in the United States and in Spain. In every case he plays fair with the user. King has personally inspected and examined every item except where otherwise noted, and indications are made that show the material that he has taken from other individuals. This personal inspection of material means that his bibliographical data are as

v

full as necessary. His devotion to bibliographical detail is apparent at every stage of this bibliography and this accuracy and detail should be of the greatest use to all interested in Ramón Sender.

Little has been known up to this point of Sender as a journalist. This bibliography shows that his interest began in writing for newspapers in the late 1920s and has continued unabated since then. The student of Sender and his work in the future should seek out these pieces to study Sender's views on the religious, political and cultural events of his time.

This bibliography will begin a new period in the study of Sender. For the first time students of his work will be provided with a guide to what he has published and what has been written concerning his life and work in both Spanish and English.

In his introduction King points to some of the gaps that he feels exist in the bibliography. These are certainly minor if they are compared with the positive features of this bibliography.

The AATSP is proud to cooperate with the Scarecrow Press in presenting this volume to all students of contemporary literature and more especially to those interested in the fiction of twentieth century Spain.

Hensley C. Woodbridge

Sept. 20, 1975
Carbondale, Illinois

CONTENTS

PART 2: WORKS ABOUT SENDER

ACKNOWLEDGMENTS

By far the largest single section in this Bibliography is IV. , F. --listed in the Contents as "Syndicated Column, 'Los libros y los días. '" It includes 667 articles published by Sender in his column syndicated by the American Literary Agency during the period, 1953-1974. I am especially indebted to Dr. Rafael Pérez Sandoval, the author of a doctoral thesis on Sender's religious thought (see item 1348), for annotating 246 of the 667 articles or "columns" appearing in section IV. , F. An asterisk follows each annotation by Pérez Sandoval. For his substantial contribution to this project Don Rafael insists that an asterisk is adequate recognition. My special thanks go also to Mrs. Jeanne M. de Juliá, Director of the American Literary Agency (until her retirement, June 30, 1975), for providing me with copies of over three hundred of Sender's articles published in the column, "Los libros y los días. "

I am also very grateful to four other individuals: Hensley C. Woodbridge, Michiko Nonoyama, José Vergés, and Ramón Sender. Woodbridge in the execution of his duties as General Editor of the joint AATSP (American Association of Teachers of Spanish and Portuguese)/Scarecrow Press bibliographical series of which this volume is a part has been not just an editor but a helpful friend and counselor. It was he who first called my attention to quite a few of the items which appear herein. It was his bibliographical enthusiasm that kept me going during the long months in which it seemed that the project would never be brought to a successful completion.

In personal correspondence and through her thesis, "El anarquismo en las obras de Ramón J. Sender" (item 1357), Michiko Nonoyama provided all the information, including the annotations, for 30 items in this Bibliography.

Mr. José Vergés, the distinguished Founder and Director of Spain's largest publishing house, Destino of Barcelona, has been very helpful by sending me clippings of many articles and reviews from Spanish publications.

Though he has never shown any enthusiasm for my bibliographical efforts, Sender has always--since my days as an undergraduate in his classes at the University of New Mexico in 1947 and 1948--in response to my requests, graciously kept me informed as to his forthcoming books and been helpful to me in other ways. I shall always be grateful to him.

My sincere appreciation goes to the American Philosophical Society and to the Council on Research and Creative Work of the University of Colorado for their grants-in-aid which have greatly facilitated the preparation of this Bibliography.

Charles L. King

INTRODUCTION

In this Bibliography I have tried to include and briefly annotate all works by and about Ramón J. Sender in Spanish and English from 1928 through the end of 1974, except for reviews, which are listed but not annotated. Sender is (August, 1975) very much alive and continuing to write. It will be necessary to compile and annotate a Supplement to this Bibliography every five years. The first such Supplement, therefore, should cover the inclusive period, 1975-1979, and include corrections of and additions to this present effort.

In New Mexico where I grew up the Indians made beautiful pottery but in each piece they left some imperfection, some slight defect. An old Indian explained, so I heard, that the imperfection was to "let the devil out." The Bibliography which follows, though perhaps not quite the same thing as an artistic piece of pottery, is incomplete and somewhat defective. I have left it that way for the following reasons:

(1) to let the "devil" out;
(2) to show that I am human;
(3) to provide reviewers who do not read the books they review negative things to write about (whereby they can demonstrate their great critical acumen); and
(4) to leave to some bright (and persistent) member of the next generation of Senderian scholar-critics the opportunity to write the "definitive" bibliography of the great Spanish author.

For the ambitious young man or woman wishing to improve upon the present unfinished work I have several suggestions:

First, obtain copies of and annotate the few items in this Bibliography which have been left unannotated ("to let the devil out");

Second, peruse the files of the Heraldo de Aragón in Zaragoza until he finds (and can copy and annotate) a short story published in that newspaper about 1915 or 1916, according to Sender's brother, Rafael;

Third, search the files of Lecturas (a magazine in Barcelona) for a long short story, "Una hoguera en la noche," published by Sender along about 1916 or 1917, and for which the young author won first prize in a contest sponsored by Lecturas;

Fourth, try to find the files of the newspaper La Tierra of Huesca for the years during which Sender acted as its editor (though his name did not appear in the masthead), 1918-1921, and see whether any articles by Sender appear therein (either under his real name or a pen name);

Fifth, attempt to locate files of the following no longer extant Madrid newspapers in which the young author wrote in 1918 and possibly in 1919 and 1920: El Imparcial, La Tribuna, El País, and España Nueva (look especially for a short story, "Las brujas del compromiso," in La Tribuna);

Sixth, go through the files of El Sol from early in 1924 until October 1930 to find articles written by Sender, the young journalist;

Seventh, search diligently the principal newspapers and journals of Spain during the period, 1930-1936, for evaluation of Senderian works by Spanish critics such as Luis Bello, Rafael Cansinos Assens (five of his newspaper articles on Sender appear in this Bibliography), Roberto Castrovido, and José Díaz Fernández;

And eighth, make an effort to locate copies of La Voz de Madrid, the propaganda journal of the Spanish Republic in Paris, for the brief period in 1938 during which Sender was its Director (he probably published some of his own work in it).

There are other things also that the younger Senderian critic might profitably do. It would be helpful, for example, were he to compile and annotate a bibliography of the numerous translations of Sender's works into languages other than English as well as of all works about Sender not in Spanish or English.

But let us look now to the present, imperfect work.

Within each division of this Bibliography (Novels, Drama, etc.) a chronological order has been followed. I have with the notable exceptions of the 246 articles or "columns" annotated by Rafael Pérez Sandoval (see my "Acknowledgments") and 30 items (including 21 from Sender's early political column, "Postal política," 329-46, 348-49, 351) provided by Michiko Nonoyama (1357) directly examined almost every item published herein, including the 516 reviews listed. An asterisk precedes each item annotated by Pérez Sandoval; and proper acknowledgment of each annotation by Nonoyama has been given in the text.

The order followed for books by Sender is as follows: first, the title of the book in its original Spanish edition, e.g., Imán (item 1), followed by the place of publication (Madrid), the publisher (Cenit), the date of publication (1930), the number of pages (272--note, I write 272 p., not 272 pp.), and series or collection in which it appears (if any); a subsequent edition is indicated by a semicolon followed by a description of any changes from the prior edition (e.g., see 4 in which the second edition of Siete domingos rojos has a prologue not in the first edition) and a listing of the data in the usual order (place, publisher, date, number of pages, series if any).

The Spanish editions of each book are listed first, then the editions of the same book in English translation whenever such translations exist. In item 1, for example, the first English version of Imán was entitled Earmarked for Hell and appeared in 1934 in London; using the same translation but under another title, Pro Patria, the novel was published the following year in Boston.

After a brief annotation of each book, reviews of it are listed. Reviews in Spanish come first, then those in English. Within each language group I have listed first--in alphabetical order--those reviews for which the names of the reviewers are known, and in second place, reviews by anonymous reviewers. For this second group the names of the publications in which the reviews appeared are listed alphabetically.

For all entries from periodicals I use the form, "34, 2 (June, 1965), 178-89," which means that the item is found in Volume 34, Number 2, published in June of 1965, and on pages 178 to 189 inclusive; if only one number is given it should be interpreted as being the volume number, e.g., "34 (June, 1965)" means Volume 34; "No. 34 (June, 1965)" or "núm. 34 (junio, 1965)" means a volume number is not used and that the number of the issue of the publication is all that is needed to find the item referred to. Some entries, especially from newspapers, merely include the date and pagination; a very few include only the date.

The classification of Sender's works into literary genres--as I have divided this Bibliography--is beset with many ambiguities. The classifications are mine; they are tentative and are principally done here as a matter of convenience. La llave, listed here as a short story, for example, was in its early editions, in both Spanish and English, staged as a play.

Part 1

WORKS BY SENDER

I. BOOKS

A. NOVELS

1   Imán (Novela de la guerra de Marruecos). Madrid: Cenit, 1930, 272 p.; Barcelona: Balagué, 1933, 112 p.

Earmarked for Hell; tr. by James Cleugh. London: Wishart, 1934, 342 p. Pro Patria; tr. by James Cleugh. Boston: Houghton Mifflin, 1935, 295 p.

The ill-starred Spanish military campaign to suppress the rebellion of the Moorish leader Abd-el-Krim in 1921 is told from the perspective of a simple Spanish soldier, Viance, who like a magnet, imán, seems to attract misfortune. In addition to English the book has been translated into German, Dutch, Portuguese, Polish, Russian, Hebrew, White Russian, Ukrainian, and Chinese.

La Libertad (Madrid), núm. 3817 (14 de junio, 1932), p. 10, col. 7.

Allen, Paul. New York Herald Tribune Books, October 6, 1935, p. 14.

Codman, Florence. Nation, 141 (October 2, 1935), p. 390.

Douglas, Frances. New York Times Book Review, January 11, 1931, p. 8.

Ferguson, Otis. New Republic, 84 (October 16, 1935), p. 275.

Kresensky, Raymond. Christian Century, 52 (November 6, 1935), p. 1421.

Kronenberger, Louis. New York Times Book Review, September 22, 1935, p. 7.

Plomer, William. Spectator, 153 (September 14, 1935), p. 374.

Pritchett, V. S. New Statesman and Nation, 8 (September 8, 1934), p. 296.

Booklist, 32 (December, 1935), p. 111.
Boston Evening Transcript, October 5, 1935, p. 5.
Saturday Review of Literature, 12 (October 19, 1935), p. 11.
Springfield Republican, October 20, 1935, p. 7e.
Times [London] Literary Supplement, October 25, 1935, p.
     734.

2   O. P. (Orden público).   Madrid: Cenit, 1931, 195 p.;
       Mexico: Publicaciones Panamericanas, 1941, 200 p.
       (Colección La novela proletaria).

       A novelization of Sender's experiences while a prisoner
for three months in 1927 in Madrid's Cárcel Modelo.   The
Wind, symbol of eternity, and the author engage in philosophical dialogue.   Brief character-sketches of a motley and rather grotesque array of prisoners along with a philosophical-
lyrical dimension constitute the book's primary values.   Except for the addition of a preface by the author the Mexican
edition is identical to the Spanish.   In a letter to me (dated
January 23, 1974) Sender states that O. P. is unworthy of inclusion in any listing of his works.   Its essence is included
in El verdugo afable (14).

Bel, G.   Orto, marzo, 1932, p. 63-64.
Somoza Silva, L.   La Libertad (Madrid), núm. 3577 (6 de
     septiembre, 1931), p. 9.

La Libertad (Madrid), núm. 3541 (26 de julio, 1931), p. 8.
     (includes photo of Sender).

3   El Verbo se hizo sexo (Teresa de Jesús).   Madrid:
       Zeus, 1931, 264 p.

       A novelized biography of the Saint of Avila with a strong
historical dimension.   In a personal letter to me (dated January 23, 1974) the author expresses the desire to suppress
El Verbo from his list of published works.   In an earlier letter to Francisco Carrasquer he refers to El Verbo as "a sin
of my childhood" (see Carrasquer, "Imán" y la novela histórica de Sender, London: Tamesis Books, 1970, p. 208),
and asks that he be judged only by his later book, Tres
novelas teresianas, 1967 (31).

La Libertad (Madrid), núm. 3559 (16 de agosto, 1931), p. 8.

Serís, Homero. Books Abroad, 6, 1 (January, 1932), p. 26.

4   Siete domingos rojos (Novela de la prerrevolución es-
      pañola)。 Barcelona: Balagué, 1932, 480 p. "Prólogo
      a la segunda edición," por el autor, p. 7-8, Nueva
      versión, revisada y corregida por el autor. Buenos
      Aires: Proyección, 1970, 248 p. (Col。 Tiempo Vital);
      1973, 274 p. Recast and rewritten with a new title,
      Las tres sorores. Barcelona: Destino, 1974, 311 p。
      (Col. Ancora y Delfín, 449)。

      Seven Red Sundays; tr. by Peter Chalmers Mitchell;
      "Translator's Introductory Note." London: Faber and
      Faber, 1936, 438 p.; New York: Liveright, 1936, 438
      p.; Harmondsworth, Middlesex, England: Penguin Books,
      1938, 308 p. (Penguin Books, 135); New York: Collier
      Books, 1961, 1969 (reissue), 286 p.

      Portrays an abortive proletarian uprising instituted by
the anarchists, syndicalists, and communists during seven
days ("Sundays") in Madrid.   Five participants in the rebellion alternate with the narrator-participant, and on one occasion with the Moon, in relating the events in the first person.
In addition to English the book has been translated into Russian, Danish, Swedish, Czech, Dutch, and French. S。 indicated (in a personal letter to the Bibliographer, dated January 23, 1974) that he regards Siete domingos rojos as unworthy of a place among his works, and that its recasting
(refundición) under a new name, Las tres sorores, should
replace the earlier work, i. e., be regarded as its definitive
edition.   Las tres sorores imposes upon the earlier work the
philosophical wisdom of Sender's mature years, a deeper mystical projection, wrestles again with the desire for absolute
dogma on the one hand and for absolute liberty on the other,
while substantially maintaining the narrative elements (and
characters) of Siete domingos rojos.

Prats y Beltrán, Alardo。 La Libertad (Madrid), 14, 3858
      (31 de julio, 1932), p. 9, cols。 6-7。

Archivos de Literatura Contemporánea. Índice Literario,
      2 (3 de marzo, 1933), p. 70-71.

Beresford, J. D. Manchester Guardian, May 1, 1936, p. 7.
Croyle, Lincoln. New Statesman and Nation, 13 (January 16,
      1937), p. 85.

Jordan, Philip. New Statesman and Nation, 11 (May 16,
     1936), p. 772.
Kazin, Alfred. New York Herald Tribune Books, October 11,
     1936, p. 10.
Marsh, F. T. New York Times Book Review, October 18,
     1936, p. 7.
Plomer, William. Spectator, 156 (May 8, 1936), p. 850.
Purdy, Theodore, Jr. Saturday Review of Literature, 14
     (September 26, 1936), p. 5.
Schneider, Isidor. New Republic, 88 (October 14, 1936),
     p. 288.
White, Leigh. Nation, 143 (October 24, 1936), p. 499.

Cleveland Open Shelf, October, 1936, p. 20.
Forum and Century, 96 (October, 1936), p. iv.
Pratt Institute Quarterly, Winter 1937, p. 42.
Saturday Review of Literature, 14, 24 (October 10, 1936),
     p. 26.
Time, 28 (September 21, 1936), p. 80.
Times [London] Literary Supplement, May 2, 1936, p. 367.

5   Viaje a la aldea del crimen (Documental de Casas Vie-
      jas). Madrid: Pueyo, 1934, 205 p.

      A novelized, though essentially factual and reportorial,
account of a peasant uprising in the Andalusian village of
Casas Viejas on January 10, 1933. Valuable for its social
realism--exposure of the unjust economic balance between
landholders and peasants in rural Spain in modern times.
See Casas Viejas (59), a collection of newspaper reports on
the suppression of the uprising.

Somoza Silva, Lázaro. La Libertad (Madrid), núm. 4377
     (1 de abril, 1934), p. 7-8.

6   La noche de las cien cabezas (Novela del tiempo en
      delirio). Madrid: Pueyo, 1934, 244 p.

      One hundred heads belonging to the most diverse repre-
sentatives of Spanish society drop into a cemetery one winter
night during a cyclone, where one by one they are examined
by Evaristo the Frogman, one of Madrid's exploited poor who
has just died from hunger and exposure to the cold. The bulk
of the book consists of satirical-philosophical commentary on
the heads by Evaristo, and the author himself. Manuel Béjar

devotes over forty pages of his doctoral thesis to a study of the work (1350), later published as an article (1298). In a letter to the bibliographer (January 23, 1974) S. states that he regards La noche as unworthy "de figurar en mi lista de obras."

Del Río, Angel. Revista Hispánica Moderna, 2, 3 (abril, 1936), p. 219.
Somoza Silva, Lázaro. La Libertad (Madrid), núm. 4572 (25 de noviembre, 1934), p. 7.

Archivos de Literatura Contemporánea. Índice Literario, 3, 9 (noviembre, 1934), p. 190-91.

Douglas, Frances. New York Times Book Review, August 25, 1935, p. 22.
_____. New York Times Book Review, April 21, 1940, p. 8.
Van Hulse, Camil. Books Abroad, 10, 1 (Winter 1936), p. 46-47.

7   Mr. Witt en el cantón. Madrid: Espasa-Calpe, 1936, 286 p. Prólogo del autor. Madrid: Alianza Editorial, 1968, 1969, 1972, 274 p. (Col. El Libro de Bolsillo, 135).

Mr. Witt Among the Rebels; tr. by Peter Chalmers Mitchell. London: Faber and Faber, 1937, 367 p.; Boston: Houghton Mifflin, 1938, 367 p.

An historical novel set in Cartagena in 1873 which relates the Murcian uprising against the First Spanish Republic. Intermeshed with the larger scene of the social struggle is the private story of Mr. Witt, a middle-aged English engineer in Cartagena who is married to Milagritos, a fiery cartagenera who is 18 years younger than he. While Milagritos becomes involved in the uprising Mr. Witt withdraws into himself and suffers from jealousy and guilt, the latter resulting from a former action of his. The novel was awarded Spain's National Prize for Literature (novel section) in 1935. In addition to English, the novel has been published in Russian, Swedish, and Finnish translations.

Conte, Rafael. Informaciones (Madrid), November 21, 1968.
Gimferrer, Pedro. Destino, November 16, 1968.
Gómez Marin, José A. Madrid, June 11, 1969. (The news-

paper Madrid is now extinct.)
Horno Liria, Luis. Heraldo de Aragón, 31 de mayo, 1969.
Pérez Cebrián, José L. Q. P., septiembre, 1971, p. 14.
Pérez Montaner, Jaime. Cuadernos Hispanoamericanos,
    núm. 285 (marzo, 1974), p. 635-44. (Listed also as
    an article [1271].)
Salcedo, Emilio. El Norte de Castilla (Valladolid), 3 de
    noviembre, 1968.
Salinas, Pedro. Archivos de Literatura Contemporánea. In-
    dice Literario, 5 (1936), p. 73-77.

Marriott, Charles. Manchester Guardian, April 23, 1937,
    p. 6.
Marsh, F. T. New York Times Book Review, January 30,
    1938, p. 8.
Pritchett, V. S. Christian Science Monitor, May 12, 1937,
    p. 10.
_____. New Statesman and Nation, 13 (April 10, 1937), p.
    596.
Purdy, Theodore, Jr. Saturday Review of Literature, 17
    (January 29, 1938), p. 20.
Rees, Goronwy. Spectator, 158 (April 16, 1937), p. 730.
Soskin, William. New York Herald Tribune Books, Febru-
    ary 13, 1938, p. 2.

Booklist, 34 (March 1, 1938).
Catholic World, 147 (May, 1938), p. 252.
Springfield Republican, June 12, 1938, p. 7e.
Time, 31 (February 7, 1938), p. 63.
Times [London] Literary Supplement, April 17, 1937, p. 291.

8   El lugar del hombre. México: Quetzal, 1939, 226 p.
    As El lugar de un hombre. México: CNT, 1958, 172
    p. El lugar de un hombre. Barcelona: Destino, 1968,
    186 p. (Col. Ancora y Delfín, 307). The Destino edi-
    tion was not released until 1974.

    A Man's Place; tr. by Oliver La Farge. New York:
    Duell, Sloan and Pearce, 1940, 280 p.; London: Jona-
    than Cape, 1941, 280 p.

    Grave repercussions occur when Sabino, a humble la-
borer who has been denied a place in his Aragonese village,
disappears into the backwoods and returns fifteen years later.
In addition to English the novel has been translated into Swedish (1965), Serbo-Croatian (1967), and Polish (1969). The

1968 edition shows considerable retouching or revising by the author of the 1939 edition. Don Jacinto, for example, becomes Don Ricardo (Don Rico=Dinero), Sabino's mother does not commit suicide, etc.

Del Río, Angel. Revista Hispánica Moderna, 8, 1-2 (enero y abril, 1942), p. 67.

Gimferrer, Pere. Destino, núm. 1930 (28 de septiembre, 1974), p. 34. (Upon the release in 1974 of the 1968 Destino edition of the novel.)

Iglesias, I. Cuadernos (París), núm. 41 (marzo-abril, 1960), p. 105-06.

Marra-López, José R. Insula, núm. 158 (15 de enero, 1960), p. 10.

Barry, Griffin. New Republic, 104 (February 3, 1941), p. 157.

Bates, Ralph. Nation, 151 (November 2, 1940), p. 424.

Boyd, Ernest. Saturday Review of Literature, 23 (December 21, 1940), p. 11.

Kazin, Alfred. New York Herald Tribune Books, November 3, 1940, p. 3.

Littell, Robert. Yale Review, n.s. 30 (Winter 1941), p. viii.

Lord, David. Books Abroad, 14, 3 (Summer 1940), p. 278.

Marsh, F. T. New York Times Book Review, November 3, 1940, p. 8.

Rankin, R. B. Library Journal, 65 (October 15, 1940), p. 874.

New Yorker, 16 (November 2, 1940), p. 86.

9   Proverbio de la muerte. México: Quetzal, 1939, 251 p.

A modified and much augmented Proverbio appeared in 1947 under a new title, La esfera (12). A narration of the metaphysical speculations and investigations of Saila, a Spanish refugee resembling S., who after the Spanish Civil War crosses the Atlantic on an oceanliner. The ship's crew and passengers form a human microcosm, and provide material for comments on the human condition.

Iduarte, Andrés. Revista Hispánica Moderna, 8, 3 (julio, 1942), p. 225-26 (also reviews 45 and 52).

Swain, James O. Books Abroad, 14, 1 (Winter 1940), p. 54.

10   Epitalamio del prieto Trinidad.   México: Quetzal,
      1943, 316 p.; Barcelona: Destino, 1966, 1968, 1970,
      1973, 304 p. (Col. Ancora y Delfín, 274); Barcelona:
      Salvat Editores, 1971, 212 p.

      Dark Wedding; tr. by Eleanor Clark. New York:
      Doubleday, 1943, 305 p.; Introduction by Arturo Barea.
      London: Grey Walls Press, 1948, 299 p.

      Black Trinidad, the boss of a penal island in the Carib-
      bean, is assassinated when he returns to the island with his
      young, virgin bride. Immediately the prisoners divide into
      factions and fight for possession of the widow, Niña Lucha,
      symbol of ideal purity. In the end Niña is saved by Darío,
      the idealistic schoolteacher on the island. Other translations
      of Epitalamio del prieto Trinidad include German, Swedish,
      Danish, Portuguese, and Czech.

      Acosta Montoro, José. El Diario Vasco, 29 de enero, 1967.
      Alvarez, Carlos Luis. Blanco y Negro, 1 de octubre, 1966,
          p. 104.
      Bosch, Andrés. Tiempo Nuevo (Madrid), 6 de abril, 1967,
          p. 48-9.
      Castroviejo, Concha. Informaciones (Madrid), 29 de octubre,
          1966.
      Doltra, Esteban. Hoja del Lunes (Barcelona), 19 de dici-
          embre, 1966.
      Mainer, José-Carlos. Insula, núm. 241, (diciembre, 1966),
          p. 8.
      Martín Abril, José L. Diario Regional (Valladolid), 5 de
          enero, 1967.
      Masoliver, Juan Ramón. La Vanguardia Española (Barce-
          lona), 27 de enero, 1967.
      Rincón, José María. La Estafeta Literaria, núm. 357 (19
          de noviembre, 1966), p. 20.
      Valencia, A. Arriba (Madrid), 27 de septiembre, 1966.
      Vázquez-Zamora, Rafael. España (Tanger), 16 de octubre,
          1966.

      Destino, 1 de octubre, 1968.
      Diario de Barcelona, 17 de septiembre, 1966.
      El Diario Vasco (San Sebastián), 2 de octubre, 1966.
      Heraldo de Aragón (Zaragoza), 21 de septiembre, 1966.
      El Norte de Castilla (Valladolid), 9 de octubre, 1966.
      S. P. (Madrid), 9 de octubre, 1966, p. 59.
      Ya (Madrid), 8 de octubre, 1966.

Gorman, Herbert. New York Times Book Review, March 28, 1943, p. 10.
Kazin, Alfred. New Republic, 108 (April 5, 1943), p. 451.
Kennedy, Leo. Chicago Sun Book Week, April 11, 1943, p. 3.
King, Charles L. Books Abroad, 41, 2 (Spring 1967), p. 205.
Kirk, Betty. Books Abroad, 17, 1 (Winter 1943), p. 45.
Redman, B. R. Saturday Review of Literature, 26 (May 15, 1943), p. 13.
Schorer, Mark. Yale Review, n. s. 32 (Summer 1943), p. vi.
Soskin, William. New York Herald Tribune Weekly Book Review, March 28, 1943, p. 4.
Stephenson, Robert C. Kenyon Review, 5, 3 (Summer 1943), p. 458-61.
Trilling, Lionel. Nation, 156 (April 24, 1943), p. 603.

New Yorker, 19 (March 27, 1943), p. 71.

11   Crónica del alba. México: Nuevo Mundo, 1942, 264 p. Textbook edition with Introduction, Notes, and Vocabulary by Florence Hall. New York: Appleton-Century-Crofts, 1946, v-xxi + 231 p. [Hall was S. 's wife, 1943-63]

Chronicle of Dawn; tr. by Willard R. Trask. New York: Doubleday, 1944, 201 p. ; London: J. Jonathan Cape, 1945, 201 p.

A first-person narrative of the adventures and cultural awakening of the boy José Garcés (obviously the author) during the eleventh year of life in his native Aragonese village. This novel has undergone several reprintings as a textbook and later became the first part of a nine-part series bearing the same title (28).

De Beck, V. F. Cuadernos Hispanoamericanos, 40, 120 (diciembre, 1959), p. 164-65.

Bates, Ralph. Saturday Review of Literature, 27 (April 15, 1944), p. 26.
Berault, Paule. Commonweal, 40 (May 26, 1944), p. 140.
Farber, Marjorie. New York Times Book Review, February 20, 1944, p. 4.
Kirk, Betty. Books Abroad, 17, 2 (Spring 1943), p. 142.
Rosenfeld, Isaac. New Republic, 110 (April 24, 1944), p. 572.
Shapiro, Leo. Chicago Sun Book Week, March 12, 1944, p. 7.

Trilling, Diana. Nation, 158 (March 18, 1944), p. 342.
Wolfe, B. D. New York Herald Tribune Weekly Book Review, March 12, 1944, p. 3.

Booklist, 40 (May 1, 1944), p. 305.
Catholic World, 159 (May, 1944), p. 187.
Kirkus' Bookshop Service Bulletin (New York), 12 (January 1, 1944), p. 31.
New Yorker, 20 (February 26, 1944), p. 86.
Newsweek, 23 (February 28, 1944), p. 92.

12   La esfera. Buenos Aires: Siglo Veinte, 1947, 300 p.
      Edición definitiva. Madrid: Aguilar, 1968, 1969,
      1970, 324 p. (Col. Novela Nueva, 18).

      The Sphere; tr. by Felix Giovanelli. New York: Hellman and Williams, 1949, 264 p.; London: Grey Walls Press, 1950, 304 p.

      An augmentation and thorough revision of Proverbio de la muerte (9) with a new title so as to be properly called a new novel. Sender's most ambitious philosophical work, La esfera narrates the metaphysical probings of Saila, a Spaniard fleeing from the Spanish Civil War (S. himself), as he crosses the Atlantic to America. Published in French translation by ediciones Robert Laffont in 1972.

      Marino, Rose Marie. Reseña de Literatura, Arte y Espectáculos, 36 (junio, 1970), p. 334-36.

      La Opinión (Los Angeles), 16 de diciembre, 1972.

      Brown, C. M. Saturday Review of Literature, 32 (June 4, 1949), p. 28.
      Krieger, Murray. Christian Science Monitor, May 24, 1949, p. 14.
      Osterhout, Hilda. New York Times Book Review, May 1, 1949, p. 6.
      Stephenson, R. C. Kenyon Review, 11, 4 (Autumn 1949), p. 703-06.

      New Yorker, 25 (May 21, 1949), p. 113.
      San Francisco Chronicle, June 19, 1949, p. 13.

13   El rey y la reina. Buenos Aires: Jackson, 1949, 256 p.; Barcelona: Destino, 1970, 179 p. (Ancora y Delfín,

341); Destino, 1973, 192 p. (Destinolibro, 5).

The King and the Queen. Tr. by Mary Low. New York: Vanguard Press, 1948, 231 p.; London: Grey Walls Press, 1948, 231 p.; Introduction by Raymond Rosenthal, p. iv-vii; New York: Grosset and Dunlap, 1968, vii + 231 p. (Universal Library edition, paperback).

As the Civil War deepens in Madrid, Rómulo, a gardener and a Republican sympathizer, protects the Duchess in an uninhabited tower on the ducal estate. Against the background of war noblewoman and plebeian encounter each other on the level of their common humanity, and their story acquires allegorical significance. Translations in addition to English include French, Slovenian, Dutch, and German. The English translation appeared before the first Spanish edition.

Catón, Gómez. Diario de Barcelona, 13 de marzo, 1971, p. 12.
Del Villar, Arturo. Alerta (Santander), 11 de agosto, 1970.
López Alvarez, Luis. Cuadernos (París), núm. 17 (marzo-abril, 1956), p. 122-23.
Martín Abril, José L. Diario Regional (Valladolid), 9 de octubre, 1970.
Mendiola, José María. El Diario Vasco (San Sebastián), 30 de agosto, 1970.
Murciano, Carlos. La Estafeta Literaria, núm. 458 (15 de diciembre, 1970), p. 410.
Nerja, Andrés. Las Españas (México), año 5, núm. 13 (29 de octubre, 1949).
Rodríguez Méndez, José M. Cuadernos Hispanoamericanos, 31, 90 (junio, 1957), p. 388-89.
Vázquez Zamora, Rafael. Destino, núm. 1715 (15 de agosto, 1970), p. 23.
Vélez, Francisco. España (Tanger), 3 de septiembre, 1970.

ABC (Madrid), 15 de septiembre, 1970.
La Actualidad Española (Madrid), 7 de octubre, 1970.
El Noticiero de Cartagena, 26 de junio, 1970.
La Vanguardia Española (Barcelona), 25 de junio, 1970.

Barr, Donald. New York Times Book Review, June 27, 1948, p. 4.
Honig, Edwin. New Mexico Quarterly Review, 18, 3 (Autumn 1948), p. 352-54.
Mayberry, George. New Republic, 118 (May 31, 1948), p. 28.

Peden, Margaret. Hispania, 55, 2 (May, 1972), p. 386.
Wolfe, B. D. New York Herald Tribune Weekly Book Review, May 16, 1948, p. 5.

Kirkus' Bookshop Service Bulletin (New York), 16 (March 15, 1948), p. 147.
New Yorker, 24 (May 29, 1948), p. 77.
San Francisco Chronicle, July 4, 1948, p. 17.

14   El verdugo afable. Santiago de Chile: Nascimiento, 1952, 427 p. Prólogo de Eduardo Naval; México: M. Aguilar, 1970, 379 p. (Col. Novela Nueva).

The Affable Hangman; tr. by Florence Hall. London: Jonathan Cape, 1954, 336 p.; New York: Las Americas, 1963, 318 p.; London: Redman, 1964, 318 p.

An executioner, in an all-night session with S., a young journalist, relates the story of his life, essentially a psychological, sentimental, moral and metaphysical probing of the forces in Spanish society which led the executioner to choose his sombre profession. Translated and published in French by ediciones Robert Laffont in 1970.

Gordón, Sigfredo. Hispanoamericano (México), 57, 1474 (3 de agosto, 1970), p. 52.

Cohen, Peter. Spectator (London), No. 7054 (September 6, 1963), p. 298.
_____. Mexican Life (Mexico), 39, 10 (October, 1963), p. 34.
Corke, Hilary. New Republic, 149 (November 30, 1963), p. 16.
Curley, Thomas. New York Times Book Review, September 8, 1963, p. 5.
Davenport, Guy. National Review, 15, 40 (October 8, 1963), p. 313.
Englekirk, John E. New Mexico Quarterly, 24, 3 (Autumn 1954), p. 341-42.
Gray, James. Saturday Review, 46 (September 7, 1963), p. 22.
Hall, Florence. Books Abroad, 27, 2 (Spring 1953), p. 153-54.
Miller, Warren. Book Week, 1 (September 29, 1963), p. 6.
_____. New York Herald Tribune, September 29, 1963, p. 6.

Peñalosa, Fernando. Library Journal, 88 (November 1, 1963), p. 4238.

British Book News, August 1954, p. 466.

15   Mosén Millán. México: Colección Aquelarre, 1953, 87 p. As Réquiem por un campesino español; Requiem for a Spanish Peasant; bilingual edition with parallel texts in Spanish and English; translation into English by Elinor Randall; prologue in English by Mair José Benardete. New York: Las Américas, 1960, vii-xxix + 123 p. (A Cypress Book). Réquiem por un campesino español; Prologue by Mair José Benardete; translated into Spanish by Ida Martínez, p. 9-45. Buenos Aires: Proyección, 1961, 142 p. (Col. Tiempo Vital). Mosén Millán; Textbook edition by Robert M. Duncan; Preface by the author. Boston: Heath, 1964, v-vx + 111 p. Réquiem, etc. Buenos Aires: Proyección, 1966, 128 p. As Réquiem para un campesino español [title change] with prologue by Julia Uceda, "Consideraciones para una estilística de las obras de Ramón J. Sender," p. 5-28, and "Ramón J. Sender, cronista y soñador de una nueva España," by Mair José Benardete (same text as in Proyección issues), p. 97-122. México: Mexicanos Unidos, 1968, 1970, 1972, 1974, 122 p. (note: although the National Union Catalog lists a 1968 edition by Mexicanos Unidos the Compiler's 1974 edition of Mexicanos Unidos lists editions only for 1970, 1972, and 1974). Buenos Aires: Proyección, 1969, 1973, 109 p. (Col. Tiempo Vital). Textbook edition by Berta Pallares with the text of the original abridged and simplified; Vocabulary and questions. Copenhagen: Grafisk Forlag A/S, 1972, 79 p. (distributed in the U.S.A. by the EMC Corporation); Barcelona: Destino, 1974, 105 p. (Col. Ancora y Delfín, 460).

A short novel or novelette first published as Mosén Millán. While waiting in the sacristy to conduct a requiem mass for a peasant, Paco, assassinated in the Aragonese village a year earlier by Fascistic agents, Mosén Millán, the priest, suffers remorse as he recalls the events leading up to the unjust execution of the villager. The work is regarded as one of S.'s very finest narratives.

Capelletti, Angel J. Universidad (Publicación de la Universidad Nacional del Litoral, Santa Fe, Argentina), 51

(enero-marzo, 1962), p. 332-34.
Carenas, F. Norte (Amsterdam), año 11, núm. 5 (1970), p. 177-81.
Carrasco, Sansón. La Voz (New York, Las Américas Publishing Co.), 5, 5 (febrero, 1961), p. 6.
Marra-López, J. R. Cuadernos (París), núm. 47 (marzo-abril, 1961), p. 121.
Maurín, Joaquín. La Voz (New York, Las Américas Publishing Co.), 5, 2 (noviembre, 1960), p. 19.
Vilas, Santiago. Hispania, 47, 3 (September, 1964), p. 678-79.

La Voz (New York: Las Américas Publishing Co.), 5, 6 (March, 1961), p. 4-5.

Bleznick, Donald W. Hispania, 44, 4 (December, 1961), p. 744.
Castellano, John R. The Modern Language Journal, 48, 8 (December, 1964), p. 538.
Duncan, Bernice G. Books Abroad, 36, 1 (Winter 1962), p. 112.
Mulvihill, E. R. Hispanic American Historical Review, 41, 2 (May, 1961), p. 307.

16   Hipogrifo violento. México: Colección Aquelarre, 1954, 223 p.

The immediate sequel to Crónica del alba (11), first published as a separate novel, and later (28) as part two of the nine-part series, Crónica del alba. It relates the experiences of Pepe (S.) in a Catholic boarding school in Reus during the academic year of 1911-12.

17   Ariadna. México: Colección Aquelarre, 1955, 267 p.

Javier (S.) and Ariadna, his lover, testify before a world organization investigating the causes and conduct of the Spanish Civil War. A surrealistic atmosphere prevails. This separate novel was later incorporated as the first "libro" in Los cinco libros de Ariadna (20).

18   Bizancio. México: Diana, 1956, 415 p.; Andorra la Vella, Principat d' Andorra: Andorra, 1968, dos tomos con unas 325 y 318 páginas respectivamente (Col. Andorra, 2).

A historical novel which narrates the expedition of the
Spanish under Roger de Flor's command in 1306 or 1307
to Constantinople to aid the Byzantine King Adronichus
II in his fight against the Turks. The book ends with
the death of the second leader of the Spanish troops, Berenguer de Rocafort, in 1309.

Iglesias Laguna, A. La Estafeta Literaria, núm. 417 (1 de
    abril, 1969), p. 129-30.

19   La "Quinta Julieta." México: Costa-Amic, 1957, 163
      p. (Col. Panoramas, 12). Originally published in the
      magazine Panoramas [México], 6, verano de 1957,
      p. 7-152 (112).

The immediate sequel to Hipogrifo violento (16). The
story begins with the arrival of Pepe to Zaragoza where his
family has moved, and continues through the summer there,
concluding with his enrollment in the Fall in the Institute of
Zaragoza. La "Quinta Julieta" later became the third part
of the long series, Crónica del alba (28).

Klibbe, Lawrence, Books Abroad, 34, 2 (Spring 1960),
    p. 167.

20   Los cinco libros de Ariadna. New York: Ibérica,
      1957, v-xvi + 584 p.

To Ariadna (17), the "libro primero," S. has added
four more "books" to form this new volume. An effort to
recreate the moral climate of the Spanish Civil War and of
the time immediately prior to it. Strongly autobiographical,
the author states that his intention in the book "es simple-
mente cumplir su deber de testigo de este tiempo de brisas
airadas y voces descompuestas." The book contains a very
important prologue by the author, p. v-xvi (95).

Ayala, Juan Antonio. Artes y Letras, julio-septiembre,
    1958, p. 97.
Ferrándiz Alborz, F. Ibérica (ed. española), 6, 2 (15 de
    febrero, 1958), p. 6-8.
Iglesias, I. Cuadernos (París), núm. 28 (enero-febrero,
    1958), p. 102-03.
Ortega y Gasset, E. El Universal (Caracas), 30 de julio,
    1957.

Guillén, Claudio.   Books Abroad, 32, 2 (Spring 1958),
     p. 137-38.
Mead, Robert G.   Hispania, 41, 3 (May, 1958), p. 234-35.

21   Emen hetan (Aquí estamos).   México: Costa-Amic,
       1958, 174 p.

In rather esperpentic scenes and with raucous humor
the author narrates the practice of necromancy or the 'black
arts" in Upper Aragon in the past.   Spain is identified as
the land of "Su Majestad el Señor Cabrón, " the devil.   The
substance of the book was later incorporated into Las criaturas saturnianas (32).

Ayala, Juan A.   Artes y Letras, julio-septiembre, 1958,
     p. 97-98.

Hispanoamericano (México), 33, 839 (2 de julio, 1958), p. 72.
Mirador (México), 4, 9 (1958), p. 42.

Klibbe, Lawrence H.   Books Abroad, 34, 3 (Summer 1960),
     p. 243.

22   Los laureles de Anselmo.   México: Atenea, 1958,
       233 p.; Barcelona: Destino, 1972, 184 p. (Col. Ancora
       y Delfín, 383).

Set in an industrial city in the United States during
present times and with other imaginative innovations this
work is essentially a recreation--in the form of a dialogued
novel--of Calderón's great work, La vida es sueño.   An-
selm, taking life to be a dream, acts with great courage.

Corbero, Salvador.   Diario de Barcelona, 13 de mayo, 1972.
Lacalle, Angel.   Las Provincias (Valencia), 7 de mayo,
     1972.
Mendiola, José M.   El Diario Vasco (San Sebastián), 4 de
     junio, 1972.

Blanco y Negro, núm. 3146 (19 de agosto), 1972.   (By M.A.
     M.)
Informaciones (Madrid), 4 de mayo, 1972.
La Vanguardia Española (Barcelona), 27 de abril, 1972.
Ya (Madrid), 20 de mayo, 1972.

Schade, George D.   Books Abroad, 34, 2 (Spring 1960),
    p. 135.

23   El mancebo y los héroes.   México: Atenea, 1960,
      205 p.

The immediate sequel to La "Quinta Julieta" (19) which
relates Pepe's adventures while working as a pharmacist's
assistant as an adolescent youth in Zaragoza.   Pepe becomes
involved in the social struggle.   This work later was incorporated into the series, Crónica del alba (28), as part three
of the first volume.

24   La tesis de Nancy.   México: Atenea, 1962, 259 p.;
      Introducción ("Presentación") por los editores, p. 9-
      12.   Madrid: Magisterio Español, 1968, 1969, 1970,
      1971, 1972, 1973, 1974 (novena edición española),
      324 p. (Col. Novelas y Cuentos, 25).

Spain and especially its gypsy subculture as seen
through the eyes of Nancy, an American university student
in Andalusia to prepare her doctoral thesis, presented in
ten chapters, each a letter of Nancy to her cousin, Betsy,
in the United States.   Marcelino C. Peñuelas classifies it
as "humorística, intrascendente, la única de este tono en
toda su obra [la de Sender]" (Conversaciones con Ramón J.
Sender, p. 17).   Its crude humor and caricatured presenta-
tion of an American female student in Spain have given it
popular appeal in Spain, where about 100,000 copies of the
novel had been sold by 1974.   Two sequels to it, Nancy,
doctora en gitanería (41), and Nancy, y el bato loco (43),
appeared in 1974.

Olstad, Charles.   Hispania, 46, 4 (December, 1963), p. 852.

25   La luna de los perros.   New York: Las Américas,
      1962, 153 p.; Barcelona: Destino, 1969, 189 p. (Col.
      Ancora y Delfín, 307).

A Spanish refugee in Paris during the German occupation in 1941 relates his strange experiences, including his
love affair with Raquel, a Czech who speaks German and
who, though treacherous, somehow comes to symbolize the
Eternal Woman.   Notable for its recreation of the bleak
moral atmosphere of the occupation and for its existentialist

tone, it reflects S. 's own experiences in Paris after the
Spanish Civil War.

Bosch, Rafael.   La Voz (New York), 7, 8 (mayo, 1963),
    p. 189.
Horno Liria, Luis.   Heraldo de Aragón (Zaragoza), 21 de
    mayo, 1969.
Parrilla, Arturo.   La Torre, año 10, núm. 39 (julio-septi-
    embre, 1962), p. 179-80.
Pérez Ollo, Fernando.   Diario de Navarra (Pamplona), 25
    de mayo, 1969.

Informaciones (Madrid), 22 de mayo, 1969.
La Prensa (Barcelona), 24 de marzo, 1970.
La Vanguardia Española (Barcelona), 24 de agosto, 1969.

Bosch, Rafael.   Books Abroad, 37, 2 (Spring 1963), p. 189.
Olstad, Charles.   Hispania, 46, 2 (May, 1963), p. 439-40.

26   Los Tontos de la Concepción.   Sandoval, New Mexico:
      Coronado, 1963, 125 p.

The story or "crónica" of two Spanish friars who minister to the Yuma Indians (the "Tontos") in Southwestern Ari-
zona at the end of the eighteenth century.   The book was
later published in a collection of S. 's short stories, El
extraño señor Photynos y otras novelas americanas (50).

Bosch, Rafael.   Revista Hispánica Moderna, 30, 2 (abril,
    1964), p. 141.
_____.   Hispania, 48, 3 (September, 1965), p. 614.

_____.   Books Abroad, 39, 1 (Winter 1965), p. 70.

27   Carolus Rex (Carolus II el Hechizado).   México: Mexi-
      canos Unidos, 1963, 172 p. (Col. Comunidad Ibérica).
      As Carolus Rex.   Barcelona: Destino, 1971, 228 p.
      (Col. Ancora y Delfín, 369).

An historical novel in which Charles II of Spain, often
called the "bewitched King," is viewed with understanding
and sympathy and Spanish court life of the epoch is endowed
with life.   The novel begins with preparations for the King's
impending marriage to María Luisa of France and concludes
with the Monarch's submission to the rites of exorcism.

Calvo Hernando, Manuel. Ya (Madrid), 26 de noviembre,
1971.
Corbalán, Pablo. Informaciones (Madrid), 9 de septiembre,
1971.
Del Villar, Arturo. Alerta (Santander), 14 de agosto, 1971,
p. 1.
Iglesias Laguna, Antonio. ABC, 19 de agosto, 1971.
Lacalle, Angel. Las Provincias (Valencia), 15 de agosto,
1971, p. 14.
Marra-López, José R. Insula, núm. 209 (abril, 1964),
p. 9.
Mendiola, José M. El Diario Vasco (San Sebastián), 26 de
septiembre, 1971.
Murciano, Carlos. La Estafeta Literaria, núm. 478 (15 de
octubre, 1971), p. 726.
Valencia, Antonio. Arriba (Madrid), 8 de septiembre, 1971.

S. P. (Madrid), 1 de septiembre, 1971, p. 56.
La Vanguardia Española (Barcelona), 14 de agosto, 1971.

28   Crónica del alba. Seis partes en dos tomos. New
York: Las Américas, 1963, I, 487 p., II, 560 p.;
nueve partes en tres tomos, Barcelona: Delos-Aymá,
1965, I, 445 p.; 1966, II, 513 p., III, 616 p.; San
Cugat del Vallés [España]: Delos-Aymá, 1965, I,
416 p.; 1969, II, 467 p., III, 601 p.; Madrid: Alianza
Editorial, 1971, I, 427 p., II, 459 p., III, 587 p.
(El Libro de Bolsillo, sección literatura, 316, 317,
318); nueve partes en dos tomos, Barcelona: Destino,
1973, I, 656 p., II, 704 p. (Col. Ancora y Delfín,
405, 406).

Before Noon; tr. by Willard R. Trask (Crónica del
alba) (11) and by Florence Hall (Hipogrifo violento and
La 'Quinta Julieta") (16, 19). Albuquerque: University of New Mexico Press, 1958, 408 p.; London:
Gollancz, 1959, 408 p. (note: this book contains in
English only the first three "parts" or "novels" of the
first six-part, then nine-part series).

Volume I of the first two-volume edition (New York)
and of all three-volume editions consists of three parts, each
of which formerly appeared as a separate novel: "Crónica
del alba" (11), "Hipogrifo violento" (16), and "La 'Quinta
Julieta'" (19).   Volume II of these editions contains "El
mancebo y los héroes" (published earlier as a separate
novel--see 23), "La onza de oro," and "Los niveles del

existir. " Volume III contains "Los términos del presagio,"
"La orilla donde los locos sonríen," and "La vida comienza
ahora. "

In the second two-volume edition (Barcelona) the first
five parts or "novels" are in Volume I; the remaining four
are in Volume II.

The first two-volume series in 1963 (New York) was
regarded by S. as the definitive edition.   Later he decided
to add a third volume; thus, the nine-part series (whether in
three or two volumes) is now considered to be the definitive
version of the work.

An autobiographical novel which purports to relate the
life of Lt. José Garcés, a Spanish Republican officer who
dies in a concentration camp in France at the conclusion of
the Spanish Civil War.   His early boyhood in his native Aragonese village, his adolescence, young manhood and eventual
participation in the Spanish conflict are all narrated.   Before dying at the age of thirty-five (the "mid-day" of life) he
records his memoirs in some notebooks.   The series is, in
its totality, a study in the sources of idealism, the idealism
that led Lt. Garcés (S. 's middle name is José and his ma-
ternal surname is Garcés) and others like him to offer their
lives in the Civil War.   For its first three-volume edition
S. was awarded the City of Barcelona Prize in 1966.

English translation of Before Noon, 1958 (Vol. I of the
      series).
   Adams, Mildred.   New York Times Book Review, Janu-
      ary 19, 1958, p. 5.
   Beales, A.   Tablet (London), 213 (May 16, 1959), p. 471.
   Blackburn, Paul.   Nation, 186 (April 19, 1958), p. 346-
      47.
   De Young, W. K.   San Francisco Chronicle, February 16,
      1958, p. 26.
   Honig, Edwin.   Saturday Review, 41 (April 12, 1958),
      p. 25.
   Phelan, Kappo.   Ibérica (English edition), 6, 2 (February,
      1958), p. 9-10.
   Stuart, Frank C.   New Mexico Quarterly, 28 (Summer-
      Autumn-Winter 1958), p. 201.
   West, Anthony.   New Yorker, 34 (April 19, 1958), p. 147.

   Times [London] Literary Supplement, April 3, 1959,
      p. 185-86.

Volumes I-II, 1963
   Otero Seco, Antonio.   Asomante (Univ. of Puerto Rico),

24, 2 (1968), p. 65-66.

Ponce de León, Luis. La Estafeta Literaria, núm. 349 (1966), p. 15.

Olstad, Charles. Hispania, 48, 1 (March, 1965), p. 179-80.

Volume I, 1965
Masoliver, Juan Ramón. La Vanguardia Española (Barcelona), 6 de enero, 1966. (Also of 30.)

Volume III, 1966
Masoliver, Juan Ramón. La Vanguardia Española (Barcelona), 22 de junio, 1967. (Also reviews 31.)
Tovar, Antonio. La Gaceta Literaria (Madrid), enero, 1968, p. 9 y 13.

King, Charles L. Hispania, 52, 1 (May, 1969), p. 161.

Volumes I-III, 1966
Cruset, José. La Vanguardia Española (Barcelona), 9 de noviembre, 1966.
Gimferrer, Pere. Destino, núm. 1916 (22 de junio, 1974), p. 50.
Salvador, Tomás. La Vanguardia Española (Barcelona), 12 de abril, 1966.

29   La aventura equinocial [sic] de Lope de Aguirre (Antiepopeya). New York: Las Américas, 1964, 362 p. As La aventura equinoccial de Lope de Aguirre; "Presentación" by Carmen Laforet, p. 7-14. Madrid: Magisterio Español, 1967, 1968, 416 p.; 1970, 403 p. (Col. Novelas y Cuentos, 1-2, sección literatura).

An historical novel of the deeds of Lope de Aguirre, "the Traitor," who rebelled against King Philip II of Spain during the Spanish expedition down the Amazon river in the sixteenth century. Background for the "adventure" is the luxuriant Amazonian region.

Allen, Richard F. Boletín Cultural y Bibliográfico, 9, 1 (1966), p. 130-32.
Cano, Lamberto A. Revista Hispánica Moderna, 33, 1-2 (enero-abril, 1967), p. 140.
Díaz-Plaja, Guillermo. ABC (Madrid), 2 de noviembre, 1967.

González-Arauzo, A.   Revista Iberoamericano, 33, 63 (enero-
        junio, 1967), p. 156-60.
Marra-López, José R.   Insula, núm. 220 (marzo, 1965), p.
        10.
Peñuelas, Marcelino C.   Revista de Estudios Hispánicos, 2,
        1 (abril, 1968), p. 143-46.
Placer, Eloy L.   Boletín del Instituto Americano de Estudios
        Vascos, 19, 75 (1968).
Sainz de Robles, F. C.   La Estafeta Literaria, núm. 383
        (18 de noviembre, 1967), p. 27.

Triunfo (Madrid), 16 de septiembre, 1967.

Allen, Richard F.   Books Abroad, 40, 2 (Spring 1966),
        p. 196.
        .   Américas (Pan American Union), 18, 3 (March,
        1966), p. 38.

Choice, 4 (March, 1967), p. 45.

30   El bandido adolescente. Barcelona: Destino, 1965,
        1969, 249 p. (Col. Ancora y Delfín, 267). Prólogo de
        Rafael Vázquez Zamora. Barcelona: Salvat Editores,
        1970, 1971, 1972, 183 p. (Biblioteca Básica Salvat de
        Libros RTV, 77); 1973, 256 p.

        A biographical novel of Billy the Kid, the notorious
bandit during the 1870's in the New Mexico Territory.   An
original interpretation of the well-known outlaw although S.
has depended on The Authentic Life of Billy, the Kid, first
published in 1882 by Pat Garrett, the sheriff who killed the
"Kid," for the factual basis for his account.   The "Kid" is
seen as a strange kind of poet, saint, and hero--the three
kinds of men which especially interest the author.

Acosta Montoro, José.   El Diario Vasco, 21 de diciembre,
        1967.
Alvarez, Carlos Luis.   Blanco y Negro, 27 de noviembre,
        1967.
Castroviejo, Concha.   Informaciones (Madrid), 27 de no-
        viembre, 1965, p. 19.
Del Río Sanz, José.   Córdoba (Córdoba), 21 de noviembre,
        1965, p. 8.
Delgado, Feliciano.   Reseña de Literatura, Arte y Espectá-
        culos, 3, 12 (abril, 1966), p. 114-15.
Fernández Almagro, Melchor.   ABC (Madrid), 23 de dici-

Books

23

embre, 1965, p. 49.

Lacalle, Angel. Las Provincias (Valencia), 19 de diciembre, 1965.

Marco, Joaquim. Destino, núm. 1526 (11 de mayo, 1966).

Masoliver, Juan Ramón. La Vanguardia Española (Barcelona), 6 de enero, 1966 (also of 28).

Ponce de León, Luis. La Estafeta Literaria, núm. 344 (21 de mayo, 1966), p. 15-16.

Roig, J. A. Razón y Fe, 175, 824-25 (septiembre-octubre, 1966), 276-77.

Valencia, A. Arriba (Madrid), 21 de noviembre, 1965.

ABC (Sevilla), 30 de diciembre, 1965.
La Codorniz (Madrid), 16 de enero, 1966 (by Ulises).
Heraldo de Aragón (Zaragoza), 20 de noviembre, 1965.
El Noticiero de Cartagena, 25 de febrero, 1966 (by J. R. C.).
El Noticiero Universal (Barcelona), 4 de enero y 15 de febrero, 1966.
La Nueva España (Oviedo), 29 de enero, 1966.
La Prensa (Barcelona), 25 de febrero, 1966.
S. P. (Madrid), 2 de enero, 1966.

King, Charles L. Hispania, 50, 2 (May, 1967), p. 389.

31   Tres novelas teresianas. Barcelona: Destino, 1967, 216 p. (Col. Ancora y Delfín, 285).

The three "novelas" or novelettes, so related as essentially to form a single novel, are "La puerta grande," followed by "La princesa bisoja" and "En la misa de Fray Hernando." Theresa's development or evolution is closely interwoven with the socio-political events and atmosphere of her time. Integrated into the first part, "La puerta grande," is an allegorical play (auto sacramental) that appears here for the first time in Spanish. (It was published in English as "The House of Lot," in the New Mexico Quarterly, 20, 1 [Spring 1950], p. 27-40; see 127.)

Acosta Montoro, José. El Diario Vasco (San Sebastián), 16 de julio, 1967.

Aguado, Emiliano. La Estafeta Literaria, núm. 373 (1 de julio, 1967), p. 25.

Alvarez, Carlos Luis. Blanco y Negro, 20 de mayo, 1967, p. 118.

Amorós, Andrés. El Libro Español, 10 (1967), p. 721.

Cerezales, Manuel. La Actualidad Española (Madrid), 20

de febrero, 1968, p. 55.
Conte, Rafael. Informaciones (Madrid), 6 de mayo, 1967,
      p. 21.
Del Río Sanz, José. Córdoba (Córdoba), 14 de junio, 1967.
Ferreres, Rafael. Levante (Valencia), 27 de agosto, 1967.
Martín Abril, José Luis. Diario Regional (Valladolid), 8 de
      octubre, 1967.
Masoliver, Juan Ramón. La Vanguardia Española (Barce-
      lona), 22 de junio, 1967. (Also of 28.)
Mico Buchón, J. L. Reseña de Literatura, Arte y Espectá-
      culos, núm. 19 (octubre, 1967), p. 269-70.
Rivas, Josefa. Insula, núm. 260-61 (julio-agosto, 1968),
      p. 16.
_____. Hispanófila, 12, 35 (enero, 1969), p. 65-67.
Tovar, Antonio. La Gaceta Ilustrada (Madrid), 2 de julio,
      1967.
Valencia, Antonio. Arriba (Madrid), 9 de julio, 1967, p. 5.
Vázquez-Zamora, Rafael. España (Tánger), 21 de enero,
      1968.

Diario de Las Palmas (Gran Canaria), 22 de enero, 1968.
Heraldo de Aragón (Zaragoza), 10 de junio, 1967.
El Noticiero (Cartagena), 16 de junio, 1967.
Razón y Fe, 177, 842 (marzo, 1968), p. 329.   (By M.B.)
S.P. (Madrid), 2 de julio, 1967.
Vida Nueva (Madrid-Barcelona), 5 de agosto, 1967.   (By
      M.C.H.)
Ya (Madrid), 14 de octubre, 1967.   (By N.G.R.)

Clements, R. J. Saturday Review, 50, 1 (July, 1967),
      p. 19.
King, Charles L. Books Abroad, 42, 1 (Winter 1968),
      p. 85-86.

Times [London] Literary Supplement, August 3, 1967, p. 712.

32   Las criaturas saturnianas. Barcelona: Destino, 1968,
      412 p. (Col. Ancora y Delfín, 300).

      An historical novel which relates the suffering and
wandering of Princess Tarakanova, niece of Catherine the
Great of Russia, late in the eighteenth century--from Italy
as an adolescent to St. Petersburg (and imprisonment there)
and back to Italy by way of Northern Spain. For much of
her journey back to Italy as a mature woman she is accompanied by Cagliostro, a fraudulent count, an adventurer

and practitioner of the occult.   An earlier novel, <u>Emen hetan</u>
(21), is incorporated into this new work.

Alperi, Víctor.   <u>Región</u> (Oviedo), 1 de septiembre, 1968.
Castaño, A.   <u>Reseña de Literatura, Arte y Espectáculos</u>,
     núm. 27 (abril, 1969), p. 113-15.
Castillo, Othón.   <u>El Sol del Norte</u> (Saltillo, Coahuila, Méxi-
     co), 4 de noviembre, 1968, p. 2-B; <u>La Estrella de</u>
     <u>Panamá</u> (Panamá, República de Panamá), 23 de octu-
     bre, 1968, p. 2; <u>El Diario de Hoy</u> (San Salvador, El
     Salvador), 27 de octubre, 1968, p. 12; <u>El Sol del</u>
     <u>Bajío</u> (Celaya, Guanajuato, México), 31 de octubre,
     1968, p. 2.   (The reviews here by Castillo are his
     syndicated column, "Libros e Ideas," and are identi-
     cal.)
Clemente, José Carlos.   <u>La Actualidad Española</u> (Madrid),
     año 17, 872 (19 de septiembre, 1966).
Doltra, Esteban.   <u>Hoja del lunes</u> (Barcelona), 14 de octubre,
     1968.
Domingo, José.   <u>Insula</u>, núm. 266 (enero, 1969), p. 5.
     (Also reviews 33.)
Gutiérrez, Fernando.   <u>La Prensa</u> (Barcelona), 8 de octubre,
     1968.
Marco, Joaquim.   <u>Destino</u>, 24 de agosto, 1968.
Marsa, Angel.   <u>El Correo Catalán</u> (Barcelona), 10 de julio,
     1968.
Tovar, Antonio.   <u>La Gaceta Ilustrada</u> (Madrid), 15 de
     septiembre, 1968.
Valencia, Antonio.   <u>Arriba</u> (Madrid), 25 de agosto, 1968,
     p. 3.

<u>Diario de Barcelona</u>, 3 de agosto, 1968.
<u>Diario de Navarra</u> (Pamploma), 8 de septiembre, 1968.
<u>El Diario Vasco</u> (San Sebastián), 19 de enero, 1969.
<u>El Noticiero</u> (Cartagena), 23 de septiembre, 1968, p. 5.
     (By J. R. C.)
<u>El Noticiero Universal</u> (Barcelona), 3 de diciembre, 1968.
<u>S P</u> (Madrid), 1 de septiembre, 1968.

King, Charles L.   <u>Hispania</u>, 52, 2 (May, 1969), p. 161.
Lord, David.   <u>Books Abroad</u>, 43, 2 (Spring, 1969), p. 234.

<u>Times</u> [London] <u>Literary Supplement</u>, November 7, 1968,
     p. 1257.

33   <u>Nocturno de los 14</u>.   New York: Iberama Publishing
      Co. , 1969, 243 p. ; Barcelona: Destino, 1970, 300 p.

(Col. Ancora y Delfín, 350).

One stormy night while alone in the house of a strange
widow, Mumú, the author-narrator is visited by fourteen suicide victims, former friends or acquaintances of the narrator. Together they ponder their difficulties, the problems of
exile, the sense and the senselessness of life, and speculate
on possible explanations for the mysterious suicide of Char-
lie, Mumú's former husband, three years earlier.

Alperi, Víctor. Región (Oviedo), 2 de mayo, 1971.
Domingo, José. Insula, núm. 266 (enero, 1966), p. 5.
    (Also reviews 32.)
Horno Liria, Luis. Heraldo de Aragón (Zaragoza), 11 de
    abril, 1971.
Lacalle, Angel. Las Provincias (Valencia), 28 de febrero,
    1971, p. 43.
Mainer, José-Carlos. Insula, núm. 481 (1 de diciembre,
    1970), p. 8.
Marsa, Angel. El Correo Catalán (Barcelona), 7 de marzo,
    1971.
Martín Abril, José L. Diario Regional (Valladolid), 26 de
    marzo, 1972.
Mendiola, José M. El Diario Vasco (San Sebastián), 30 de
    mayo, 1971.
Murciano, Carlos. La Estafeta Literaria (Estafeta libros,
    suplemento bibliográfico), núm. 481 (1 de diciembre,
    1971), p. 774.
Pujol Galindo, Félix. La Vanguardia Española (Barcelona),
    17 de abril, 1972.
Tovar, Antonio. La Gaceta Ilustrada, 1 de agosto, 1971,
    p. 8.
Vázquez-Zamora, Rafael. Destino, 19 de junio, 1971.

ABC (Madrid), 27 de marzo, 1971.
Diario de Barcelona, 22 de mayo, 1971. (By S. C.)
La Vanguardia Española (Barcelona), 25 de marzo, 1971.

Olstad, Charles. Books Abroad, 46, 1 (Winter 1972), p. 85.

34   En la vida de Ignacio Morel. Barcelona: Planeta,
     1969, 261 p. (Col. Autores Españoles e Hispanoameri-
     canos, 236).

     Winner of the Planeta Prize for 1969 (1,100,000 pese-
tas). Fifty-five thousand copies of the first edition were

published.

There are strange repercussions when Madame Saint-
Julien expires (probably from a heart attack) while making
illicit love to Ignacio Morel, a Spaniard teaching in a lycée
in the Parisian suburb of Argenteuil, in a downtown hotel in
Paris. Characterization of Ignacio (the author) is drawn with
a masterly hand and is the source of keen humor. Poetic
philosophizing meshes well with the narrative elements, lend-
ing a lyrical dimension at times. Each of the first seven
chapters relates one day in Ignacio's life; the final two chapters deal with the aftermath of Madame Saint-Julien's death.

Díaz-Plaja, Guillermo. ABC (Madrid), 22 de enero, 1970,
    p. 105.
Iglesias Laguna, Antonio. La Estafeta Literaria, núm. 439
    (1 de marzo, 1970), p. 273.
Zumarriego, Tomás. Reseña de Literatura, Arte y Espectá-
    culos, núm. 34 (abril, 1970), p. 210-11.

Alvarez, Elsa. Sagitario (Western Michigan University), 1,
    2 (February, 1971), p. 35-36.
King, Charles L. Books Abroad, 44, 3 (Summer 1970),
    p. 446-47.

35   Tánit. Barcelona: Tánit, 1970, 327 p.

While awaiting orders to embark on a secret and dangerous mission to assassinate Sagittarius, the hated dictator
of an unnamed island, Enrique, the protagonist-narrator,
meets and falls in love with Thanit, a 23-year old beauty,
who comes in the story to symbolize the ancient goddess
whose name she bears. Their wedding reception, held in a
New York apartment, and attended by such notables as the
poets Wallace Stevens and Carl Sandburg, becomes the occasion for conversations (and musings by Enrique) and ac-
counts for the bulk of the book, pages 99 to the end (323).
On page 322 Enrique gets notice that his mission has been
canceled.

Domingo, José. Insula, núm. 291 (febrero, 1971), p. 5.
Peñuelas, Marcelino C. Cuadernos Americanos, año 31,
    180, 1 (enero-febrero, 1972), p. 219-24.

Garbo, 18, 922 (4 de noviembre, 1970).

36   Zu, el ángel anfibio.   Barcelona: Planeta, 1970, 231 p.

Zu, a blue whale, rebels against the myths of whale-
dom, and begins an odyssey in search of truth and beauty
after his young bride, Zetania, dies when trapped beneath a
cross-Atlantic cable. In the end he is killed by whalers.
Zu's story is told by an omniscient author in the third person. An imaginative work with some lyrical force, it is not
one of Sender's better novels.

Iglesias Laguna, A. La Estafeta Literaria, núm. 464 (15
    de marzo, 1971), p. 497-99.

King, Charles L. Books Abroad, 46, 1 (Winter 1972),
    p. 85.

Booklist, 68 (February 1, 1972), p. 453.

37   La antesala. Barcelona: Destino, 1971, 244 p. (Col.
      Ancora y Delfín, 377).

While Nazaria, a 48-year old teacher of defective
children who hides her baldness with a wig, waits one after-
noon in the outer hall to see the military commander of her
district in Madrid during the final days of the Civil War,
she reviews in memory her impoverished life. Her memories create a second plane of action to the primary one of
waiting in the antechamber. In the end, unsuccessful in her
efforts to see the Commander, she wanders out into the
street to be killed by machine gun fire--the door (death) into the inner chamber had finally opened for her.

Alperi, Víctor. Región (Oviedo), 2 de febrero, 1972.
Doltra, Esteban. Hoja del Lunes (Barcelona), 28 de febrero,
    1972.
Domingo, José. Insula, núm. 304 (marzo, 1972), p. 5.
Horno Liria, Luis. Heraldo de Aragón (Zaragoza), 12 de
    enero, 1972.
Lacalle, Angel. Las Provincias (Valencia), 19 de diciembre,
    1971, p. 49.
Murciano, Carlos. La Estafeta Literaria (Estafeta libros,
    suplemento bibliográfico), núm. 500 (15 de septiembre,
    1972), p. 1074.
Tovar, Antonio. La Gaceta Ilustrada, 30 de julio, 1972.
Valencia, Antonio. Arriba (Madrid), 15 de enero, 1972.
Vázquez Zamora, Rafael. Destino, núm. 1804 (29 de abril,

1972).

Peden, Margaret. Hispania, 57, 3 (September, 1974),
    p. 602-03.

Diario de Barcelona, 22 de julio, 1972.
Diario de Cádiz, 30 de abril, 1972.
La Vanguardia Española (Barcelona), 10 de enero, 1972.

38   El fugitivo. Barcelona: Planeta, 1972, 190 p. (Bibli-
      oteca Universal Planeta, 5).

Joaquín, the narrator-protagonist, a "fugitive" for no
explicit reason in the uncertain early days of the Spanish
Civil War, hides in the clock-tower of his native Aragonese
village church. While there he muses and meditates on life
and its enigmas in typical Senderian fashion (throughout most
of the book) until he is discovered and sentenced to be
hanged. As the story ends, he is under psychiatric care
and awaiting an undetermined future.

Abreu, F. de. Reseña de Literatura, Arte y Espectáculos,
    núm. 63 (marzo, 1973), p. 18.
Carandell, J. M. Fotogramas (Barcelona), 26 de mayo,
    1972, p. 54.
Carrasquer, F. Camp de L'arpa (Barcelona), núm. 3
    (septiembre, 1972), p. 21-22.
Hornia Liria, Luis. Heraldo de Aragón (Zaragoza), 25 de
    mayo, 1972.
Rivas, Josefa. Insula, núm. 318 (mayo, 1973), p. 8.

El Día (Santa Cruz de Tenerife), 17 de agosto, 1972.
Proa (León), 27 de abril, 1972.
Las Provincias (Valencia), 27 de octubre, 1972.   (By L. B.
    J.)
Triunfo (Madrid), 6 de mayo, 1972.   (E. H. T.)
La Verdad (Murcia), 7 de mayo, 1972.   (A. C.)

Olstad, Charles. Books Abroad, 47, 4 (Autumn 1973),
    p. 732-33.

Booklist, 69 (February 1, 1973), p. 513.

39   Túpac Amaru. Barcelona: Destino, 1973, 202 p.
      (Col. Ancora y Delfín, 414).

An historical novel relating the uprising of the "last
Inca," José Gabriel Túpac Amaru, "inca por la gracia de
Dios, rey del Perú, de Santa Fe, Quito, Chile, Buenos
Aires y continentes de los mares del Sur," in 1780 against
the Spanish colonial rulers who were, according to the Rebel, thwarting the wishes of the Spanish Throne. A mixture
or fusion of documentary evidence and imagination, the book
reveals the author's lifelong and passionate interest in social
justice.

Alperi, Víctor. Región (Oviedo), 12 de agosto, 1973.
Gómez López-Egea, Rafael. Arbor (Madrid), 88, 342 (1973),
    p. 150-51.
Lacalle, Angel. Las Provincias (Valencia), 2 de septiembre,
    1973, p. 49.
Mendicutti, Eduardo. La Estafeta Literaria, núm. 538 (15
    de abril, 1974), p. 1682-83.
Salvador, Tomás. La Prensa (Barcelona), 23 de septiembre,
    1973.
Sordo, Enrique. La Estafeta Literaria, núm. 527 (1 de
    noviembre, 1973), p. 1508. (Also reviews 50.)

Blanco y Negro, núm. 3218 (5 de enero, 1974), p. 74.   (By
    L. E.)
El Diario Vasco (San Sebastián), 7 de octubre, 1973.
Hierro (Bilbao), 9 de agosto, 1973.
La Vanguardia Española (Barcelona), 16 de agosto, 1973.

Espadas, Elizabeth. Journal of Spanish Studies: Twentieth
    Century, 2, 3 (Winter 1974), p. 204-05.
King, Charles L. Books Abroad, 48, 2 (Spring 1974),
    p. 340-41.

40   Una virgen llama a tu puerta. Barcelona: Destino,
    1973, 217 p. (Col. Ancora y Delfín, 433).

A work of great imaginative-lyrical force in which the
narrator, a retired sixty-two-year-old professor of nuclear
physics, is led--through his interest in Sandra, a twelve-
year-old girl (and virgin), to discover a secret circle of
men--mostly scientists--who are plotting the overthrow of
all national governments in favor of a single, all-powerful
but benevolent world government. The action occurs during
three days and three nights--with a kind of epilogue on the
morning of the fourth when the narrator-participant is briefly reunited with Sandra (symbol of youth, hope)--and apparently, though not explicitly, is laid in California.

From a plane of realism the novel subtly shifts its
ground to include the phantasmagorical, the symbolic, and
abstract metaphysical-lyrical levels.

Horno Liria, Luis.   Heraldo de Aragón (Zaragoza), 29 de
    marzo, 1974.
Lacalle, Angel.   Las Provincias (Valencia), 9 de junio, 1974.
Pombo, A. F.   Ya (Madrid), 25 de abril, 1974.
Sánchez-Ocaña, Esteban.   Región (Oviedo), 26 de marzo,
    1974.

La Vanguardia Española (Barcelona), 28 de febrero, 1974.

Johnson, Roberta.   Books Abroad, 48, 4 (Autumn 1974),
    p. 746.

41   Nancy, doctora en gitanería.   Presentación (por los
        editores), p. 9-17.   Madrid: Magisterio Español,
        1974, 288 p. (Col. Novelas y Cuentos, 144).

        A sequel to La tesis de Nancy (24).   In a university in
California, professors Sender and Blacksen, members of
Nancy's doctoral thesis committee, read, discuss, and finally approve her study of gypsy lore--not, however, without many digressions of a poetic-philosophical nature along
the usual Senderian lines.   The trilogy is completed with
Nancy, y el Bato loco (43).

42   La mesa de las tres moiras.   Barcelona: Planeta,
        1974, 225 p. (Col. Autores Españoles e Hispanoameri-
        canos).

        In one long chapter ("Capítulo cero") Jack, a retired
commercial pilot and citizen of the United States, listens,
and occasionally gets a word in "edgewise," to an extended
monologue by Mitchell, a schizophrenic war veteran, as he
expounds upon his strange adventures and the absurd world
in which we live today.   Hitler, Stalin, the sombre and perhaps apocalyptic future of mankind (dominated by technology),
and other ponderous themes, including the author's unortho-
dox religious views--all balanced by a kind of grim humor--
constitute the substance of the "monologue," and the novel.

43   Nancy, y el Bato loco.   Madrid: Magisterio Español,
        1974, 239 p.

The last member of the "Nancy" trilogy, of which the first two were La tesis de Nancy (24) and Nancy, doctora en gitanería (41), this volume relates, in letters Nancy sends to Professor Sender (the most influential member of her doctoral committee), the experiences of the young American woman while on a visit to the Balearic Islands and a return visit to Andalusia, this time with her recently acquired husband, a wealthy and bizarre but exceptionally cultured thirty-year old American, Laury, known to the Gypsies as the "Bato loco," or the "crazy Powerful One." Conversations between Laury and an old Spanish Duke in Seville, Nancy's own reflections and impressions, notes from Laury's secret notebook, etc., all allow for commentary, not without humor, upon familiar Senderian themes: Atlantis, love, death, mystery, religion, cultural differences between Americans and Europeans, etc.

44   Cronus y la señora con rabo. Madrid: AKAL, 1974, 147 p. (Col. Manifiesto. Serie: Narrativa, 4).

Cronus (in Latin, Saturno), obviously the author's alter ego, here identified as a middle-aged doctor and anthropologist--well-known in professional circles--returns to Recife, Brazil (after an absence of forty years), to read a paper at a scientific conference. On the plane enroute he becomes friendly with one of the stewardesses, Susan, with whom he has some unusual conversations both in the air and later in Recife. Written as one long chapter the book is replete with familiar Senderian themes: Atlantis (Cronus "se consideraba más o menos en broma descendiente de los atlantes"), the mysterious "chakras" ("centros de consciencia"), the role of quixotic illusion in life, etc.

B.   SHORT STORIES

45   Mexicayotl. México: Quetzal, 1940, 255 p.

A collection of nine stories united by the common theme expressed by the title, Mexicayotl, which is Nahuatl for "song of Mexico." Together they constitute, writes S., "la definición de la naturaleza virgen mexicana tal como yo la siento." The stories are: "Tototl o el valle," "El puma," "El águila," "Los peces," "Xocoyotl o el desierto," "Nanyotl o la montaña," "Ecatl o el lago," "El zopilote," and "Navatl o el volcán." The last five, shortened and re-cast, appeared later in Novelas ejemplares de Cíbola (47).

Iduarte, Andrés.   Revista Hispánica Moderna, 8, 3 (julio, 1942), p. 225-26.   (Also reviews 9 and 52.)

Lord, David.   Books Abroad, 16, 2 (Spring 1942), p. 200.

46   La llave.   Montevideo: Alfa, 1960, 137 p. (Col. Cara-bela, 1); New York: Las Americas, 1963, 108 p.   As La llave y otras narraciones and with a 4-page "Pre-sentación" by an anonymous writer.   Madrid: Magi-sterio Español, 1967, 225 p. (Col. Novelas y Cuentos, 14).

The first two editions (Montevideo and New York) in-clude two stories, "La hija del doctor Velasco," and "La fotografía del aniversario," in addition to the lead-story, "La llave."   In the Madrid edition two stories, "El pelagatos y la flor de la nieve," and "Mary-Lou," are added to the three found in the first two editions.   "La llave" first appeared in print in English as "The Key," in 1943 in The Kenyon Re-view (100).   "La fotografía" was published earlier in Cua-dernos Americanos (109) and in Deslinde (113).   In "La llave," Fau, an idiot, thinking that his unconscious father, Avelino, is dead, rips open his stomach in search of a key needed to open a recently discovered treasure chest, while Rosenda, Avelino's mistress who possesses the coveted key, knowingly stands by.   Except for "Mary-Lou" the remaining stories in the collection have a similar grotesque and night-marish atmosphere.

Aguado, Emiliano,   La Estafeta Literaria, núm. 390 (2 de febrero, 1969), p. 30-31.
Barce, R.   Indice de Artes y Letras (Madrid), núm. 148 (mayo, 1961), p. 24.
Lamana, M.   Cuadernos (París), 46 (enero-febrero, 1961), p. 116.
Schraibman, J.   Revista Hispánica Moderna, 32, 1-2 (enero-abril, 1966), p. 106-07.

Meridiano (Madrid), núm. 302 (1968), p. 127.

Schwartz, Kessel.   Hispania, 48, 1 (March, 1965), p. 180-81.

47   Novelas ejemplares de Cíbola.   New York: Las Améri-
      cas, 1961, 322 p. ; Santa Cruz de Tenerife (Canarias):
      Romerman Ediciones, 1967, 417 p. (Col. Flor de Ro-
      mero, 3).

      Tales of Cibola; tr. by Florence Sender, Elinor Ran-
      dall, Morse Manley, and the staff of Las Américas
      Publishing Co. New York: Las Américas, 1964, 383
      p. (changes from Novelas are noted below).

      The common denominator of these "novelas" (stories)
      is that they are all set in the American Southwest (Cibola) or
      in Mexico, and that they reflect the local color and flavor of
      this area. The Spanish edition (Novelas ejemplares) contains
      twelve stories: "La madurez del profesor St. John," "El
      cetro," "El padre Zozobra," "El lago," "La terraza," "El
      buitre," "Aventura en Bethania," "El desierto," "Delgadina,"
      "La montaña," "Los invitados del desierto," and "El caria-
      marillo." Five of the stories ("El cetro," "El lago," "El
      buitre," "El desierto" and "El cariamarillo") formerly ap-
      peared in Mexicayotl (45), although they were recast for this
      new book. Tales of Cibola contains only seven stories from
      Novelas ejemplares (omitting "El cetro," "El lago," "La
      montaña," "El desierto," and "El cariamarillo") and adds
      two stories: "The Tonatiu" (see 48 and 50), appearing for
      the first time in print here, and "The Red Light," published
      previously in the Southwest Review (118, see also 50 ["La
      luz roja"]).

Novelas ejemplares de Cíbola
Tovar, Antonio. La Gaceta Ilustrada, núm. 366 (12 de
      octubre, 1963), p. 43.
Vilar, Sergio. Destino, núm. 1437 (20 de febrero, 1965),
      p. 36.
      .   Papeles de Son Armadans, 31, 93 (1963), p. 330-
      32.

Adam, Carole. Hispania, 46, 1 (March, 1963), p. 164-65.
Duncan, Bernice G. Books Abroad, 39, 2 (Spring 1965),
      p. 227.
Lacayo, H. Hispanic American Historical Review, 43, 3
      (August, 1963), p. 460.
Myers, Oliver T. Nation, 202 (January 17, 1966), p. 75-
      76.
Olstad, Charles. Hispania, 48, 4 (December, 1965), p. 940.
Thorne, M. Library Journal, 89, 22 (December 15, 1965),
      p. 4933.

Booklist, 61 (May 1, 1965), p. 862.
Choice, 2 (March, 1965), p. 26.

48   Cabrerizas Atlas.   México: Mexicanos Unidos, 1965,
      176 p.

Three stories, "Cabrerizas Atlas," "El tonatiu," and
"Las rosas de Pasadena," all published here for the first
time except for the second, which appeared in English-trans-
lation in Tales of Cibola (47).   In "Cabrerizas" (86 pages in
the book) Alfonso, a Spanish corporal in a disciplinary bat-
talion in Melilla during the Moroccan campaign, narrates his
unfortunate love affair with a tavern waitress.   "El tonatiu"
is based on the Mexican legend that Tonatiu, the sun god,
descends to earth to walk disguised among men on cloudy
days.   "Las rosas de Pasadena" tells of strange incidents
that occur when the criminal, Caryl Chessman, and other inmates of death row in San Quentin prison watch the Pasadena
Rose Parade on television.   This last story as well as "El
tonatiu" (under a new title, "El extraño señor Photynos")
are included in the collection, El extraño señor Photynos y
otras novelas americanas (50).

Mainer, José-Carlos.   Insula, núm. 240 (noviembre, 1966),
      p. 8.

Clements, R. J.   Saturday Review, 50 (February 4, 1967),
      p. 38.
King, Charles L.   Hispania, 51, 2 (May, 1968), p. 367-68.

49   Las gallinas de Cervantes y otras narraciones parabó-
      licas.   México: Mexicanos Unidos, 1967, 180 p. (Col.
      Comunidad Ibérica).

In addition to the lead story, "Las gallinas de Cervantes," the volume contains "El sosia y los delegados" (119)
"Parábola de Jesús y el inquisidor" and "Aventura del Ange-
lus I."   In "Las gallinas de Cervantes" the wife of the great
author undergoes a grotesque and surrealistic transformation
into a hen-woman, in scenes reminiscent of Franz Kafka.
"El sosia" relates what Sender imagines would happen were
Stalin's double, posing as the former dictator, to appear at
a Soviet Congress.   "Parábola," an adaptation of Dostoyevsky's The Brothers Karamazov, appeared earlier in the
journal Política (see 120).   In the last the narrator-protago-

nist visits Mars and Jupiter and comments on the human condition. All four stories in this collection appear later in Novelas del otro jueves (51). They are reviewed in an article by Josefa Rivas (1265).

King, Charles L.   Books Abroad, 52, 2 (Spring 1968),
    p. 245.

50   El extraño señor Photynos y otras novelas americanas.
      Barcelona: Delos-Aymá, 1968, 273 p.; Barcelona:
      Destino, 1973, 279 p. (Col. Ancora y Delfín, 409).

      Contains five stories: "El extraño señor Photynos"
      ("The tonatiu," see 48), "Los Tontos de la Concepción" (26),
      "El amigo que compró un Picasso," "La luz roja" (47,118),
      and "Las rosas de Pasadena" (48). The only previously un-
      published story in this collection is "El amigo que compró
      un Picasso," in which the author-narrator, inspired by a
      Picasso painting at a dinner party one evening, narrates to
      his hosts the story of his strange love affair with a beauti-
      ful and elusive Spanish woman.

Gimferrer, Pere.   Destino, 29 de septiembre, 1973, p. 26-
    27.
Sordo, Enrique.   La Estafeta Literaria, núm. 527 (1 de no-
    viembre, 1973), p. 1508. (Also reviews 39.)

El Diario Vasco (San Sebastián), 4 de noviembre, 1973.
La Gaceta Ilustrada (Madrid), 2 de diciembre, 1973.
Heraldo de Aragón (Zaragoza), 4 de octubre, 1973.

51   Novelas del otro jueves. México: M. Aguilar, 1969,
      347 p. (Col. Novela Nueva).

      The four stories in Las gallinas de Cervantes y otras
      narraciones parabólicas (49) are reprinted here along with
      three previously unpublished stories: "El regreso de Edel-
      miro," "El urucurú," and "El viaducto." Edelmiro suffers
      humiliation and outrage when he returns to his native Span-
      ish village after an absence of twenty-one years in America.
      "El urucurú" is an allegorical tale set on an island in a
      Venezuelan lake during the time of the German naturalist,
      Humboldt. The action of "El viaducto" occurs at a viaduct
      in Madrid during the Spanish Civil War.

C.   DRAMA

52   <u>Hernán Cortés</u>.   México: Quetzal,   1940,   168 p.

A dramatic re-enactment of history in eleven scenes in which, beginning in Cuba with preparations for the expedition to Mexico and ending in Mexico City a year after its conquest, Hernán Cortés is seen "as a very complex character, religious, Machiavellian, idealistic, arrogant," according to James O. Swain. Realistic and fantastic planes intersect. Theater to be read more than to be staged.

Iduarte, Andrés.   <u>Revista Hispánica Moderna</u>, 8, 3 (julio, 1942), p. 225-26 (also reviews 9 and 45).

Swain, James O.   <u>Books Abroad</u>, 15, 1 (Winter 1941), p. 74.

53   <u>El diantre</u> (Tragicomedia para el cine según un cuento de Andreiev). México: Ediciones de Andrea, 1958, 131 p. (Col. Los Presentes, 65). As "Comedia del diantre" in book entitled <u>Comedia del diantre y otras dos</u>, and with a one- or two-page introduction by S. to each of the three plays. Barcelona: Destino, 1969, 268 p. (Col. Ancora y Delfín, 330).

When the millionaire Charles Reinhardt dies, the Devil inhabits his body and uses it to debate with Logus, a scientist who is "diabolically" seeking the secret formula needed to destroy the Universe. For the second edition Sender changed the title, reduced the number of acts from seven to six, and made other minor changes.

Two additional "comedias" are included in the edition by Destino: "Los antofagastas (Misterio en tres actos)" and "Donde crece la marihuana [sic] (Drama en cuatro actos)." The second of these had earlier appeared in <u>La Estafeta Literaria</u> (130), and was later published separately (56).

<u>El diantre</u>
      Bleznick, Donald W.   <u>Hispanoamericano</u> (México), 34, 863 (17 de noviembre, 1958), p. 46.
      González, Emilio.   <u>Revista Hispánica Moderna</u>, 26, 3-4 (julio-octubre, 1960), p. 157.

<u>Comedia del diantre y otras dos</u>
      Mendiola, José M.   <u>El Diario Vasco</u> (San Sebastián), 15

de marzo, 1970.

ABC (Madrid), 6 de mayo, 1970.
Blanco y Negro, núm. 3029 (23 de mayo, 1970), p. 102.
Diario de Barcelona, 21 de marzo, 1970. (By S. C.)
Hispanoamericano (México), 34, 863 (17 de noviembre, 1958),
    p. 46.
Las Provincias (Valencia), 3 de mayo, 1970. (By L. B.)
La Vanguardia Española (Barcelona), 19 de febrero, 1970,
    p. 48.

Lord, David. Books Abroad, 45, 3 (Summer 1971), p. 491.

54   Jubileo en el Zócalo (Retablo conmemorativo). Text-
      book edition by Florence Hall with a "Preface" (in
      English), "Nota preliminar del autor," "Notas," "Ejerci-
      cios," and "Vocabulario. " New York: Appleton-Cen-
      tury-Crofts, 1964, v-vi + 215 p. Definitive edition.
      Barcelona: Delos-Aymá, 1967, 240 p. (Nueva Colec-
      ción Aymá, 1). "Nota preliminar del autor" and "Notas. "
      Barcelona: Destino, 1974, 227 p. (Col. Ancora y Del-
      fín, 420).

For the definitive edition (those of 1967 and 1974) the
author added two short chapters and made other slight modifications. The setting for the "retablo conmemorativo" is
the Zócalo in Mexico City in 1536 after the Spanish conquest of
Mexico. Among those present to view the "retablo" are
Cortés, Pedro de Alvarado, Father Bartolomé, and the common soldier, Bernal Díaz del Castillo. To the bibliographer's knowledge, the work has never been staged.

Bradford, Carole A. Hispania, 48, 1 (March, 1965), p. 203-
    04.
Tatum, Terrell. Books Abroad, 39, 1 (Winter 1965), p. 73.

55   Don Juan en la mancebía (Drama litúrgico en cuatro
      actos). México: Mexicanos Unidos, 1968, 128 p.
      With no sub-title and with a 26-page preface, "Consi-
      deraciones sobre Don Juan, " by the author. Barcelona:
      Destino, 1972, 173 p. (Col. Ancora y Delfín, 399).

An aging Don Juan (seventy) discovers one night in a
brothel in Seville that an attractive 24-year-old prostitute is
his daughter--conceived by Doña Inés on the night of her

violation by the notorious libertine. Later that evening on a
visit to the cemetery Don Juan is killed by an unknown enemy, perhaps out of jealousy by his rival, Miguel de Mañara.
From beyond death, Don Juan observes what is occurring in
life, makes comments, and thus continues to act in the play.

Gimferrer, Pere. Destino, núm. 1822 (2 de septiembre,
    1972), p. 32-33.
Mendiola, José M. El Diario Vasco (San Sebastián), 17 de
    septiembre, 1972.
Salvat, Ricard. Tele eXprés (Barcelona), 26 de septiembre,
    1972.

Hoja del lunes (Barcelona), 12 de septiembre, 1972.
La Vanguardia Española (Barcelona), 27 de julio, 1972.

Williamsen, Vern G. Books Abroad, 47, 2 (Spring, 1973),
    p. 334.

56   Donde crece la marihuana [sic]. Madrid: Escelicer,
      1973, 88 p.

    A comedy in four acts. Don Luis, an Arizona ranch-
er, tests the love of his wife for him in much the same
way as did the "curioso impertinente" in the story inter-
calated in Don Quijote. The color and flavor of the Southwest lend atmosphere to the play. In the end Don Luis
learns the impossibility of his absolute demands. The play
had formerly appeared in La Estafeta Literaria (130), and
in Comedia del diantre y otras dos (53).

D.   ESSAYS, JOURNALISM AND PERSONAL NARRATIVE

57   El problema religioso en Méjico; católicos y cristianos.
      Prólogo de Ramón del Valle-Inclán. Madrid: Cenit,
      1928, 230 p.

    Articles previously published in El Sol, the well-known
newspaper in Madrid during the 1920's, were gathered together and reprinted as S. 's first book. The young author
reveals a sound understanding of the relations between
Church and State in Mexico. S. now regards the book as
unworthy of a place in his bibliography.

58   Teatro de masas. Valencia: Orto, 1932, 117 p.

        In thirteen short chapters (some published previously
in the Madrid newspaper, La Libertad; possibly others in El
Sol), S. maintains that the current "teatro burgués" in Spain
is false and should be supplanted by a new theater that would
confront national realities and truly express "la entraña popular."

59   Casas Viejas (Episodios de la lucha de clases). Ma-
        drid: Cenit, 1933, 103 p.

        A journalistic report of the brutal repression of an up-
rising of Andalusian peasants in Casas Viejas, January 9-12,
1933, consisting of articles published separately and earlier
in La Libertad, the Madrid newspaper. This book, in addition to some new material, forms the factual basis for Sender's novel on the same incident, Viaje a la aldea del crimen
(5). S. now (1974) considers the book not significant enough
to be included in his bibliography (personal letter to Charles
King, January 23, 1974).

60   Madrid-Moscú (Narraciones de viaje). Madrid: Pueyo,
        1934, 238 p.

        S. reports simply and directly on the conditions of life
in Moscow during his stay in the Soviet Union in 1933 (June-
October) as a guest of the Unión Internacional de Escritores,
revealing himself as a critical observer of Soviet life. Most
if not all of the book's contents formerly appeared as articles in La Libertad (although titles of the articles do not
correspond to those of chapters in the book).

Somoza Silva, L. La Libertad (Madrid), núm. 4377 (1 de
        abril, 1934), p. 7-8. (Also of 5.)

Oppenheim, Sydney. Books Abroad, 8, 3 (July, 1934),
        p. 333.

61   Carta de Moscú sobre el amor (A una muchacha es-
        pañola). Madrid: Pueyo, 1934, 141 p.

        A long letter-essay that attacks the dualist concept that
attributes evil to matter and good to that which is spiritual

or immaterial. According to the author this dualism has been fostered or imposed by the Catholic Church in Spain and is responsible for the anomalies in the sexual development of many Spanish men and women. On the other hand, he argues, sexual attitudes in the Soviet Union seem to him to be much more natural, human, and healthful. Much of the substance of this book was later incorporated into the last chapter of Tres ejemplos de amor y una teoría (68).

Somoza Silva, L. La Libertad (Madrid), núm. 4395 (22 de abril, 1934), p. 8.

Archivos de Literatura Contemporánea. Índice Literario. año 3, núm. 4 (abril, 1934), p. 90-91.
La Libertad (Madrid), núm. 4385 (11 de abril, 1934), p. 3.

Putnam, Samuel. Books Abroad, 9, 4 (Autumn 1935), p. 452.

62   Proclamación de la sonrisa. Madrid: Pueyo, 1934, 223 p.

The fifty-eight short chapters of this book consist of commentary on a wide diversity of subjects--social, political, or literary. Thirty-eight chapters appeared earlier as articles in La Libertad. A key source for understanding S.'s outlook and views during the turbulent Thirties in Spain.

Somoza Silva, Lázaro. La Libertad (Madrid), núm. 4448 (24 de junio, 1934), p. 9.

Archivos de Literatura Contemporánea. Índice Literario. 3, 5 (mayo, 1934), p. 107-08.

63   Contraataque. Madrid-Barcelona: Nuestro Pueblo, 1938, 305 p.

The War in Spain, tr. by Peter Chalmers Mitchell. London: Faber and Faber, 1937, 328 p.; Counter-Attack in Spain, tr. by Peter Chalmers Mitchell. Boston: Houghton Mifflin, 1937, 288 p.

A personal narrative of Sender's experiences and impressions--with propagandistic dimensions deriving from the author's attraction to Communism--during the first six

months of the Civil War as an active combatant on the Republican side.   Towards the end of the book S. relates in
restrained tone the execution of his wife by Rebel forces in
Zamora.   Its English translations were published before the
Spanish edition appeared.

Dorta, Antonio.   Blanco y Negro, mayo, 1938, p. 7.

Adams, Mildred.   Nation, 145 (November 13, 1937), p. 536.
Bates, Ralph.   Saturday Review of Literature, 17 (November
    13, 1937), p. 10.
Carter, W. H.   Manchester Guardian, August 13, 1937,
    p. 5.
Curtis, E. R.   Boston Evening Transcript, December 11,
    1937, p. 1.
Garnett, David.   New Statesman and Nation, 14 (July 31,
    1937), p. 187.
Steer, G. L.   Spectator, 159 (August 13, 1937), p. 283.
Stowe, Leland.   New York Herald Tribune Books, November
    21, 1937, p. 2.
Swain, James O.   Books Abroad, 13, 1 (Winter 1939),
    p. 104.
Woolbert, R. G.   Foreign Affairs, 16 (January, 1938),
    p. 11.
Ybarra, T. R.   New York Times Book Review, February 6,
    1938, p. 19.

Booklist, 34 (December 15, 1937), p. 144.
Catholic World, 146 (December, 1937), p. 371.
Christian Science Monitor, December 31, 1937, p. 20.
Cleveland Open Shelf, November, 1937, p. 21.
Times [London] Literary Supplement, July 31, 1937, p. 551.

64   Unamuno, Baroja, Valle-Inclán, y Santayana (Ensayos
      críticos).   México: Andrea, 1955, 170 p. (Col. Stu-
      dium; segunda serie, 10).

      Four essays: "Unamuno, sombra fingida," "Valle-
Inclán y la dificultad de la tragedia," "Baroja y las contradicciones latentes," and "Santayana y los castellanos interiores." A valuable source of S.'s unique views as a literary critic.

Earle, Peter G.   Nueva Revista de Filología Hispánica, 10,
    3-4 (julio-diciembre, 1956), p. 445-47.
Peñuelas, Marcelino C.   Hispania, 39, 2 (May, 1956),

Books

43

p. 240-42.
Placer, Eloy L. Symposium, 11, 1 (Spring 1957), p. 163-
67.

Chase, Kathleen. Books Abroad, 31, 2 (Spring 1957), p. 151.

65 Examen de ingenios; los noventayochos (Ensayos críticos). New York: Las Américas, 1961, 326 p. Prólogo de Eduardo Naval. México: M. Aguilar, 1971,
446 p. (Col. Estudios Literarios).

In this book S. has slightly revised the chapters from
Unamuno, Baroja, Valle-Inclán y Santayana (64) on three of
its four authors, left the chapter on Valle-Inclán untouched,
and added three chapters: "Azorín, el espejo y la inútil
cautela," "Maeztu, víctima expiatoria," and "La lisis lírica
y la boca del dragón," the last being primarily a criticism
of Juan Ramón Jiménez.

Acevedo Escobedo, Antonio. El Universal, Revista de la
Semana (México), 13 de febrero, 1972.
Amorós, Andrés. Cuadernos Hispanoamericanos, 68, 199-
200 (julio-agosto, 1966), p. 550-52.
Marra-López, José R. Insula, núm. 185 (abril, 1962),
p. 8.
Valenzuela, Victor M. La Voz (New York), 5, 5 (February
1961), p. 5.

Valenzuela, Victor M. Books Abroad, 36, 1 (Winter 1962),
p. 65.

66 Valle-Inclán y la dificultad de la tragedia. Madrid:
Gredos, 1965, 150 p. (Biblioteca Románica Hispánica,
7. Campo Abierto, 16).

The chapter on Valle-Inclán in 64 and 65 above has
been trebled in length to form a book-length essay. Among
the new material in this book is a long and praiseful study
of the Galician's novel, Flor de santidad, as well as a rather detailed explanation for the absence of true tragedy in
Spanish letters today and specifically in the case of Valle-
Inclán.

Bosch, Rafael. Hispanófila, núm. 29 (enero, 1967), p. 64-
65.

44 Works by Sender

Fernández de la Mora, Gonzalo. ABC (Madrid), 8 de febrero, 1966.

King, Charles L. Revista Hispánica Moderna, 32, 3-4 (julio-octubre, 1966), p. 263-64.

Mainer, José-Carlos. Insula, núms. 236-37 (julio-agosto, 1966), p. 16.

Míguez, Alberto. El Alcázar (Madrid), 1 de enero, 1966.

Ponce, Fernando (FP). La Estafeta Literaria, núm. 339 (12 de marzo, 1966), p. 18.

Rodríguez Cepeda, E. Revista de Literatura, 28, 55-56 (julio-diciembre, 1965), p. 300-02.

——. Segismundo (Madrid), 2 (1966), p. 232-34.

Valencia, A. Arriba (Madrid), 21 de noviembre, 1965.

Allen, Richard F. Books Abroad, 40, 4 (Autumn 1966), p. 447.

——. Duquesne Hispanic Review, 6, 2 (1967), p. 45-47.

Amor y Vázquez, J. Modern Language Notes, 82, 5 (December, 1967), p. 652-655.

Brooks, J. L. Bulletin of Hispanic Studies (Liverpool), 46, 86 (January, 1969), p. 68.

King, Charles L. New Mexico Quarterly, 36, 3 (Autumn 1966), p. 294-95.

Lima, Robert. Hispania, 50, 2 (May, 1967), p. 388-89.

67   Ensayos sobre el infringimiento cristiano. México: Mexicanos Unidos, 1967, 187 p. (Col. Comunidad Ibérica).

A collection of six essays, preceded by a "Nota Bene" of three pages by the author. The six chapters are: "La cruz y las vírgenes migratorias," "Magia blanca y magia negra," "Simposium negativo y eudemonología cristiana," "El fecundo prodigio cristiano," "El eficaz infringimiento 'en la libertad,'" and "Física del infringimiento último." The book constitutes the best source for Sender's religious viewpoint. Much of the substance of chapter 1 had previously been published in an article, "La migratoria cruz" (Cuadernos [Paris], núm. 68, enero de 1963, p. 14-25; see 440). Ensayos has aroused little critical attention. No reviews in the United States, at least, have been found.

Gordón, Sigfredo. Hispanoamericano (México), 52, 1335 (22 de abril, 1968), p. 49-50.

68 Tres ejemplos de amor y una teoría. Madrid: Alianza Editorial, 1969, 1970, 287 p. (Col. El Libro de
Bolsillo, Sección, Literatura, 171).

S. imaginatively examines the relationships of three
great novelists, Balzac, Tolstoi, and Goethe, with their re-
spective lovers, Madame Hanska, Sofía Andreievna, and
Carlota. To each pair he devotes an anecdotal chapter followed by a chapter of highly personal and intuitive commentary on the sex-love relationship just narrated. The seventh
and final chapter expresses in revised and condensed form
the substance of the author's earlier book on sex, Carta de
Moscú sobre el amor (61). Narrative and essay or personal
comment are inextricably mixed in this volume.

El Correo Gallego (Santiago de Compostela), 10 de diciembre,
        1969.
El Meridiano (Barcelona), enero, 1970, p. 128.

King, Charles L. Books Abroad, 44, 3 (Summer 1970),
        p. 449-50.

69 Ensayos del otro mundo. Barcelona: Destino, 1970,
        267 p. (Col. Ancora y Delfín, 357).

Eighteen essays which had formerly appeared in periodicals throughout North and South America were selected by
the author for this book. S. 's comments on Somerset
Maugham, D. H. Lawrence, and others alternate with such
varied topics as "El ensayo como obra de arte," "Probabilidades lunares," the "hippies" in American society, pre-
Columbian Indians, and "Miserias y grandezas del viajar."
The book demonstrates once again S. 's prodigious culture,
deep participation in the leading literary events of his time,
keen observation of the current social scene, and great skill
as a writer.

Calvo Hernando, Manuel. Ya (Madrid), 16 de diciembre,
        1970.
Carrillo, Germán D. Hispania, 55, 3 (September, 1972),
        p. 593.
Lacalle, Angel. Las Provincias (Valencia), 22 de noviembre,
        1970, p. 47.
Mendiola, José M. El Diario Vasco (San Sebastián), 13 de
        diciembre, 1970.
Murciano, Carlos. La Estafeta Literaria, núm. 459 (1 de

enero, 1971).

_____. La Estafeta Literaria, núm. 469 (1 de junio, 1971),
p. 583.

ABC (Madrid), 18 de febrero, 1971.
La Vanguardia Española (Barcelona), 26 de noviembre, 1970.

70   Relatos fronterizos. México: Mexicanos Unidos, 1970,
352 p. ; Barcelona: Destino, 1972, 335 p. (Col. Ancora y Delfín, 390).

The "relatos" are a diversified collection of seventeen
anecdotes, narrative-essays, personal commentary, and es-
says--many of which had previously appeared in print. The
common theme that seems to lend some unity to the book is
that of "frontier"--frontiers more cultural, intellectual, or
spiritual than merely geographical. "Frontier" characters
include the criminal Caryl Chessman, and the French painter Utrillo. "Frontier" experiences or personal impressions
in different chapters occur in places such as Moscow, El
Paso, London, the Grand Canyon, Paris and Acapulco. An
interesting book which reveals S.'s lifelong interest in new
ways of perceiving reality.

Castillo, Antonio. El Diario Vasco (San Sebastián), 25 de
marzo, 1973.
Lacalle, Angel. Las Provincias (Valencia), 4 de febrero,
1973, p. 47.
Marsa, Angel. El Correo Catalán (Barcelona), 21 de diciembre, 1972.
Mendiola, José M. El Diario Vasco (San Sebastián), 24 de
diciembre, 1972.
Murciano, Carlos. La Estafeta Literaria, núm. 532 (15 de
enero, 1974), p. 1586-87.
Tovar, Antonio. La Gaceta Ilustrada (Madrid), 8 de julio,
1973.
Valencia, Antonio. Arriba (Madrid), 7 de octubre, 1973.

Región (Oviedo), 31 de diciembre, 1972.
La Vanguardia Española (Barcelona), 29 de marzo, 1973.

E. POETRY

71   Las imágenes migratorias.   México: Atenea, 1960,
       324 p.

    Seventy-eight poems, seventeen of which are "gozos"
(couplets, glees) in praise of the Dame of Elche, symbol of
ideal feminine virginity, and eighteen are so-called "sylla-
bas." (There is a "syllaba cándida," "vehemente," "eró-
tica," "tremens," "idílica," "saudosa," "memorable," "ascé-
tica," "vivida," "alegórica," "figurativa," "nostáligica,"
"insistente," "íntima," etc.) Rafael Bosch is the author of
a perceptive article on Las imágenes migratorias (1232).
Many poems reappear in 72.

Bosch, Rafael.   Cuadernos (París), núm. 64 (septiembre,
       1962), p. 93-94.
Uceda, Julia.   Insula, núm. 183 (febrero, 1962), p. 9.

72   Libro armilar de poesía y memorias bisiestas.   Méxi-
       co: Aguilar, 1974, 717 p. (Col. Literaria, Poesía).

    In this volume S. has reprinted without change some
poems from his earlier volume of poetry, Las imágenes
migratorias (71), has retouched some pieces from the
earlier volume, and has added many new poems to make a
total of 177, one of which, number LXXXIX, "Memorias bisiestas," is one hundred pages in length, and consists of
short, aphoristic statements in poetic prose with only an occasional use of verse.   The book will probably stand as
Sender's definitive work of poetry.   Contains an illuminating
prologue (on poetry) by the author (99).

F. ANTHOLOGY

73   Páginas escogidas.   Selección y notas introductorias
       por Marcelino C. Peñuelas.   Madrid: Gredos, 1972,
       343 p. (Col. Biblioteca Románica Hispánica. VI. Anto-
       logía Hispánica, 31).

    Selections from the novels: Los cinco libros de Ari-
adna, Imán, Crónica del alba, Epitalamio del prieto Trinidad,

La esfera, and Réquiem por un campesino español; and publication in their entirety of three short stories: "La llave"
(46), "El buitre" (45, 47, 86, 89, 103), and "El padre Zozobra" (47); and twenty-one pages of poems taken from
Crónica del alba and Las imágenes migratorias.

In a short (1-1/2 pages) note, "Al lector," Peñuelas
explains that he had simply chosen those stories or passages
which had been to him most memorable, while at the same
time seeking to make his selections sufficiently varied and
representative of the author's total work.

II. PAMPHLETS AND OTHER SHORT
SEPARATE PUBLICATIONS

A. DRAMA

74   El secreto. Madrid: Tensor, 1935, 16 p.
On the eve of a popular uprising in Barcelona two political prisoners who know the secret plans of the revolu-
tionaries are tortured by the police in an effort to get them
to confess "el secreto. " The second prisoner, sensing that
his companion is weakening, promises the police to reveal
the "secret" in exchange for their execution of the first
prisoner. His request is carried out and the second prisoner, who now alone knows the "secret," resolutely faces
death rather than betray the uprising. Published later in
English translation (90, 126).

B. JOURNALISTIC ESSAYS

75   América antes de Colón. Valencia: Cuadernos de
Cultura, 1930, 67 p. (Col. Historia y Geografía, 2).
Consisting of articles formerly published in La Libertad, this pamphlet-length work is a popular "history" of the
pre-Columbian Indians in America--their common character-
istics, customs, beliefs, crafts, etc. The work ends with
a strong criticism of the exercise of Spanish power, especially of their two kinds of terror, "el religioso y el militar," during the Conquest and the Colonial period.

76   Crónica del pueblo en armas (Historia para niños).
Madrid-Valencia: Ediciones Españolas, 1936, 46 p.
The author relates (and interprets according to his own
views) the struggle of the Spanish "pueblo" through the

centuries to achieve and keep their liberties. The three
chief enemies of those liberties since the Middle Ages until the
present time have been three forces--the Monarchy, the
Church, and the Aristocracy. A historical-essay intended
for children or unsophisticated adults.

77   Primera de acero. Madrid: Quinto Regimiento, 1937,
      30 p.
      A chapter from Contraataque (63) issued as a propa-
gandistic pamphlet by the Republican forces in the midst of
Civil War.

78   El sosia y los delegados. México: Costa-Amic, 1965,
      61 p.
      A narrative-essay which appeared in the Mexican maga-
zine, Panoramas (119), at about the same time that the present booklet or pamphlet was issued. Three years after
Stalin's death the man who had served as the dictator's
double appears before a Soviet Congress (which had just re-
pudiated the deceased dictator and his cult of the individual)
and declares himself to be Stalin himself. An imaginative
story which tells not what happened but what "very well
could have happened," and which is meant to be a political
lesson for those who wish to remain free. Republished
later as a story in Las gallinas de Cervantes y otras narraciones parabólicas (49) and in Novelas del otro jueves (51).

(Part 1, cont.)

III. CONTRIBUTIONS IN BOOKS

A. FICTION

79 "The Journey," tr. by Warre B. Wells. Great Spanish
Short Stories, ed. by Henry Barbusse. Boston:
Houghton, Mifflin Co. , 1932, p. 321-42.
Chapter eight of the novel, El Verbo se hizo sexo (3),
which relates what happens when a farmer places an eagle's
egg under a brooding hen. The eaglet which emerges into a
world of chicks finds itself, as did Saint Theresa (according
to S.), a "bird of a different feather," and flies off on a
journey--as did the Saint of Avila (on a mystical "journey").

80 "The Dancing Witch," tr. by Oliver La Farge. Heart
of Europe, ed. by Klaus Mann and Hermann Kesten.
New York: L. B. Fischer, 1943, p. 175-83. The
Best of Modern European Literature. Philadelphia:
Blakiston, 1954, p. 175-83.
An excerpt from the novel, A Man's Place (8), relating
the antics of a witch in an Aragonese village.

81 "The Buzzard," tr. by Paul Bowles. A Night with
Jupiter and Other Fantastic Stories, ed. by Charles H.
Ford. New York: published by View Editions, distributed by the Vanguard Press, 1945, p. 53-65.
A buzzard flying over a battlefield reflects upon the
absurdities of human behavior. (In 45 as "El zopilote," in
47 as "El buitre" and "The Vulture"; see also 86, 89, and
103.)

82 "The Clouds Did Not Pass." The Pen in Exile, 2 vols
ed. by Paul Tabori. London: International Pen Club
for Writers in Exile, 1954, Vol. I, p. 126-33.
A Spanish peasant woman goes berserk on the third
anniversary of the assassination of her brother-in-law whom

52 Works by Sender

she had betrayed to the Civil Guard.   (See 111.)

83   "The Terrace," tr. by Florence Sender.   The World of
      Modern Fiction, Vol. 2, ed. by Steven Marcus.   New
      York: Simon and Schuster, 1966, p. 399-428.
      A short story reprinted from Tales of Cibola (47).
      See also 88 and 104a (Spanish) and 47 and 115 (English).

84   "El padre Zozobra" from Novelas ejemplares de Cíbola
      (47).   Literatura española, tomo 2.   Introducción y
      notas por Diego Marín.   New York: Holt, Rinehart
      and Winston, 1968, p. 401-28.
      Contains three-page introduction (in Spanish) to S. by
      Diego Marín, in addition to "El padre Zozobra" which beauti-
      fully characterizes a Spanish alcoholic priest who is spending
      time in a rehabilitation home in New Mexico for wayward
      clerics.

85   "Las gallinas de Cervantes," from Las gallinas de
      Cervantes y otras narraciones parabólicas (49).   Narra-
      ciones de la España desterrada, comp. por Rafael Conte.
      Barcelona: Edhasa, 1970, p.   47-82 and 246-48 (El
      Puente Literario).
      Conte's anthology includes fiction by F. Ayala, J. R.
      Arana, Max Aub, P. Masip, S., and others.   Reprints S.'s
      "Las gallinas de Cervantes" (p.   47-82 from item 49 of this
      Bibliography), and contains a brief "ficha biobibliográfica"
      (p.   246-48).

86   "El buitre," from Novelas ejemplares de Cíbola (47).
      Visiones de hoy, ed. for student use by Robert B.
      Brown and Barry J. Luby.   New York: Harcourt
      Brace Jovanovich, 1971, p.   179-200.
      See "The Buzzard" (81).   First published as "El zopi-
      lote" in 45.   See also 47, 81, 89, and 103.

87   "La fotografía de aniversario," from La llave (46).
      Antología de autores españoles antiguos y modernos,
      ed. by Fernando Ibarra and Alberto Machado da Rosa.
      New York: Macmillan, 1972, p. 386-98.
      Short, general introduction to S. and a reprinting (with
      editing for student use) of 109 and 113.   Could be classified
      as a play rather than a short story.

88   "La terraza," from Novelas ejemplares de Cíbola (47,
      104a).   Spanish Literature Since the Civil War, ed.
      (with Introduction) by Beatrice P. Patt and Martin

Nozick for use in American universities. New York: Dodd, Mead, 1973, p. 311-45.

A two and one-half page general introduction in English to S. (p. 311-13). Erroneously reports that S. was born in Alcolea de Cinca in 1902, rather than in Chalamera de Cinca in 1901. Reproduces intact the short story, "La terraza" (47, 83, 115), with translation into English of difficult words and expressions in notes placed at the bottom of pages. Mr. Arner, a lawyer, dances on the terrace of an insane asylum with Matilda, one of the inmates. She intrigues him with her fantastic stories.

89 "El buitre," from Novelas ejemplares de Cíbola (47; and from Mexicayotl [45] in 1940 in which its title was "El zopilote"). Misterio y pavor, 13 cuentos, ed. by Douglas R. McKay with a Preface to the book and an introduction to each author. New York: Holt, Rinehart and Winston, 1974, p. 73-88.

The pagination includes an excellent two and one-half page introduction to S., and three pages of "Preguntas" for intermediate students of Spanish in American universities. See also 81, 86, and 103.

B. DRAMA

90 "The Secret." Drama I, ed. by Marjorie Wescott Barrows. New York: Macmillan, 1961, p. 81-98. Reprinted from One-Act Play Magazine (126), the English version of El secreto (74).
See 74 for annotation.

C. ARTICLES

91 "Pío Baroja y su obra." Baroja y su mundo, tomo II, ed. por Fernando Baeza. Madrid: Arion, 1961, p. 339-43. (Col. Hombre y Mundo).

A discussion of the lyricism as well as the antibourgeois attitude of Pío Baroja who was, according to S., at the same time "un esclavo de las convenciones." The chapter here is reprinted from an article in Cuadernos (425).

92   "Estudio preliminar: Escolios al margen de las sona-
      tas." Sonatas (Memorias del marqués de Bradomín) de
      Ramón del Valle-Inclán. New York: Las Américas,
      1961, p. vii-xli.
      Comments on each of the four "Sonatas," especially on
their lyrical dimension or projection, serving as an introduction to a book in which the four works are reprinted.

93   "Valle-Inclán, la política y la cárcel." Valle-Inclán
      visto por ..., comp. por José Esteban. Madrid:
      Gráficas Espejo, 1973, p. 281-88 (Col. Ediciones de
      El Espejo; serie: literatura).
      Reprinted (43 years later) from Nueva España (Madrid),
March, 1930 (327).

94   "Flor de santidad y la dificultad de la tragedia." Ra-
      món del Valle-Inclán: An Appraisal of His Life and
      Works, A. N. Zahareas, general editor. New York:
      Las Américas, 1968, p. 267-72.
      Fragments selected and edited from Sender's book,
Valle-Inclán y la dificultad de la tragedia (66). The excerpt
here is divided into three sections: "Los personajes," "La
tragedia," and "El pueblo."

D.   PROLOGUES   (only the more important and longer prologues by Sender to his own works are included in this section)

95   "Prólogo." Los cinco libros de Ariadna. New York:
      Ibérica, 1957, p. v-xvi.
      A very important (and often quoted) statement in which
S. gives a succinct portrayal of himself as a Spaniard living
in painful exile from his Country, and emphasizes once again
his broad human view as opposed to a narrow, political outlook. "Nuestra religión [la de los españoles] es el hombre."

96   "Preface by the Author." Textbook edition of Mosén
      Millán. Boston: Heath, 1964, p. v-vii. (See 15.)
      Those who "leen el libro con atención," says S., "no
sólo conocerán la vida rural española en sus aspectos más
típicos sino que podrán decir que conocen también una de
las causas fundamentales del problema nacional español
desde la remota Edad Media."

97   "Prólogo de Sender. "   "Imán" y la novela histórica de
Sender, por Francisco Carrasquer.   2d ed.   (of "Imán"
y la novela histórica de Ramón J.   Sender [Primera incursión en el "realismo mágico" senderiano], Amsterdam, 1968, see 1137).   London: Tamesis Books,
1970, p. ix-xiii.
An important discussion of the so-called "magic realism" attributed to Sender's works by Carrasquer.   For S.
such "realism" consists "sencillamente, en la dimensión
lírica de un escritor que tiene ante la realidad la tendencia
iluminativa (no constructiva) de los seres con tendencias
panteístas. "

98   "Carta Prólogo de Ramón J. Sender. "   La obra narrativa de Ramón J. Sender, por Marcelino C. Peñuelas.
Madrid: Gredos, 1971, p. 7-12 (Biblioteca Románica
Hispánica.   II.   Estudios y Ensayos, 153).
Comments on the creation of myths by men and especially by novelists.   Man has shown his superiority over
animals by the myths, religious, literary, and cultural,
that he has created through the centuries.   (See 1139.)

99   "Prólogo del autor. "   Libro armilar de poesía y
memorias bisiestas.   México: Aguilar, 1974, p. 7-
24 (Col. Literaria.   Poesía).
A very important statement of Sender's conception of
the nature of poetry and of "la razón de este libro, en cuyas
páginas nostálgicas, ligeramente nuevas, yo quisiera que
hubiera ese acento personal trascendente que lo es todo en
el arte póetico. "   (See 72.)

IV. CONTRIBUTIONS IN PERIODICALS

A. FICTION

100 "The Key. " Kenyon Review, 5 (Winter 1943), 201-18.
Republished as the lead story in the collections, La
llave and La llave y otras narraciones (46), despite its first
publication in English as a play.

101 "The Eagle," tr. by Julia Davis. Partisan Review, 10,
4 (July-August, 1943), 306-13.
An old Indian feels guilty when forced by hunger to rob
an eagle's nest.

102 "Tale from the Pyrenees," tr. by Florence Hall.
Quarterly Review of Literature, 1, 2 (Winter 1944),
119.
Witches ("lamias") attempt to kill men (through causing
snow avalanches) as they push through the Pyrenees, en
route to France.

103 "The Buzzard. " View--The Modern Magazine, Series
5, No. 2 (May, 1945), 10-11, 28, 44-46.
After a battle a buzzard fearfully approaches a dead
soldier and begins his meal. Originally in Spanish in
Mexicayotl (45) as "El Zopilote," later as "El buitre" in
Novelas ejemplares de Cíbola (47) and as "The Vulture" in
Tales of Cíbola (47). Also in 81 (in English) and 86 and 89
(in Spanish).

104 "The Broken Bell," tr. by Martha Allen. Pacific
(Mills College, Oakland, Cal.), 1, 4 (May, 1946), 27-
31.
"A story of three bells in a small church tower, the
sexton, and a stranger who attends mass being held for the
dead Efrain Barrios"--D. Domenicali (1197).

104a "La terraza." Cuadernos Americanos, 39, 3 (mayo-junio, 1948), 264-85.
Republished later in the collection of short stories, Novelas ejemplares de Cíbola (47, Spanish) and in 88 (Spanish). Published in Tales of Cibola (47, English) and in 83 and 115. See 88 for annotation.

105 "Tale of the Hot Land," tr. by Edwin Honig. Partisan Review, 16, 3 (March, 1949), 272-76.
An allegory on the frustrated search of the Indians for a proper place in life after their conquest by Europeans.

106 "El gato negro." Cuadernos Americanos, 44, 2 (marzo-abril, 1949), 268-78.
A cat seems to confirm a friar in his disbelief in the reality of the Devil--thus aiding the cause of evil. For English translation see 47 (Tales of Cibola) and 116.

107 "Miss Slingsby." Las Españas, Suplementos (once cuentos) (México), 3 (abril, 1949), 7 p. (s. n.).
Characterization of a Puritan spinster from New England.

108 "Cocktail Party in Santa Fe." The American Mercury, 73, 331 (July, 1951), 20-26.
Humorous portrayal of some colorful members of Santa Fe's artistic and intellectual colony at a cocktail party. Incorporated later in "Los invitados del desierto," in Novelas ejemplares de Cíbola (and in Tales of Cibola, as "Desert Guests"), item 47 in this Bibliography.

109 "La fotografía," Cuadernos Americanos, 60, 6 (noviembre-diciembre, 1951), 276-93.
Upon their twentieth wedding anniversary Rosario and Teodosio dress to have their photograph taken. Only then does Teodosio notice that Rosario is pregnant--a pregnancy he begins to relate to the "accidental death" of the madcap, Gustavo, a month earlier. Republished in La llave (46), and as items 87 and 113 of this Bibliography.

110 "The Old Wetback." Southwest Review, 40, 4 (Autumn 1955), 311-22.
Characterization of an old Mexican in New Mexico who had changed his name upon entering the United States illegally many years before and who was worried lest death not knowing his name might not "come" for him.

111   "The Clouds Did Not Pass. " New Mexico Quarterly,
        27, 1-2 (Spring-Summer 1957), 17-26.
        Formerly published in The Pen in Exile, Volume I (82).

112   "La 'Quinta' Julieta. " Panoramas (México), núm. 6
        (verano de 1957), 7-152.
        An autobiographical novelette republished first as a
separate "novel" (19), and then several times as part two of
the nine-part series, Crónica del alba (28).

113   "La fotografía de aniversario. " Deslinde (Montevideo),
        núm. 12 (septiembre, 1959), 10-14. (Deslinde sus-
        pended publication with its number 16, June 1961 issue.)
        The same as 109 above--with slightly altered title.
Appears later in 46, and 87.

114   "Delgadina, " tr. Morse Manley. New Mexico Quarter-
        ly, 30, 3 (Autumn 1960), 226-61.
        There are strange repercussions when Delgadina,
daughter of a shepherd working for the rich Aranda family
in Cíbola (New Mexico), is seduced by young Pepe Aranda,
heir to the ranch.   Republished in Novelas ejemplares de
Cíbola (47).

115   "The Terrace, " tr. Florence Sender. Partisan Review,
        27, 4 (Fall 1960), 652-89.
        Republished in Novelas ejemplares de Cíbola (Tales of
Cibola) (47), in The World of Modern Fiction (83), and
Spanish Literature Since the Civil War (88, in Spanish).
Appeared earlier in Spanish (104a).

116.   "The Black Cat, " tr. George D. Schade. Texas
        Quarterly, 4, 1 (Spring 1961), 240-48.
        A black cat seems to confirm a priest's unbelief in
the Devil and thus contributes toward his impending moral
delinquency.   English translation of "El gato negro" (106).

117   "Lo mejor que Dios ha hecho: un día después del
        otro, " Cuadernos (París), núm. 58 (marzo, 1962), 57-
        62.
        S. recalls in memory his semi-fantastic relations with
animals during his visit to Puerto Rico, and a conversation
about Hemingway with a dwarf who was a barber.

118   "The Red Light, " Southwest Review, 48, 3 (Summer
        1963), 259-69.
        The ironic story, told by old Jelinek, tavern-keeper in

an American industrial city, of a rich prostitute who had
herself buried in a costly mausoleum.   Right after her death
the city installed a red traffic light at the street corner next
to her tomb.   Published in Spanish in a book of Sender's
short stories: El extraño señor Photynos y otras novelas
americanas (50) and in English in Tales of Cibola (47).

119   "El sosia y los delegados." Panoramas (México), 3,
      18 (noviembre-diciembre, 1965).
      A narrative-essay later (1965) published separately (78),
and then in 1967 and in 1969 in two books (49, 51).

120. "Al margen de Dostoiewski. Parábola de Jesús y el
      inquisidor." Política (Caracas), 4, 46 (febrero, 1966),
      59-85.
      An adaptation of a chapter from The Brothers Karama-
zov by Dostoyevski.   During the Inquisition Jesus visits Seville where he is jailed for having raised a dead girl to life.
In jail where Torquemada visits him Jesus expresses his
lack of conformity with the Roman Catholic orthodoxy.   Republished in 49.

121   "El fugitivo." El Urogallo, núm. 13 (enero-febrero,
      1972), 25-32.
      An advance printing of the first chapter of the novel,
El fugitivo (38).   The narrator-protagonist, fleeing from unknown crimes, hides in the clocktower of the church in
which he, as a lad, had served as altar boy, and reflects
on the mysteries of human existence.

122   "La risa." Destino, núm. 1838 (23 de diciembre,
      1972), 37-39.
      When Bukska, an Eskimo, hears from Ivan Ivanovitch,
a Russian dealer in contraband furs, of past wars and the
continuing war-making policy of the Soviet Union, the ab-
surdity of it all causes him to laugh so much that he suffers
a hernia.

123   "Para una psicología del mal." El Urogallo (Madrid),
      4, 24 (noviembre-diciembre, 1973), 49-59.
      A certain Professor Thomas relates the grotesque
story of a Jew of unbalanced mind who, as a cruel practical joke, was proclaimed by the Nazis in Warsaw during
World War II as King David II.   The Jew accepted his coro-
nation seriously, married a Jewess in a grotesque mock
wedding ceremony, and was finally hanged by the Nazis.
Since most of his "subjects" (six million Jews) had passed

to the Other World, it was, the Nazis said, his obligation to
follow them. One of Sender's "crónicas" or columns bears
the same title as this fictionalized account (1071).

124   "La mesa de las tres moiras. " Vórtice (Stanford Uni-
       versity), 1, 1 (Primavera 1974), 23-29.
       An excerpt from the manuscript of the novel by the
same title, published later in 1974 (42). An extended "monologue" by Mitchell, a schizophrenic patient and veteran of
World War II, is broken occasionally by responses from
Jack, a retired pilot, to communicate a peculiarly Senderian
view of reality.

125   "El gitano como entidad frenética. " Norte, año 14,
       núms. 2-4 (marzo-agosto, 1973), 29-34.
       The first chapter of the novel, Nancy, doctora en gi-
tanería (41).

B.   DRAMA

126   "The Secret. " One-Act Play Magazine, 1 (November,
       1937), 612-26.
       Originally published as El secreto (74), later repub-
lished in Drama I (90).

127   "The House of Lot. " New Mexico Quarterly Review,
       20, 1 (Spring 1950), 27-40.
       A peculiarly Senderian interpretation of the Biblical
story of Lot in Sodom and Gomorrah. Incorporated later as
an auto sacramental or morality play in the first of the
three parts of Tres novelas teresianas (31).

128   "Los héroes. " Between Worlds, 1 (Summer 1960), 171-
       83.
       A one-act drama, complete in itself although stated to
be the first act of an unpublished three-act drama.

129   "The Wind, " tr. Elinor Randall. New Mexico Quarter-
       ly, 33, 2 (Summer 1963), 185-212.
       A dignified fifty-year old Protestant minister is con-
vinced that God has told him to kill his son, a thirty-year-
old cripple. Alone in their isolated home overlooking the
sea, father and son desperately converse about death while,
outside, the wind, symbolic of dark fatalistic forces, moans

and shrieks. In the end the son is saved by the timely appearance of Pamela, a symbol of ideal love.

130 "Donde crece la marihuana [sic]." La Estafeta Literaria, núm. 362 (28 de enero, 1967), 19-22; 363 (11 de febrero, 1967), 16-24; 364 (25 de febrero, 1967), 17-21.
Republished in Comedia del diantre y otras dos (53) and as a separate book (56).

C. POETRY

131 "Pastoral." Las Españas (México), 19-20 (mayo, 1951), 15.
A series of three sonnets representing (I) life and love in youth, (II) middle age, and (III) old age.

132 "Syllaba cándida." Cuadernos (París), 18 (mayo-junio, 1956), 56-57.
Sixteen sonnets addressed to the mythical Senderian woman.

133 "Syllaba idílica." Papeles de Son Armadans, año 4, 12, 36 (marzo, 1959), 305-18.
Fourteen sonnets.

D. ARTICLES IN LA LIBERTAD

In 1930 Sender abandoned his position on the editorial staff of El Sol and devoted himself to freelance journalism and the writing of novels. Below are listed 193 articles published by him in the Madrid newspaper, La Libertad, during the period, 1930-1936. For a more complete bibliographical entry one may add the year number to the references given below--calendar year 1930, e.g., is Año 12; 1931, Año 13, etc. In July 1936 La Libertad ceased to exist.

134 "Defensa del público," núm. 3270 (11 de septiembre, 1930), 3.
The Spanish public, "el mejor espectador de teatro y el más apto para recibir y asimilar el nuevo arte escénico,"

stays away from the theater. S. finds it outmoded and too abstract, ignoring the Spanish tendency to materialize--to see--ideas, "dándoles valor plástico." "La idea le entra al español por los ojos."

135   "El público de los toros y la educación teatral," núm. 3284 (27 de septiembre, 1930), 3.
Republished as Chapter 2 of Teatro de masas (58). Calls bullfighting the "auténtico teatro nacional," albeit an anti-literary one, and as such sees in the reactions of the Spanish public to it valuable lessons in what makes good theater.

136   "Los dos axiomas de Moscú," núm. 3320 (8 de noviembre, 1930), 3.
It is axiomatic in "todos los teatros verdaderamente renovadores" that the stage be in the central position (as in a bullring) and that the action be a harmonious fusion or "synthesis" of script ("al servicio de una acción de verdadero relieve"), the interpretation given by the actors, music, lights, stage scenery, etc.

137   "El realismo de una escuela de títeres," núm. 3343 (6 de diciembre, 1930), 1.
Republished in Teatro de masas (58) as Chapter 4. A discussion of the puppet theater created by Stanislavsky and Nemirovich Dantchenko at the end of the last century (and which reached the zenith of its success in Moscow in 1921 and continued in 1930 to be successful).

138   "El Volksbühne," núm. 3353 (18 de diciembre, 1930), 3.
A discussion of the founding (in about 1890) of the German theater of the people (Volksbühne), its great growth and influence, and its current decline. "La masa propulsora que le hizo extenderse y arraigar la ha perdido ya."

139   "El proletariado y la escena moderna," núm. 3389 (29 de enero, 1931), 12.
Appears later in Teatro de masas, (58, p. 101-06). "El teatro proletario es la única modalidad que responde a las íntimas características de nuestra época."

140   "El Oriente revolucionario y el teatro español," núm. 3417 (3 de marzo, 1931), 3.
From the East have come "las corrientes religiosas, ideológicas, que hicieron cambiar al Mundo." The Spanish

theater might well be revitalized by learning today from the East.

141 "El Viento en la Moncloa (Prólogo en la primera galería), I," núm. 3425 (12 de marzo, 1931), 3.
Part I of a series of three articles in La Libertad. Republished in the novel, O. P. (2). Introduces the Wind, not the wind of the city, but "ese viento de las alturas," the wind that was imprisoned in Madrid's jail, the Moncloa.

142 "El viento en la Moncloa, II," núm. 3430 (18 de marzo, 1931), 3.
Part II of a three-part series in La Libertad. Republished in O. P. (2). Observations on life in jail and its prisoners by an omniscient author.

143 "El Viento en la Moncloa, III," núm. 3443 (2 de abril, 1931), 3-4.
Part III of a three-part series in La Libertad--all of which was republished in O. P. (2). The imprisoned Journalist discovers that he enjoys more real freedom (an inner freedom) than those who are "esclavos de sí mismos, presos de todos," whether in or out of jail.

144 "Del cerro del Pimiento al de los Mártires," núm. 3682 (7 de enero, 1932), 1.
Republished in Proclamación de la sonrisa (62, p. 102-06). In praise of Fermín Galán who was shot by reactionary forces in the closing days of the Dictatorship, and buried on the Hill of the Martyrs on the outskirts of Huesca, Aragón.

145 "El republicano clásico y el socialista," núm. 3695 (22 de enero, 1932), 1.
Classic republicanism has opposed two kinds of "latifundio: el agrario, de orden económico, y el latifundio cultural." The Republicans of today are restricted by public opinion, and are in danger of being outwitted by the Socialists.

146 "Impopularidad de la iglesia," núm. 3701 (29 de enero, 1932), 1.
The Spanish people are "irreligioso," nearer to Pantheism than to any "inclinación religiosa y confesional [sic]," asserts S.
"Desde los godos, la religión católica estaba ligada a la autoridad civil y militar y a la conciencia feudal de la aristocracia. En España nunca fué popular."

147   "¿Dónde está la fe?," núm. 3706 (4 de febrero, 1932),
      1.
        S. finds faith still alive in "un sector importante de la
clase media," in what he also calls "la gran masa católica
española." "Indefinida como clase, ya que por lo general
vive de su trabajo, y, sin embargo, niega su condición social de asalariado...."

148   "Presencia y coacción de la iglesia," núm. 3716 (16
      de febrero, 1932), 1.
        In broad outline S. reflects on the growing union of
State and Church in Spain, especially since the "concordato
de 1851, en el que la aristocracia hacía concesiones im-
portantes a la Iglesia, una realidad más patente que el mismo Estado." The Church came to pervade and influence, if
not control, all sectors of Spanish life.

149   "Posición anticlerical de la República," núm. 3728 (1
      de marzo, 1932), 1-2.
        Comments on the expulsion of Cardenal Seguro by
Alcalá Zamora's Government, and the dissolution of the
Jesuits. Warns that "la substancia mística, transformada
en fuerza política por la Iglesia, será un arma con la cual
no podrá dejar de contar la República en el porvenir."

150   "Epitafio a la camarada Francis Mains," núm. 3731
      (4 de marzo, 1932), 1.
        Republished in Proclamación de la sonrisa (62, p. 61-
63). Thoughts upon the death of the young correspondent for
the English Workers' press-in Madrid, and the epitaph for
her: "Duermes, camarada Frances Mains, en la belleza de
mañana."

151   "Goethe, 22-III-1932," núm. 3746 (22 de marzo, 1932),
      1.
        Republished in Proclamación de la sonrisa (62, p. 128-
32). Commemorates the centenary of Goethe's death. "Su
obra es maravillosa."

152   "Domingo de resurrección," núm. 3751 (27 de marzo,
      1932), 1.
        Republished in Proclamación de la sonrisa (62, p. 22-
26). Regards Easter as "el mito de la primavera que los
pobres judíos de Palestina adoptaron e intercalaron en la
historia poemática de uno de los suyos, del más pobre y del
más rebelde," an uninformed and superficial view which dis-
mays the reader.

153   "El vagabundo en la puerta," núm. 3758 (5 de abril,
      1932), 1.
      Republished in Proclamación de la sonrisa (62, p. 57-
61). Discusses the "vagabundos" in the novels of Traven,
O'Flaherty, and Istrati and in a film then being shown in
Madrid, "Viva la libertad," by René Clair, all of which go
counter to Spanish bourgeois society.

154   "Vuelta a Maquiavelo y al renacimiento," núm. 3771
      (20 de abril, 1932), 1.
      Mussolini and Hitler do not create; they simply return
to the past.   There is nothing new in their Machiavellism.
"Hitler cede, transige al parecer.   Promiscúa y mistifica. "
History repeats itself.

155   "La semana del libro," núm. 3774 (23 de abril, 1932),
      1.
      Republished in Proclamación de la sonrisa (62, p. 73-
75). Laments that the "Semana del Libro" in Spain lacks
"un sentido industrial animado por el espíritu del autor.
Una colaboración estrecha y una compenetración moral entre
el editor y el hombre de letras. "

156   "El dictador, el 'ultraje' y el delirio," núm. 3786 (8
      de mayo, 1932), 1-2.
      S. attributes the recent nationalistic campaign in Portu-
guese newspapers to the desire of the Portuguese dictator,
General Carmona, to persuade the Spanish Government that
Portuguese political exiles in Spain should be returned to
their homeland.   Many of these exiles are personal enemies
of General Carmona, asserts S.

157   "Cinco negros a la silla eléctrica," núm. 3791 (14 de
      mayo, 1932), 1.
      Reflections upon the sentencing of five blacks to the
electric chair in Scottsborough, Alabama, for rape, a crime
S. regards as less serious than economic and financial
"rape," though the latter crime usually goes unpunished.

158   "El domingo madrileño y la incongruencia," núm. 3798
      (22 de mayo, 1932), 1-2.
      Republished in Proclamación de la sonrisa (62, p. 132-
36). "El descanso durante el régimen burgués no satisface,
porque el trabajo del cual se descansa es un trabajo que no
basta. " S. observes several "incongruencias" during a "domingo burgués" in Madrid.

159   "La chilaba, el 'habus' y el 'guembri'," núm. 3803
      (28 de mayo, 1932), 1.
      Republished in Proclamación de la sonrisa (62, p. 63-
66).   Comments on Islam and its integration into the politi-
cal-social organization of Morocco.   "El berberisco ... ¿es
musulmán?   ¿Seguirá siéndolo much tiempo?"

160   "El 'socialismo' chileno," núm. 3812 (8 de junio,
      1932), 1.
      The new Chilean Government, headed by Dávila and
Grove, is not really Socialist, and the workers are too radi-
calized to lend to it their support.

161   "Libros sobre Rusia: el de un intelectual socialista,"
      núm. 3820 (17 de junio, 1932), 1.
      Comments on the book, Rusia al día, by Julián Zugaza-
goitia, who is seen to be a writer "con grandes afinidades
sentimentales e intelectuales hacia la Unión de Repúblicas
Socialistas Soviéticas; pero en absoluto fuera de la dialéctica,
de la lógica, de la línea comunistas."   A new book on Russia is needed, one "que nos cuente cómo es el nuevo espíritu de las gentes."

162   "Contra la guerra," núm. 3827 (25 de junio, 1932), 1.
      Comments upon the convoking by Romain Rolland and
Henri Barbusse of a World Congress against war.   The effectiveness of the Congress is doubtful.   "Sobre la eficacia
inmediata de este Congreso no hay que cifrar tantas ilusi-
ones como pueden cifrarse en los acuerdos de las distintas
Internacionales obreras."   Praises the Republican Constitu-
tion for its express declaration against war.

163   "Los visigodos, el nacionalismo y el moro Marmita,"
      núm. 3836 (6 de julio, 1932), 1.
      Republished in Proclamación de la sonrisa (62, p. 124-
28).   "Pegarles a los moros es una manía visigótica, pro-
longada hasta Alfonso XIII y Berenguer y Silvestre por la
red de la aristocracia y de la Iglesia."

164   "La cigüeña en el ayuntamiento," núm. 3843 (14 de
      julio, 1932), 1.
      Republished in Proclamación de la sonrisa (62, p. 99-
102).   A baby stork falls from the tower of the municipal
building.   By action of the town council it is restored to its
nest in the tower.   This incident later appears in El lugar
de un hombre (8).

165   "Un tiro en la quinta galería," núm. 3849 (21 de julio,
      1932), 1.
      Upon the "accidental" shooting of a prisoner, a Commu-
nist youth, in Madrid's Model Jail, S. asks why it is always
either an Anarchist or a Communist who is the victim of a
"lamentable incidente." He deplores the recent removal of
Victoria Kent from her position as head of Spanish prisons,
and argues for a maximum of freedom for prisoners. "Si
en algo pudo y debió demostrar su horror al negro pasado
español de la aristocracia, el cepo y golilla, fué en esto de
las prisiones."

166   "Oro y mercurio de Almadén," núm. 3858 (31 de julio,
      1932), 1.
      Republished in Proclamación de la sonrisa (62, p. 176-
78).   "Si del mercurio [de las minas de Almadén] se pudiera
sacar oro, España tendría un porvenir risueño." Observations on the elusive "philosopher's stone."

167   "1921--Memorándum," núm. 3862 (5 de agosto, 1932),
      1.
      On the occasion of the eleventh anniversary of the
crushing defeat of the Spanish Army in Morocco by Rif
tribesmen, S. reflects on the senselessness of the conflict,
"gracias a la cual pueden dormir tranquilos doce mil
muertos."

168   "Espere usted seis semanas," núm. 3866 (10 de agosto,
      1932), 1.
      The title is from Hitler's answer to a journalist who
inquired as to the next move by the Nazis in their drive to
power in Germany: "Espere usted seis semanas y verá."
The events of that period--transpiring at the time--speak
eloquently for Hitler. Observations on Germania by Tacitus
and the Germanic character.

169   "Terror blanco," núm. 3868 (12 de agosto, 1932), 1.
      Republished in Proclamación de la sonrisa (62, p. 90-
93). Upon the premature and mysterious death of Lasarte,
"jefe del servicio secreto de investigación y represión del
sindicalismo" during the Dictatorship, S. comments on the
dangers in the use of terror tactics.

170   "Sobre el patriotismo de verano," núm. 3871 (16 de
      agosto, 1932), 1 y 2.
      S. protests the Republican Government's continuing in
positions of authority certain military officers, "patriotas de

verano," who had been important leaders during the Monarchy and Dictatorship.

171   "Los creadores de atmósferas," núm. 3881 (27 de
       agosto, 1932), 1.
The different segments of Spanish socio-political life--
Socialists, conservatives, Catholics, etc. --produce moral
atmospheres. So do the people (el pueblo) themselves, and
in this fact S. sees hope for a better Spain. "El pueblo
español manda y mandará más cada día por el procedimiento
de asimilar o de suscitar y producir atmósferas morales."

172   "La dula de Coscullano," núm. 3887 (3 de septiembre,
       1932), 1.
       Republished in Proclamación de la sonrisa (62, p. 66-
69). When the dulero of the mountain village of Coscullano
tarries too long among a rich man's flocks and herds, he
not only loses his dula (the few, scraggly animals entrusted
to him by his poor fellow-villagers) but also his very humanity.   A lesson for the poor everywhere, asserts S.

173   "La sierra niña," núm. 3891 (8 de septiembre, 1932),
       1.
       Republished in Proclamación de la sonrisa (62, p. 218-
21). On vacation in the "sierra de Guarra," S. poetizes on
the nature of the mountain--"es infantil y dice cosas de
niño."

174   "La virgen de Fabana," núm. 3899 (17 de septiembre,
       1932), 1.
       Appears later in Proclamación de la sonrisa (62, p. 83-
86). "La virginidad fisiológica y la mental, fomentada por
las viejas religiones para el uso de los poderosos, han
creado mitos y ritos: el de la Virgen de Fabana."

175   "Carta a un pastor," núm. 3901 (20 de septiembre,
       1932), 1.
       Republished in Proclamación de la sonrisa (62, p. 43-
46). A letter to a shepherd is the pretext for observations
on politics in Madrid.

176   "Dinamococo," núm. 3906 (25 de septiembre, 1932), 1.
       Republished in Proclamación de la sonrisa (62, p. 69-
72). The title is the word S. proposes for a kind of "infección moral, de epidemia del espíritu, con su microbio y
todo" which may account for the increasing suicide rate. "El
papel del dinamococo no está claro aún."

177 "El buitre en la ex corte," núm. 3912 (2 de octubre, 1932), 1.
Republished in Proclamación de la sonrisa (62, p. 155-58). A vulture visits Madrid. Why? "El pobre buitre ha olido la vieja atmósfera moral que ha intentado prolongarse sobre el 14 de abril e imprimir a lo nacional el sello de su agonía."

178 "Sobre la próxima guerra," núm. 3919 (11 de octubre, 1932), 1.
Asserting that "el capitalismo europeo prepara una nueva guerra" and that Spain will become involved, S. "como español movilizable" voices his opposition to serving in such a war.

179 "La raza," núm. 3920 (12 de octubre, 1932), 1.
Republished in Proclamación de la sonrisa (62, p. 114-17). Observations on the celebration of the "fiesta de la raza" in Spain. "La República no debe seguir prohijando esas manifestaciones [the "fiesta de la raza"] seniles y tiernas con las que la España caduca todavía quiere consolar reprimidos impulsos imperialistas."

180 "El ex Kronprinz, resentido," núm. 3927 (20 de octubre, 1932), 1.
Commentary on the reported preparations of Frederick William of Prussia (ex-Imperial Crown Prince) to regain the throne of Prussia, seen by S. to threaten "la paz de un continente."

181 "Alfar, cuero y tul," núm. 3929 (22 de octubre, 1932), 1.
Republished in Proclamación de la sonrisa (62, p. 35-38). Comments on an Exposition of Hispanic-Moroccan crafts in the Retiro, and of the condition of the medieval craftsmen: "El maestro en artesanía era siempre un esclavo."

182 "Crónica frustrada del melancólico otoño," núm. 3932 (26 de octubre, 1932), 1.
Republished in Proclamación de la sonrisa (62, p. 110-14). Superficial observations on the grape harvest--and wine drinking.

183 "André Gide en el cenit," núm. 3939 (3 de noviembre, 1932), 1.
Republished in Proclamación de la sonrisa (62, p. 148-

51). "Gide, en el cenit. Sería bueno estar en el cenit si
no existiera el nadir.   Pero ya que existe es necesario re-
cordar que pasar el cenit es comenzar a caminar hacia su
sombría contraafirmación: hacia el nadir. "

184   "Seis reales de risa," núm. 3943 (8 de noviembre,
       1932), 1.
Comments on Grock, a comic currently performing in
Madrid, and on the art of making people laugh--exposing our
hidden self-deceptions.   "El público de los seis reales, el
de la galería, ríe lo mismo que el intelectual y el político. "

185   "En El Escorial," núm. 1932 (16 de noviembre, 1932),
       1.
       Republished in Proclamación de la sonrisa (62, p. 86-
90).   Visiting El Escorial history "deja de ser letra muerta
y descompuesta. "

186   "Spengler y el dolor de morir," núm. 3956 (23 de no-
       viembre, 1932), 1.
       The demise of technological civilization gloomily pre-
dicted in Spengler's book, El hombre y la técnica, is but the
prelude to a bright new revolutionary world, according to S.
(who affirms faith in the masses, a faith Spengler lacks).

187   "Interrogaciones sobre un libro," núm. 3963 (1 de di-
       ciembre, 1932), 1-2.
       Comments on Nosotros los marxistas; Lenin contra
Marx (Editorial España), a book by Antonio Ramos Oliveira
in which its young author "afronta crudamente, con un valor
a veces heroico, las cuestiones más arduas que la realidad
política española ha planteado al socialismo. "   In one thing,
"en el espíritu anarquista de los revolucionarios españoles.
De todos los campos [aún el comunista], " S. declares his
agreement with Ramos.

188   "Peregrinos del hambre en el país de Roosevelt, " núm.
       3969 (8 de diciembre, 1932), 1-2.
       Comments on a "hunger march" on Washington soon
after Franklin Roosevelt's overwhelming victory in the presi-
dential elections.   "No parece que hayan hecho mucha impresión a los electores de Mr. Roosevelt. "

189   "Marte y el general," núm. 3977 (17 de diciembre,
       1932), 1.
       Republished in Proclamación de la sonrisa (62, p. 136-
40).   S. recounts interviewing a general who had just viewed

Mars from the astronomical observatory.

190   "3 obispos, 3," núm. 3985 (27 de diciembre, 1932), 1.
       Republished in Proclamación de la sonrisa (62, p. 75-
79).   To impress readers with the importance of a religious
function a notice in a Portuguese newspaper states in large
print: "3 obispos, 3." S. finds this, and other contents of
the paper "triste."

191   "El realismo y la novela," núm. 3994 (6 de enero,
       1933), 1.
       Republished in Proclamación de la sonrisa (62, p. 140-
44).   "Para hacer novela y, sobre todo, para continuar la
tradición novelesca del realismo español, hay que desnudarse.
Quedarse en pura y simple hombría."

192   "1933 de la era cristiana," núm. 4007 (14 de enero,
       1933), 1.
       Republished in Proclamación de la sonrisa (62, p. 172-
76).   Criticizes inconsistencies in the Catholic Church's policies and practices.

193   "Primera jornada del camino a Casas Viejas," núm.
       4005 (19 de enero, 1933), 3.
       Republished in Casas Viejas (59). S. reports on his
flight from Madrid to Seville, the first stage of his trip to
Casas Viejas. "¿Habremos ganado cuatro días al tiempo?"
--by flying.

194   "Medina Sidonia, Medina Coeli y María Maímol," núm.
       4006 (20 de enero, 1933), 3.
       Reflections upon visiting the Andalusian town of Medina
Sidonia enroute to report on the peasant uprising and its suppression in Benalup (Casas Viejas).

195   "El que tenía jaca cortaba tierra, según 'Seisdedos',"
       núm. 4008 (22 de enero, 1933), 3-4.
       Republished in Casas Viejas (59). The old peasant
"Seisdedos" used to "explain" why some people were rich
and others poor. "Al principio tó era de nadie. Uno que
tenía una jaca ligera salió al campo y cortó tierra. Otro
que sólo tenía un caballejo, cortó menos.... Luego salie-
ron seis u ocho a pie. Pero nuestros pobres agüelos eran
baldaos."

196   "En la noche del día 10, todos 'al avio'," núm. 4009
       (24 de enero, 1933), 3-4.

S. visits Seisdedos, the peasant leader, in his miserable hut in Casas Viejas and relates the first day after the proclamation by Seisdedos of the reign of "comunismo libertario"--a reign soon to be cruelly crushed by Government Assault Guards. Reprinted--at least in essence--in Casas Viejas (59).

197   "Las primeras bajas: dos de cada bando," núm. 4010
       (25 de enero, 1933), 3-4.
       Republished in Casas Viejas (59). Narrative of the beginning of the violence in Casas Viejas (Benalup) early on the morning of January 11, 1933: "Con las 'primeras luces, los primeros tiros'."

198   "Totalmente incinerados," núm. 4012 (27 de enero,
       1933), 3-4.
       Republished in Casas Viejas (59). Narrates the attack upon and burning of the "choza" of the leader of the uprising, "Seisdedos," by Assault Guards.

199   "Permiso para constriur un ataúd," núm. 4013 (28 de
       enero, 1933), 3-4.
       Republished in Casas Viejas (59). Commentary on the restlessness and fear in the area of Casas Viejas two weeks after the "triunfo" of the upper classes. A woman received permission to build a coffin for her husband killed by Government forces but a carpenter refused to build it for her.

200   "Donde aparecen, por fin, 'los responsables'," núm.
       4014 (29 de enero, 1933), 3-4.
       Republished in Casas Viejas (59). The "crime" of Casas Viejas would not have "existed" had it not been made known to the rest of Spain. "En Casas Viejas no sucedió nada hasta que nosotros lo hemos contado."

201.   "Una carta de Sender--Los sucesos de Casas Viejas"
       (Una carta al director de La Libertad), núm. 4018 (3
       de febrero, 1933), 3.
       S. objects to a statement by Antonio de la Villa attributing undue influence of the Confederación Nacional de Trabajo (CNT) on S.'s reporting of the incidents at Casas Viejas.

202   "Un ayuntamiento en fuga," núm. 4024, viernes (10 de
       febrero, 1933), 1.
       Commentary on the news that all the councilmen, including the mayor, of the Extremaduran town of Nogales had left their town for "six months," declaring that it was im-

possible "afrontar el problema social, adaptar las leyes re-
publicano--socialistas a la realidad económica de Nogales"--
despite the fact that they were all Republicans.

203 "Zeben Provincien, el acorazado rojo," núm. 4029 (16
     de febrero, 1933), 1.
Discussion of the recent suppression of a mutiny of the
crew members of a Dutch cruiser, the "Zeben Provincien,"
with criticism of the Dutch colonial policy.

204 "Un atentado contra míster Roosevelt," núm. 4034 (22
     de febrero, 1933), 1.
     Republished in Proclamación de la sonrisa (62, p. 50-
53). Commentary on the "responsibility" of the American
middle class for the attempt on President Roosevelt's life by
a member of the working class. Reveals a poorly informed
and distorted view of the United States.

205 "Las evidencias de Casas Viejas," núm. 4035 (23 de
     febrero, 1933), 3.
     S. concludes three days after the "crime of Casas
Viejas": "Los pocos propietarios que hay en Medina Sidonia
y Casas Viejas son monárquicos de tipo feudal. La República que representan Azaña y los socialistas puso a su
servicio todo el aparato de represión de un régimen votado
por los enemigos del feudalismo y de la monarquía."

206 "Carta a los campesinos de Casas Viejas," núm. 4037
     (25 de febrero, 1933), 3.
     Though the Government was "rápido, cruel, implacable"
in its suppression of the uprising in Casas Viejas (and thus
was obviously informed of the event) it has long delayed in
becoming "informed" of the facts of the suppression. "Todo
queda en pie," S. writes to the peasants, "menos vuestros
veintitrés muertos."

207 "El incendio del Reichstag," núm 4043 (4 de marzo,
     1933), 1-2.
     Hitler, according to S., is using the burning of the
Reichstag as a pretext to justify suppression of the press
(and especially the Communist press) which opposes him in
the election now underway. "Sabe [Hitler] que estas elecciones tienen una fuerza decisiva, sobre el porvenir de la
política alemana."

208 "Responsabilidad en pequeñas dosis," núm. 4047 (9 de
     marzo, 1933), 1.

Responsibility for the excessive reaction of Government forces at Casas Viejas will be passed around from one level to another, from one part of the Government to another. "El Congreso de Diputados creerá salvarse sacrificando al presidente, " etc.

209   "Casas Viejas y el parlamento: La denuncia, el informe y la responsabilidad, " núm. 4050 (12 de marzo, 1933), 3.

In a series of articles in La Libertad, S. denounced the Republican Government for its brutal repression of the peasant uprising in Casas Viejas. But, laments S. , "el Gobierno de la República no entiende el lenguaje de la 'denuncia' ni mucho menos el de la 'acusación' ... sólo entiende al lenguaje oficinesco del informe 'por conducto regular'. " But the Government cannot so easily evade its responsibility, asserts S.

210   "La responsabilidad y las Cortes, " núm. 4052 (15 de marzo, 1933), 3.

Comments on the day that the Commission established to determine the Central Government's responsibility for the bloody suppression of a peasant uprising in Casas Viejas (ordered perhaps to teach the rebels a lesson: "el de la responsabilidad") is to reveal its findings.

211   "Comité nacional de la caza de judíos, " núm. 4063 (28 de marzo, 1933), 1.

Republished in Proclamación de la sonrisa (62, p. 181-85). Comments on the establishment of an anti-Semitic "Comité nacional" in Nazi Germany, calling it "una afrenta para la cultura alemana, que tanto debe a los judíos. "

212   "Veinte mil duros, " núm. 4069 (4 de abril, 1933), 1.

Republished in Proclamación de la sonrisa (62, p. 144-48). A proposal of the "Cámara del Libro" to award annually 100,000 pesetas for the best literary work is attacked. "Lo creo poco eficaz como estimulante de talentos. "

213   "Un esteta en la U. R. S. S. , " núm. 4076 (12 de abril, 1933), 1.

Republished in Proclamación de la sonrisa (62, p. 39-42). Commentary on Waldo Frank's new book, Aurora rusa.

214   "Amigos de la U. R. S. S. , " núm. 4085 (22 de abril, 1933), 1.

A recent manifiesto sponsored by the incipient "Asocia-

ción de Amigos de la U. R. S. S. , " urging Spain to take more
interest in promoting cultural and scientific exchange with
the Soviet Union "ha sucedido recelos, como no podía menos
de suceder.   ... Ese aldeanismo, esa resistencia hacia lo
que se desconoce, " asserts S. , "era una de las características del viejo régimen [the Spanish Monarchy]. "

215   "El pobre Kerenski, " núm. 4088 (26 de abril, 1933), 1.
Republished in Proclamación de la sonrisa (62, p. 121-
24). Reviews the troubled tenure of Alexander Kerensky as
President of the Provisional Government of the Russian Republic (February-October, 1917).

216   "Los muchachos de la F. U. E. , " núm. 4094 (3 de mayo,
1933), 1.
S. applauds the protest against traditional Spanish
"puritanism" represented by the actions of the "Primeras
Jornadas Eugénicas Españolas" (which appear to be the work
of the "F. U. E. "--Federación Universitaria Estudiantil ?).

217   "Reflexiones sobre el amor, I, " núm. 4096 (5 de mayo,
1933), 1-2.
First of a series of four articles on love and sex.   "En
torno a lo físico y sensual existe una zona cuyos límites se
desconocen, una zona de voluptuosidades que enlaza el sexo
con el espíritu. " "El amor comienza en el instinto sexual
y nadie sabe donde termina. "

218   "Reflexiones sobre el amor, II, " núm. 4099 (9 de
mayo, 1933), 1.
The early religious training of children in Spain tends
to cause children to equate sex or the body with evil and the
incorporal with good or love; thus sex and love become anti-
thetical one to the other.

219   "Reflexiones sobre el amor, III, " núm. 4107 (18 de
mayo, 1933), 1-2.
The dualism--sex and love--as propagated by Catholicism in Spain contributes to difficulties in the mature sexual
adjustment of married couples.

220   "Reflexiones sobre el amor, y IV, " núm. 4112 (24 de
mayo, 1933), 1-2.
Concluding a series of four articles on the subject of
love.   S. insists that human instincts, and specifically the
sexual instinct, must be "rehabilitated" or given their natural and rightful role in life.   What he calls "la vieja cultura

infestada de espiritualismo" has had pathological repercussions in the sexual adjustment of many Spaniards--male and female.   The substance--if not the letter--of this series of articles is found in Carta de Moscú sobre el amor (61).

221   "Getafe-el Ruhr a través de Francia en fiestas," núm. 4115 (27 de mayo, 1933), 5-6.
    S. reflects on the mechanization of life in the large cities, recalls flying over Aragón and Catalonia ("Nos sentimos más en nuestra casa en Cataluña que en Castilla") and a conversation with a reactionary and rigid Frenchman on the train from Paris to Berlin.

222   "Kolh-Berlin-Zoo en tres intervius," núm. 4117 (30 de mayo, 1933), 5-6.
    S. relates his experiences and thoughts while traveling by train from Paris to Berlin.   Between trains in Cologne he visits the famous cathedral in that city.

223   "Paréntesis en Berlín. La calle," núm. 4119 (1 de junio, 1933), 5.
    Reflections on antisemitism in Berlin ("Pero," writes S. , "la fiebre antisemita ha remitido bastante.   Hasta se echa un poco a broma el antisemitismo") and on the possible consequences of the passionate Nazi indoctrination of young Germans which, from "la calle," S. observes.

224   "Paréntesis en Berlín. Alexanderplatz," núm. 4120 (2 de junio, 1933), 5.
    S. reflects upon the Nazis, and German manners and customs in general, upon the occasion of his visit to Alexander Square.

225   "Paréntesis en Berlín. Hitler," núm. 4121 (3 junio, 1933), 5-6.
    S. notes the growing racism in Nazi Germany as well as that country's increasing adherence to Italy, and gives his own impressions of Hitler who, he writes, "no es un genio. . . .   Ni un loco. . . .   Hitler es un peón de albañil que aspiró toda su vida a incorporarse a la pequeña burguesía y que llevó a ella su conciencia política natural de proletario. "

226   "En Varsovia reina la paz; pero. . . ," núm. 4128 (11 de junio, 1933), 5.
    Appears to have been republished in Madrid-Moscú (60) under the title, "El silencio de Varsovia. "   S. describes his impressions of the Polish capital during an overnight

stay there while awaiting a train to Moscow.

227   "Llegamos a la capital de la Unión Soviética," núm.
      4132, (16 de junio, 1933), 5-6.
      S. relates the last leg of his journey by train to Mos-
cow--from the Polish border to the Soviet capital (customs,
checking of passports, changing currency, language difficulties, etc.)--and recalls incidents and conversations during
the trip from Berlin to Warsaw.

228   "Moscú, campamento general," núm. 4133 (17 de junio,
      1933), 5-6.
      After ten days in Moscow, S. concludes that the Rus-
sian city may be characterized as "un campamento en pie de
guerra. " Paris, for example, S. says, could be called "un
inmenso cafe. "

229   "En Moscú amanece más temprano," núm. 4134 (18 de
      junio, 1933), 5-6.
      Moscow continues its dynamic activity day and night.
"Moscú no duerme. Yo, que soy un pequeño burgués en
medio del dinamismo socialista de estas gentes, me voy a
dormir, porque a la una y media amanece, y si veo el día
antes de acostarme," writes S. , "me desmoralizo un poco. "

230   "De cómo los niños son los tiranos de Rusia," núm.
      4136 (21 de junio, 1933), 5.
      Homeless children (los "bisprichiornys") roam the
streets of Moscow, stealing and committing other annoying
acts, knowing that the police will not apprehend them. "Los
niños aquí son unos tiranos indiscutibles, absolutos. "

231   "12, Día de Reposo y 'Fiskultur'," núm. 4140 (25 de
      junio, 1933), 5-6.
      S. describes a day in Moscow dedicated to physical
culture in which 600,000 Russian athletes participate--be-
ginning with a huge parade to the Red Square.

232   "Interiores de la ciudad. Armas y letras," núm. 4146
      (2 de julio, 1933), 5-6.
      S. relates his experiences and impressions of Soviet
life while riding streetcars through the streets of Moscow,
and comments on the critical housing problem in the Soviet
capital.

233   "Strasnaya; o sea, plaza de las pasiones," núm. 4150
      (7 de julio, 1933), 5-6.

Apparently republished in Madrid-Moscú (60) with a
new title, "Hablando español en la Strasnaya. --¿Qué es eso
de las 'pasiones'?" S. gives his impressions of the Strasnaya, a plaza in Moscow, which he finds to be "una síntesis
de Moscú," and Moscow, he adds, "lo es de Europa y Asia,
incluyendo, naturalmente, en el Asia, a las razas islámi-
cas."

234   "Noches blancas y noches rojas," núm. 4155 (13 de
       julio, 1933), 5-6.
       Apparently republished in Madrid-Moscú (60) under the
title "Noche roja, o sea la nueva noche blanca, la de la
producción." S. describes his impressions during a recent
trip to Leningrad. "Cerca de Leningrado, la noche es como
el día en Madrid, en invierno, a las cuatro de la tarde."

235   "Aquí todo el mundo tiene quince años," núm. 4161 (21
       de julio, 1933), 5-6.
       S., while attending the funeral of an old and respected
Bolshevist, Clara Zentkin, sings the praises of the youthful
"pioneers," who "Si hoy tienen quince años, tienen la edad
misma que conocemos aquí entre los rusos. Clara Zentkin
misma no parece tener más de quince años."

236   "El librito rojo y la 'Chiska'," núm. 4164 (23 de julio,
       1933), 5-6.
       Seeing many people reading a little red book, upon in-
quiry S. learns that it is the history of the Bolshevik Party
and that throughout the U.S.S.R. the "Chiska" (purging of
all "unworthy" members from the Communist Party) is occurring. "Los Consejos analizan en público la historia de
los militantes de conducta no satisfactoria. Su origen. Si
fué burgués o hijo de burgueses...."

237   "La muerte y la nueva vida," núm. 4166 (26 de julio,
       1933), 5-6.
       S. affirms that in the U.S.S.R. "el Estado es el mis-
mo proletariado," while in Spain the State is "el aparato de
defensa de una clase." The "órganos" of the Soviet State
are "el cuartel, la fábrica y el 'koljos'."

238   "Preguntas sobre España," núm. 4168 (28 de julio,
       1933), 6-7.
       S. relates some of the questions about Spanish life
asked him by Soviet workers (from among a crowd of three
or four hundred workers) during his recent visit of the fac-
tory "A.M.O.," questions such as "¿Cuándo hareis vuestro

'Octubre'?," "¿Tú crees que los guardias civiles, como algunos cosacos, se negarán a luchar contra los obreros?," etc.

239   "Pequeñas notas que se nos habían perdido," núm. 4173
      (3 de agosto, 1933), 5-6.
      Miscellaneous impressions--none of which in itself
merits an article, says S. (datelined "Moscú, julio de 1933")
--of life in the Soviet Union: the northern sun of Russia,
the violence of the summer rains in Moscow, the urban unity
in Moscow ("no es la casa, sino la manzana"), etc.

240   "Notas sobre la 'Crasne-Arm'," núm. 4196 (30 de
      agosto, 1933), 5-6. (Datelined "Moscú, agosto, 1933.")
      S. seems impressed with the egalitarianism of the
Soviet army. "La camaradería que hemos visto en la fábrica, en el taller, en el campo, se prolonga en el cuartel, y
en esta Casa Central del Ejército Rojo." Relates the occupation of five Chinese border towns four years earlier in
which the "Crasne-Arm" (Red Army) took 3000 Chinese prisoners and treated them so well that in three days' time the
"confianza y camaradería" between the Red soldiers and
their prisoners "eran absolutas."

241   "Camino de Leninski Pat," núm. 4202 (6 de septiembre,
      1933), 5-6.
      Enroute to Leninski Pat, S. visits a small "koljos"
(collective farm), and meditates on the misery and humiliation of the country folk before the Revolution, "A veces
llegaba allí el Estado con sus jinetes cosacos a cobrar, a
llevarse los mozos para la guerra o a castigar a los campesinos."

242   "De la 'obchtchina' al 'kiljos' en una aldea de setenta
      familias," núm. 4218 (24 de septiembre, 1933), 5-6.
      (Datelined "Moscú, septiembre, 1933.")
      S. observes the arrival of the mail in a village of
seventy families, which includes a few copies of the official
newspaper published in Moscow for people in the country,
"Kristianskata Gatseta," subtitled "Diario de los Campesinos."
Also relates a visit to the village library, called the "isba."

243   "El Soviet, el suicidio y el incendio," núm. 4220 (27
      de septiembre, 1933), 5-6. (Datelined "Moscú, septiembre de 1933.")
      S. spends a day on a collective farm and quotes abundantly from a Communist leader (Stansni) who accompanies
him and points out the virtues of the Soviet system, the

apparent happiness of the farm workers, their educational
advantages under Communism, etc.

244   "Regreso a Moscú a bordo del 'Vostok'," núm. 4222
        (29 de septiembre, 1933), 5-6.
            In Gorki S. takes the excursion boat, Vostok, for Mos-
cow. On board he has some interesting conversations with
Bagritski, who professes to be a moral anarchist, and Kus-
ter, a woman who is in charge of a section of the "Editorial
del Estado de Moscú." In discussing love, S. says: "No
hay más que uno. Parte de los instintos.... El instinto en
los animales es ciego. En nosotros es clarividente y lo
alcanza y lo comprende todo."

245   "Ultimas horas en Moscú," núm. 4229 (7 de octubre,
        1933), 5-6. (Datelined "Vienna, septiembre, 1933.")
            S. talks all night in a bar with a Russian general be-
fore departing the Soviet Union. Asked by the general what
in his Russian visit he most disliked, S. replied: "Lo más
desagradable ha sido encontrarme en el ambiente intelectual
una posición servil en relación con la cultura burguesa de
Occidente." Denied by the German Embassy a visa to re-
enter Germany, S. chose to return to Spain by way of Poland, Czechoslovakia, and Austria.

246   "Tres Fronteras," núm. 4234 (13 de octubre, 1933),
        4.
            S.'s experiences (reading, conversation, etc.) while
traveling by train from Russia through Poland to Vienna via
Czechoslovakia.

247   "Viena, lago de Zurich y fin de ruta en París," núm.
        4238 (18 de octubre, 1933), 5-6. (Datelined "Madrid,
        octubre, 1933.")
            Returning from the Soviet Union, S. relates his very
pleasant stopover in Vienna ("Cuando nos fuimos de Viena lo
sentimos como si estuviéramos identifacados con la ciudad a
través de largos años de permanencia"), his passage through
Switzerland, and a short stay in Paris--a city in which he
found a lack of sincerity, even among the self-proclaimed
"revolucionarios."

248   "Pormenores de la 'razzia' (I)," núm. 4247 (28 de
        octubre, 1933), 5.
            A reconstruction of the bloody events of the beginning
of the repression of the uprising of peasants in Casas Viejas.

249   "Pormenores de la 'razzia' (II), " núm. 4250 (1 de
      noviembre, 1933), 5-6.
         S. continues his report upon the cruelties imposed upon
      the peasants of Casas Viejas during their uprising in January
      1933.

250   "Pormenores de la 'razzia' (III), " núm. 4252 (3 de
      noviembre, 1933), 5.
         A further report on the crushing defeat of the peasants
      (by Assault Guards) in the village of Casas Viejas.   In the
      ashes of the ruins of the miserable hut of the peasant-leader,
      "Seisdedos, " were "seis cuerpos abrasados. " Reprinted
      later in Casas Viejas (59) and in substance, if not textually,
      in Viaje a la aldea del crímen (5).

251   "Los vencidos y la tierra yerma, " núm. 4254 (5 de
      noviembre, 1933), 5-6.
         S. continues his narration of the brutal repression (by
      Assault Guards) of the peasant uprising in Casas Viejas,
      January 12-14, 1933.   Republished in Casas Viejas (59).

252   "La cárcel de Medina Sidonia, " núm. 4256 (8 de novi-
      embre, 1933), 5.
         Relates the miserable conditions in Casas Viejas and
      the arrest of a peasant woman from Casas Viejas by the
      Civil Guard and her detainment in the jail in Medina Sidonia.
      Jail officials denied S. permission to interview her in jail.

253   "El poeta soviético y la singularidad, " núm. 4263 (16
      de noviembre, 1933), 1.
         Discusses the position of the literary artist and the in-
      tellectual in Soviet society.   "Ni allí [in the U. S. S. R.] ni en
      ninguna otra parte se puede evitar--ni en Rusia se trata de
      evitar--que el artista que tiene talento se sirva libremente
      de él, con brillantez y hasta con provecho económico. "
      Cites the case of the Soviet poet Démian Bedny whose talents
      have been amply recognized and rewarded in the U. S. S. R.

254   "El teatro realista de Moscú y el nuevo teatro de
      Tiflis, " núm. 4272 (26 de noviembre, 1933), 5.
         The success of the "teatro realista" ("un teatro sin
      escenario, donde los actores carecen de un fondo y un de-
      corado" and directed to the masses with a political message)
      in Moscow has been so great, writes S. , that it has had
      repercussions even in Tiflis (on the periphery of the Soviet
      Union) where a new theater is under construction.

255 "Garcilaso y el Danubio Azul," núm. 4278 (3 de diciembre, 1933), 8.
     Republished in Proclamación de la sonrisa (62, p. 14-
18). A biography of Garcilaso de la Vega by Manuel Altolaguirre (as the last volume in the series, "Vidas extraordinarias," published by Espasa-Calpe) evokes praiseful comments on the poet who celebrated in verse the Blue Danube.

256 "La cultura y las nacionalidades," núm. 4282 (8 de diciembre, 1933), 5-6.
     A bit of the cultural and linguistic history of the Russian Empire upon the occasion of the sixteenth anniversary of the Constitution of the Soviet Union, with praise for the extent of "las tareas culturales llevadas a cabo" by the Soviet Government since the Revolution.

257 "Palacio del Libro de la R. S. F. S. R.," núm. 4290 (17 de diciembre, 1933), p. 5.
     S. describes a visit to the Palacio del Libro on Novinski boulevard in Madrid with comments on the rich collections of the works of Pushkin, Tolstoi, and others, the "Manifiesto" of Marx, the condensed history of the Revolution (the last translated and printed in sixty-two languages). The "Palacio," built in 1818 was first a private aristocratic home and then a private hotel until taken over by the Russian Government.

258 "Van der Lubbe," núm. 4293 (21 de diciembre, 1933), 1.
     Comments upon the impending sentencing of Van der Lubbe, the Dutch bricklayer, who after expulsion (apparently) from the Dutch Communist Party went to Germany where he became implicated in the burning of the Reichstag. S. argues that Van der Lubbe's condition of mental abnormality should be given weight in the sentence to be made by the Fascist Court in Leipzig but he writes: "No saben los 'Nazis' lo que es la generosidad."

259 "Ha muerto Macià," núm. 4301 (30 de diciembre, 1933), 1.
     S. eulogizes the Catalonian Republican leader, Macià, who "Sabía sentir como un anarquista transido, soñar como un castellano y creer como un niño, en lo absoluto."

260 "Lunatcharsky," núm. 4303 (2 de enero, 1934), 1.
     Republished in Proclamación de la sonrisa (62, p. 204-

07). Laments the death of Lunatcharsky, Soviet ambassador-
designate to Spain and author of the drama, Don Quixote Li-
berted.

261   "Garrote 'según la calidad de su persona'," núm. 4310
      (10 de enero, 1934), 1-2.
      Comments on "el bandolerismo andaluz como un fe-
nómeno social que se desprende de la estructura feudal de
la propiedad," and relates the public garroting of an Andalusian robber (as told by Bernaldo de Quirós and Luis Ardila
in their recent book, El bandolerismo).

262   "El tiro de alarma," núm. 4238 (31 de enero, 1934),
      1.
      Republished in Proclamación de la sonrisa (62, p. 192-
95). The slaying of the French financier and swindler Sta-
visky by the police (though called suicide) "ha sido un tiro
de alarma de hondas consecuencias políticas."

263   "Hacia el 'anti-Toledo'," núm. 4276 (31 de marzo,
      1934), 1.
      Republished in Proclamación de la sonrisa (62, p. 211-
14). "Va forjándose un Toledo nuevo. O, si se quiere, un
'anti-Toledo'." The times require not "la destrucción del
Toledo tradicional, sino su reajuste en nuestro tiempo y su
completación."

264   "Villa Malta, en Roma," núm. 4381 (6 de abril, 1934),
      1.
      Republished in Proclamación de la sonrisa (62, p. 208-
11). Mariana Beccadelli di Bologha, Princess of Camporeale,
who died recently in Villa Malta, married von Bülow, German ambassador to Italy. The two of them changed history
through their influence upon Wilhelm II, the German Kaiser.

265   "El señor verdugo," núm. 4389 (15 de abril, 1934),
      1-2.
      Republished in Proclamación de la sonrisa (62, p. 195-
200). An expression of S.'s opposition to the imposition of
the death penalty--for any reason whatsoever.

266   "El rescate de la República," núm. 4394 (21 de abril,
      1934), 1.
      After reviewing the near-chaotic condition of Spanish
political parties, S. asks: "¿qué quiere decir cada organización cuando habla de rescatar la República? Tendríamos
tantas respuestas como partidos políticos."

267   "El diá de los libros quemados," núm. 4399 (27 de
      abril, 1934), 1.
      Commenting on the upcoming "Feria del Libro," spon-
sored by the "Cámara del Libro," S. suggests that part of
the celebration of books (May 10, 1934) be dedicated to the
"rehabilitación del 'libro quemado'," in regretful memory of
the burning of thousands of books in several German capitals
one year earlier.

268   "Inadaptados en el banco azul," núm. 4408 (9 de mayo,
      1934), 1.
      S. comments on the recent appointment to the Ministry
of Justice by the Republican Government of two men who
during three years of the Republic "No se han adaptado. Se
conservan al margen." Perhaps now, S. writes ironically,
we may hope to see Pío Baroja as "presidente de las Cortes,
o al pintor Solana de Presidente de Comisión de Códigos."

269   "Libros y críticos de libros," núm. 4413 (15 de mayo,
      1934), 1.
      S. deplores the tendency in Spain to prefer foreign
literary works over the work of Spanish authors, and sati-
rizes Spanish critics for whom "la vida parece que habría
de ser una inmensa biblioteca aislada, sin conexión con el
Mundo." S. points out that Spaniards downgrade the importance of their own country, not realizing that in Moscow,
Rome, Berlin, and Paris "España es un tema de primer
orden."

270   "Rabelais e Ignacio, en el pinar," núm. 4415 (17 de
      mayo, 1934), 1.
      Republished in Proclamación de la sonrisa (62, p. 200-
04). The Franciscan, Rabelais, would be content today in
the Jesuit seminary in Aranjuez with its splendid kitchens.

271   "El 'político del buen sentido'," núm. 4419 (22 de
      mayo, 1934), 1.
      A discussion of the life, political views, and accom-
plishments of Thomas G. Masaryk, who at 84 had just been
re-elected President of Czechoslovakia. Masaryk has shown
good sense and "cree que se han de llegar a realizar todas
las aspiraciones del socialismo, pero sin privarlas de las
conquistas morales de la cultura. Por un ideal de humanidad
más que por la economía política."

272   "Casas Viejas y los delincuentes," núm. 4422 (25 de
      mayo, 1934), 1.

Comments on the continuing investigation of those responsible for the killing of several peasants at Casas Viejas in January of 1933. "La realidad de Casas Viejas," writes S., "es que allí no hubo oro, sino plomo. Que cayeron campesinos sin color político, ... y que los agresores cometieron los desmanes defendiendo de un riesgo más o menos imaginario a los terratenientes enemigos de la República."

273   "La cosecha y los campesinos," núm. 4426 (30 de mayo, 1934), 1.

Though a bountiful crop in all parts of Spain is predicted it will not benefit either the consumer in the city or the jornalero (dayworker) on the farms. The Spanish economic "monstruo" on the one side "trata de esquilmar al trabajador del campo y por otro al consumidor de la ciudad."

274   "Los escritores soviéticos," núm. 4441 (16 de junio, 1934), 1.

The Congress of Soviet Writers is to convene at the end of June in Moscow. The younger Soviet writers in general advocate "realismo socialista," and S. predicts that this tendency will prevail at the meeting of the Congress. S. discusses the differences between "realismo socialista" and "la primitiva escuela realista francesa," with special reference to Zola.

275   "Arte de dejar estar," núm. 4449 (26 de junio, 1934), 1.

Quoting Baltasar Gracián's aphoristic statement that in medicine one should often do nothing but "dejar hacer a la Naturaleza," S. agrees with Gracián but insists that in socio-politico-economic matters one cannot stand by passively and "dejar estar." To do so is "un medio seguro de prolongar y complicar la dificultad."

276   "Un refrán junto al manantial," núm. 4452 (29 de junio, 1934), 1.

On vacation, S. roams through the countryside talking with country folk, including a goatherd whom he met beside a spring. "Hemos cruzado tres aldeas. En la montaña las aldeas son tristes. Los viejos son todos reumáticos."

277   "Por la noche en la plaza," núm. 4456 (4 de julio, 1934), 1.

On vacation in a village in the Sierra of Aragon, S. comments on the differences between the mountain people--los montañeses--and people from the plains--los hombres

d'abaxo--as well as the reactions of the villagers towards
visitors from the cities. "En el fondo ... el aldeano de la
montaña esconde un rencor resentido contra la ciudad. "

278 "Noticias de Madrid y de Berlín, " núm. 4459 (7 de
     julio, 1934), 1.
     From Berlin S. comments on the news (from Madrid)
that while eleven Spanish peasants are still in jail for possession of firearms the year before petitions are being made
to exempt two members (diputados) to the Spanish Parlia-
ment--Lozano and Primo de Rivera's son--from being tried
for illegal possession of firearms.

279 "Los siglos y la muerte airada, " núm. 4466 (15 de
     julio, 1934), 1.
     While on vacation S. reads a book by a French author,
Verdinois, which reports on the number of people killed by
war in recent centuries, and reflects on the grave conse-
quences facing mankind in this century if a sweeping change
does not occur. "La cuestión ha sido siempre en engañar
de arriba abajo, unas veces con la religión, otras con el
idealismo. "

280 "Materialismo y misticismo en el pinar, " núm. 4469
     (19 de julio, 1934), 1.
     While on vacation in a Spanish village S. spends two
hours lying under the pine trees and conversing with the
village doctor and the village priest. Though he rejects ma-
terialism the doctor argues for "libertad de pensamiento"
which is rejected by the priest. "El cura lo [the doctor or
his position] combate sin espíritu cristiano alguno. "

281 "Divagación sobre lo concreto, " núm. 4473 (24 de
     julio, 1934), 1.
     Vacationing in northern Spain S. reflects on the "con-
creteness" of life one finds in the country among the rural
folk whose minds are unaffected by abstractions so dear to
the so-called cultured and intellectual classes. "Hoy es
verdaderamente excepcional la mente orientada 'al concreto, '
por la gran cobardía difusa ... que invade libros, periódicos y asambleas. " Politicians are neither men of "concre-
ciones, " nor "abstracciones, " but "gente de vaguedades. "

282 "Con un campesino, entre dos valles, " núm. 4479 (31
     de julio, 1934), 1.
     While vacationing in the country, S. talks with some
campesinos and learns that after more than two years of

Republican Government the peasants have received little, if anything, more than unfulfilled promises.

283   "Un Cristo tallado por los ángeles," núm. 4496 (19 de agosto, 1934), 1.
While on vacation, S. visits a hermitage where there is a wooden image of Christ ("una blasfemia de una gran plasticidad") supposedly sculptured by some angels who stopped there disguised as "caminantes" (travelers). Comments on various kinds of superstition--free versus that "organized" or "exploited" by the Church or political organizations.

284   "Alemania y el plebiscito," núm. 4501 (25 de agosto, 1934), 1.
The recent election in Germany in which about five million votes were cast against the Nazis "no tiene valor ninguno como función democrática." The Nazis play only to win, and "no conciben la ganancia sino en la proporción de ciento por uno." The elections were to demonstrate to the outside world Hitler's popularity in Germany. Comments on the recent demand by the Nazi Government for the abolition of the German "frente del Trabajo."

285   "Los jóvenes y la indecisión," núm. 4505 (30 de agosto, 1934), 1.
S. laments the indecision and fear of the future which Spanish youth of twenty years of age reveal. "Esa angustia frente al porvenir es malsana. No alcanza a todos los jóvenes--afortunadamente--sino al sector intelectual."

286   " 'Salvar a Telman'," núm. 4508 (2 de septiembre, 1934), 1.
In a Spanish village S. finds that someone has written on a white wall "Salvar a Telman." Thaelmann was a German worker unjustly threatened with execution by the Nazis. S. sees in the "letrero" perhaps the "núcleo palpitante de cierta conciencia palpitante," despite the subhuman conditions in which the Spanish villagers live.

287   "A. E. A. R.," núm. 4514 (11 de septiembre, 1934), 1.
The Asociación de Escritores y Artistas Revolucionarios has just been established in Spain. "Pasan del millar los jóvenes entusiastamente adheridos. Obreros, empleados, estudiantes, jóvenes intelectuales--periodistas, profesores, poetas--artistas--pintores, dibujantes, grabadores, escultores, músicos ... Salud ... a la A. E. A. R. Y mi adhesión,

satisfecho de poder adherirme sin reservas, confiado e
ilusionado. "

288 "Los años decisivos," núm. 4522 (19 de septiembre,
      1934), 1.
      A negative commentary on Spengler's latest book, Los
años decisivos. "Spengler, a través de mil contradicciones, "
writes S. , "... nos plantea las más recientes conclusiones
del fascismo imperialista. "

289 "Thaelmann y el 'Tribunal popular'," núm. 4526 (23
      de septiembre, 1934), 1.
      Commenting on the recent announcement by the German
Government that the revolutionary leader, Thaelmann, would
not receive the death penalty, S. attributes this decision
mainly to the force of public opinion in and out of Germany.
"Tienen que tomar en cuenta en la Alemania actual a la
callada, pero activa oposición de dentro y de fuera. "

290 " 'Canguro' y el individualismo," núm. 4529 (27 de
      septiembre, 1934), 1.
      "Gran libro 'Canguro' [Kangaroo] es una epopeya del
individualismo de nuestro tiempo en liquidación.... " Lawrence, one of those individualists "hypersensibles del sentimiento de sí mismos" should have stayed in England rather
than going off to another island, Australia. "Pero en dos
circunstancias se muestra fiel Lawrence a su individualismo. "

291 "Sobre unas palabras de Gorki, " núm. 4532 (30 de
      septiembre, 1934), 1.
      Quoting from Gorki, S. argues that though D. H. Law-
rence is a genius, his latest book, Canguro, is "una expo-
sición lenta y segura de la esterilidad del conocimiento de
sí mismo.... " When man neglects the fact that he is a social creature he turns inward in his aloneness to ask "preguntas ociosas y perturbadoras: '¿Quién soy? ¿Qué soy?' "

292 "En el aniversario de Emilio Zola," núm. 4534 (3 de
      octubre, 1934), 1.
      It is ironic that today Zola is "exaltado y conmemo-
rado por la crema de la burguesía francesa contra la que
dirigió sus diatribas más apasionadas.... Zola se indigna-
ría mucho si leyera hoy las críticas políticas que se hacen
de sus libros. "

293 "Ataraxia," núm. 4547 (27 de octubre, 1934), 1.
      Ataraxia (tranquillity of soul) is needed today in Spain,

especially by the Monarchists who clamor feverishly for revenge. "La dolencia [in Spain] ha hecho crisis. Ahora, en estos momentos, apelar a la venganza es querer suscitar una nueva enfermedad, cuyos alcances nadie puede predecir."

294   "El hombre y el tiempo," núm. 4561 (13 de noviembre, 1934), 1.
Instead of asking what kind of man will be "el hombre de mañana," we should ask "¿cuál es la esencia perdurable del hombre, lo que ha de permanecer y prolongarse hacia el porvenir? ... Del hombre esclavo del tiempo pasamos al hombre señor del tiempo: al hombre en eternidad."

295   "Hacia el 'hombre nuevo'," núm. 4568 (21 de noviembre, 1934), 1.
Because of modern means of communication we are moving towards the future and the "new man" at an accelerating rate. "No sólo filosóficamente, sino prácticamente, nuestro presente está henchido de porvenir y se desprende cada día más apresuradamente del pasado, conservando sólo la esencia perdurable, la levadura de lo eterno."

296   "Algunos síntomas," núm. 4575 (29 de noviembre, 1934), 1.
S. sees two symptoms of the "decadencia del individualismo": "... por un lado, en la aproximación social de los dos sexos, en la despreocupación sexual, que viene ganando a las generaciones actuales.... Por otro, en la frecuencia y desvalorización moral del heroísmo y el héroe."

297   "Sobre el sentimiento de lo heroico," núm. 4580 (5 de diciembre, 1934), 1.
Hero worship is diminishing today as some men are beginning to think not " 'en individuo,' sino 'en especie,' que es como pensaría la propia naturaleza físico." S. would destroy the old idea of individualism (with its hero worship) in favor of "la idea de lo social y de lo colectivo."

298   "Hablemos del estilo, si usted quiere," núm. 4584 (9 de diciembre, 1934), 1.
S. reveals his disdain for "style" as understood in the academies. "No faltan los que, desdeñando los conceptos de estilo y estilismo, poseen una manera personal, aislada y distinta. El verdadero estilo."

299   "Una manera de entender el estilo," núm. 4592 (19 de diciembre, 1934), 1.

A reader penetrates the true "style" of an author only
by seeking "en la composición y en la expresión objetiva la
posición totalizadora del autor ante la Naturaleza, ante el
Mundo, ante la sociedad." It is in this "cuarta dimensión"
of art that true style is born. In the true artists expression "tomaba ... la forma que le daban imperiosamente la
temperatura, el ritmo y el ímpetu interiores."

300   "Cervantes, el estilo y un capítulo apócrifo," núm.
       4602 (30 de diciembre, 1934), 1.
       S. affirms that he will never believe that Chapter V of
the second part of Don Quijote was written by Cervantes--
because its style is not Cervantine at all. S. speculates
that perhaps Cervantes carelessly permitted "que metiera la
pluma en su obra una inteligencia tosca."

301   "Sexta Representación de 'Yerma'," núm. 4607 (5 de
       enero, 1935), 1.
       A review of Lorca's play, Yerma. S. praises very
highly "la escena de las lavanderas y la bacanal de la ere-
mita" but views Act One as "peor que malo."

302   "Con motivo de una flauta berberisca," núm. 4612 (11
       de enero, 1935), 3.
       Reflections on Moorish music, singing, dancing, and
poetry inspired by the gift of a flute sent to S. by a friend
from Ifni.

303   "Los diletantes," núm. 4619 (19 de enero, 1935), 1, 3.
       Reflections on dilettantism--in philosophy, art, politics,
revolution. "El pobre diletantismo no hace nada. Se limi-
ta a contemplar."

304   "Balzac y madame Hanska," núm. 4624 (25 de enero,
       1935), 1.
       Reflections upon the discovery in the National Library
in Warsaw of a letter from Madame Hanska to her brother,
Henryk Rsewuski, shedding light on her love for the great
writer, Balzac. Two chapters of Tres ejemplos de amor y
una teoría (68) are devoted to Balzac and Madame Hanska.

305   "El bandido sentimental," núm. 4632 (3 de febrero,
       1935), 1-2.
       Reflections on the romantic sentimentalism often asso-
ciated in the popular mind with bandits. "El bandolerismo
se ha dado en todo el Mundo; pero el carácter sentimental
y heroico de los bandoleros florecía en España mejor que

en ningún sitio. "

306   "El 'logos,' de chaqué," núm. 4638 (10 de febrero, 1935), 1.
Commentary on Keyserling (who at the time was giving lectures in Madrid) revealing Sender's admiration for the man and his work. Summarizes Keyserling's basic message, which is essentially an exaltation of intuitive knowledge.

307   "La vida literaria y la otra," núm. 4657 (5 de marzo, 1935), 1.
Discusses the "atmósfera moral" ("más turbia aún con la influencia del cine alemán y americano") in Spain which militates against literary work.

308   "La necesidad de aturdirse," núm. 4662 (10 de marzo, 1935), 1-2.
Reflections on man's need to "aturdirse"--find release through unconventional and irrational behavior in public (as during carnival, for example; "walking on all fours," etc.).

309   "Wells y Stalin," núm. 4669 (19 de marzo, 1935), 3.
Comments on an interview H. G. Wells had with Stalin. S. finds Wells in his efforts to reconcile British and American intelligence and technology with state capitalism (Communism) not taking all the facts into account.

310   "La 'anti-España' y los municipios," núm. 4683 (4 de abril, 1935), 5.
Only in the town (and city) governments, "los municipios," have the Spanish people been able to retain political power. "Las Constituciones democráticas no han podido quitarle [al Concejo] prerrogativas. "

311   "Panait Istrati," núm. 4700 (24 de abril, 1935), 1-2.
Reflections on the life and ideology of the humanitarian (and author of Kira Kyralina), Panait Istrati, on the occasion of his death. Some elements in his thought separate him from S.; others unite him.

312   "Gaudeamus, sed...," núm. 4712 (9 de mayo, 1935), 1-2.
Comments on the lecture by a Catholic priest (P. Laburu) in praise of bullfighting. S. suspects the Church of using its priest to incorporate the Church and its followers "a una corriente general de defensa contra-revolucionaria. "

313   "Ludendorf y Hitler," núm. 4737 (7 de junio, 1935), 2.
      Reflections on why Hitler recently chose to honor the
Prussian general Ludendorf, and on a book by Wilhelm Reich,
Psicología de masas del fascismo. S. views Ludendorf as
simply "un servidor técnico del espíritu rapaz e imperialista."

314   "Los Ayuntamientos de elección popular," núm. 4743
      (14 de junio, 1935), 1-2.
      Pleads for a return to election of city and town govern-
ments (ayuntamientos) by popular vote. Apparently the Republican Government had suspended some (or all?) popularly
elected ayuntamientos.

315   "Sobre un desdichado acuerdo," núm. 4749 (21 de junio,
      1935), 1-2.
      S. objects to the members (and their attitudes) of the
new "Patronato del teatro Español," and the Government's
selection of the members of that Board or "Patronato."
"Cada día se explica uno con más dificultad la conducta del
Estado, la Provincia y el Municipio con aquellas manifestaciones del arte y del pensamiento en las que les es dado
intervenir."

316   "Yen Wang," núm. 4756 (29 de junio, 1935), 1-2.
      In Chinese "Yen Wang" means "king of hell." Though
the idea of hell and of cruelty may have come from the
Orient, the Western World "vive su infierno" and has its
laws, codes of repression, and instruments of cruelty "en
nada inferiores a los de China."

317   "Dicen Caillaux y Paul Valéry," núm. 4773 (19 de
      julio, 1935), 1.
      Takes issue with statements by Caillaux (ex-president
of the French Council) and Paul Valéry blaming science for
the ills of the World, especially its economic problems.
For a large proportion of the World's population the era of
science and technology, which could improve their living
standard, has not yet arrived.

318   "Recordando lo de Osa de la Vega," núm. 4781 (28 de
      julio, 1935), 1-2.
      Recalls the torturing of two peasants, León Sánchez
and Gregorio Valero, by the Civil Guard a decade earlier
(during the days of Primo de Rivera) to extract from them
a confession of an assassination they did not commit, their
serving time in prison for the same "crime," subsequent
release, and non-acceptance by society. Served, it appears,

as the inspiration for El lugar de un hombre (8).

319   "Un antecedente del Congreso de escritores," núm.
      4788 (6 de agosto, 1935), 1.
      Recalls an antecedent to the International Congress of
Writers recently held in Paris, a Congress held in June,
1878, to which Turgenev was a delegate. Discusses the
great writer and quotes from his speech to the Congress.

320   "La tradición: escoria y herencia," núm. 4797 (16 de
      agosto, 1935), 1.
      Discussion of tradition. One must distinguish between
the living part of tradition and its dead part, the "eco inerte
de las sombras de un tiempo sin continuidad posible." The
"herencia mejor de los tiempos está viva en la calle."

321   "La guerra," núm. 4846 (12 de octubre, 1935), 3.
      Comments on the Italian attack upon Abyssinia. "El
capitalismo italiano va a enterrarse vivo en Abisinia." No
capitalist country will come to Mussolini's aid--at least for
the moment.

322   "El Delator," núm. 4864 (2 de noviembre, 1935), 1-2.
      Discussion of a new (the second) film of O'Flaherty's
novel, El delator, and of the novel itself.

323   "A propósito de Monipodio," núm. 4893 (6 de diciembre,
      1935), 1-2.
      Comments on Monipodio, a charming old pícaro in Cer-
vantes' Rinconete y Cortadillo, and on Spanish life then and
now.

324   "P. E. N. Club, crepúsculos y otras evasivas," núm.
      4899 (13 de diciembre, 1935), 7.
      Having been invited to join the P. E. N. Club, S. ex-
amines its purpose and program and concludes that the Club
"carece de base," and is perhaps evasive. "En un tiempo
agitado y erizado de problemas la evasiva es una actitud
inmoral."

325   "Fermín Galán," núm. 4914 (31 de diciembre, 1935), 7.
      S. urges the Republican Government to bring to Madrid
the remains of Fermín Galán, the "héroe de Jaen," in whom
the people found incarnate "la protesta contra una monarquía
abyecta." Accuses the Government (of the last two years)
of obstructing the full expression of the popular will. But
in the end "La fuerza popular seguirá su curso y su proceso,

a pesar de todo. "

326   "Glosa a un decreto," núm. 4979 (15 de marzo, 1936),
      1-2.
      S. criticizes the Government's decree obligating busi-
ness enterprises to rehire (with indemnification for lost
time) employees who were discharged during a recent struggle of the Bloque Popular against "las derechas. "

E. ARTICLES IN PERIODICALS OTHER THAN LA LIBERTAD
AND NOT AS SYNDICATED COLUMN,
"LOS LIBROS Y LOS DIAS"

327   "Valle-Inclán, la política y la cárcel," Nueva España
      (Madrid), marzo, 1930.
      Republished in Valle Inclán visto por... (93), compiled
by José Esteban in 1973. Relates the two occasions on
which the Galician author was jailed during the Dictatorship
of the twenties. Interesting observations on Valle-Inclán's
political interests, home life, and colorful personality.

328   "Diatriba del arte puro," Mañana (Madrid), junio,
      1930, 14.
      "Dice Sender con gran ironía que no puede concebir el
arte puro excepto en 'el balbuceo del niño ante cada nueva
cosa.' Lo que le interesa al hombre maduro es 'la vida,
la esperanza, la desesperación, el placer, el dolor, el individuo y la sociedad' " (Nonoyama, 1357).

329   "Postal política," Solidaridad Obrera (Barcelona), 1 de
      octubre, 1930. ("Postal política" was the title of a
      column written by S. and published in Solidaridad
      Obrera, the organ of the Confederación Nacional de
      Trabajo, from October 1929 until mid-1932. All anno-
      tations of "Postal política" are direct quotations from
      Michiko Nonoyama's doctoral thesis [item 1357 of this
      Bibliography] or based directly upon her thesis. The
      compiler has not examined these items directly.)
      S. comments on a large Republican meeting in Madrid's
Plaza de Toros on September 28. Supporting the meeting he
writes: "La serenidad y la fe en la eficacia de esta revolución política [against the Dictatorship] es tal que son capa-
ces de reunirse 40,000 hombres sin una voz disonante, sin
un grito subversivo" (quoted from Nonoyama's thesis [item
1357]).

330   "Postal política," Solidaridad Obrera (Barcelona), 18 de octubre, 1930.
S. "se burla de los socialistas que quieren gobernar con el rey" (Nonoyama, 1357).

331   "Postal política," Solidaridad Obrera (Barcelona), 5 de abril, 1931.
"Celebra [S.] los esfuerzos de los republicanos [to establish the Republic through legal channels, without violence] y dice que por primera vez en la historia del mundo se quiere derrocar por la persuasión una monarquía militar de 20 siglos de existencia" (Nonoyama, 1357).

332   "Postal política," Solidaridad Obrera (Barcelona), 23 de abril, 1931.
S. approves of the newly established Republic "como un paso de avance con respecto a la monarquía. Dice: 'Es un régimen posible, más fácil que durante la monarquía. El próximo paso será la revolución en nombre del trabajo y la producción' " (Nonoyama, 1357).

333   "Postal política," Solidaridad Obrera (Barcelona), 30 de abril, 1931.
Irritated, S. asks the Republican Government: "¿Qué plan se va a seguir con los latifundios? ¿Qué normas van a regir en los contratos de arrendamiento?" (Nonoyama, 1357).

334   "Postal política," Solidaridad Obrera (Barcelona), 9 de mayo, 1931.
S. "propone el Frente Unico [de los trabajadores] como la única posición revolucionaria de las izquierdas y recomienda su dirección a la CNT [Confederación Nacional de Trabajo] como la única organización obrera de clase" (Nonoyama, 1357).

335   "Postal política," Solidaridad Obrera (Barcelona), 17 de mayo, 1931.
Commenting on "la guerra de los conventos e iglesias que ocurrió el 11 de ese mes en Madrid, [S.] protesta contra la movilización de la guardia civil, de la policía, del ejército, hasta del parque de bomberos" (Nonoyama, 1357).

336   "Postal política," Solidaridad Obrera (Barcelona), 10 de junio, 1931.
S. distinguishes the CNT from the UGT (Unión General de Trabajadores) as follows: "En la CNT, sin existir una

disciplina existe la confianza en los dirigentes y por lo tanto, un conjunto orgánico consciente, mientras que en la UGT donde se pretende mantener una dictadura burocrática y una disciplina cuartelaria, ni existe la confianza ni la disciplina, ni hay jefes que pueden responder de la voluntad de los trabajadores" (quoted by Nonoyama, 1357).

337   "Postal política," Solidaridad Obrera (Barcelona), 27 de junio, 1931.
S. "parece apoyar la posición del anarquismo clásico individualista contra el sindicalismo" (Nonoyama, 1357).

338   "Postal política," Solidaridad Obrera (Barcelona), 24 de julio, 1931.
S. protests against the Government's suppression of agitation by the CNT in Seville ("semana sangrienta, 18 de julio--25 de julio, 1931") "y declara que la batalla contra la CNT es la batalla contra el pueblo español" (Nonoyama, 1357).

339   "Postal política," Solidaridad Obrera (Barcelona), 9 de diciembre, 1931.
S. defends the CNT "a la que tienden a culpar los conservadores ministeriales de la amenaza terrorista.
... Identifica lo que caracteriza a los sindicatos con lo que honra a cualquier democracia europea: limpieza moral y educación societaria, cultura y dignidad de clase" (Nonoyama, 1357).

340   "Postal política," Solidaridad Obrera (Barcelona), 11 de marzo, 1932.
S. "dice que la CNT sin caudillos ni jefes tiene ventajas y peligros, peligros porque hay dificultades para orientarse. El espíritu y la idealidad que se distribuyen en centenares de miles de trabajadores tarda demasiado en hallar el organismo vivo a través del que debe actuar.... ([S.] se acerca más a la línea realista de los sindicalistas [comments Nonoyama, p. 17])" (Nonoyama, 1357).

341   "Postal política," Solidaridad Obrera (Barcelona), 12 de marzo, 1932.
Revealing disillusionment with the fruits of recent anarchist efforts S. recommends that anarchists "llenar con algo sólido y firme el vacío eterno de la buena fe, del espíritu de sacrificio, del entusiasmo, que nos han llevado al gran triunfo moral pero al estancamiento en la lucha" (quoted by Nonoyama, 1357).

342   "Postal política," Solidaridad Obrera (Barcelona), 22
de marzo, 1932.
S. attacks the Socialists "por su oportunismo; por vo-
tar con Miguel Maura y colaborar con Primo de Rivera"
(Nonoyama, 1357).

343   "Postal política," Solidaridad Obrera (Barcelona), 27
de marzo, 1932.
S. persists "en la actitud antagónica contra el republi-
canismo afirmando la necesidad de la revolución en lugar de
la reforma, al decir: 'Nada resuelve porque no suprime el
interés privado, el capitalismo y la explotación' " (Nonoyama,
1357).

344   "Postal política," Solidaridad Obrera (Barcelona), 29
de marzo, 1932.
S. criticizes "el federalismo iniciado por Proudhon y
heredado por Bakunín que introdujo en España Pi y Margall,
por su falta de coordinación" (Nonoyama, 1357).

345   "Postal política," Solidaridad Obrera (Barcelona), 1 de
abril, 1932.
S. "critica violentamente a los comunistas del partido
diciendo que España es el primer país del mundo 'donde de
momento es posible la democracia [no en el sentido político, dice
S., sino " 'en el absoluto de la filosofía' "] ... y que ... el
proletariado español es adversario de todo lo que sea coacción y dictadura de minorías' " (Nonoyama, 1357).

346   "Postal política," Solidaridad Obrera (Barcelona), 2 de
abril, 1932.
S. "califica negativamente a las actividades anarquistas
realizadas bajo la segunda República. Llama a los militantes de la Federación Anarquista Ibérica [FAI] fanáticos"
(Nonoyama, 1357).

347   "Presión del superestado católico," Cultura Libertaria
(Barcelona), 3 de abril, 1932.
"Ve [S.] que por el concordato de 1851 el superestado
católico adquiere una realidad más potente que el estado
civil, que la enseñanza cayó en el poder del clero, que se
establecío una división territorial de España por metropoli-
tanos, diócesis y parroquias pagados por el Estado. Todas
las ventajas jurídicas fueron otorgadas a la iglesia" (Nonoyama, 1357).

348   "Postal política," Solidaridad Obrera (Barcelona), 8 de

abril, 1932.
Insisting on the need to unify "la propaganda y la lucha
legal contra el Estado en la ofensiva, expone [S.] la utilidad
y las limitaciones del municipio libre.... Es una adverten-
cia severa contra la tendencia del espontaneísmo y la exalta-
ción individual" (Nonoyama, 1357).

349   "Postal política," Solidaridad Obrera (Barcelona), 10
      de abril, 1932.
      Reflecting his recent shift in viewpoint away from ex-
treme individualistic anarchism and towards the syndicalist
group in the CNT, S. "dice que la sociedad de mañana tiene
su porvenir asegurado porque se basa en los camaradas
albañiles y metalúrgicos y panaderos y campesinos, en
hechos económicos infalibles" (Nonoyama, 1357).

350   "Literatura proletaria," Orto (¿Valencia?), 2, 3 (mayo,
      1932), 11-12.
      S. "llama camaradas a los escritores de la Unión In-
ternacional de Escritores Proletarios y les agradece el
haberlo titulado escritor proletario por la publicación de
Imán" (Nonoyama, 1357).

351   "Postal política," Solidaridad Obrera (Barcelona), 29
      de junio, 1932.
      S. asserts that "el Frente Unico va contra la constitu-
ción y las líneas generales de la República" (Nonoyama,
1357).

352   Article in La Lucha (Madrid), 30 de enero, 1934.
      ("Al nacer La Lucha, suprimido Mundo Obrero [news-
paper of the Communist Party], durante las elecciones
de noviembre de 1933," writes Nonoyama [1357, p. 8],
S. "llegó a ser su director. Con la confiscación de
este periódico fue arrestado.")
      S. "critica a Largo Caballero por excluir a los campe-
sinos de la dictadura del proletariado," and says that "la
huelga general es un movimiento inconcluso y que antes de
ella deben existir los órganos de lucha por el poder. Estos
órganos durante la huelga revolucionaria podrían crear in-
mediatamente la dualidad de poder: el poder de los obreros,
campesinos y soldados frente al de la burguesía" (Nonoyama,
1357).

353   Article in La Lucha (Madrid), 9 de febrero, 1934.
      S. "critica a los socialistas y a los anarquistas que
creen que el único frente popular es el contacto de hombres

en la calle. Elogia al partido comunista por su posición
certera a este respecto y por la eficacia de su campaña,"
writes Nonoyama in her thesis (1357).

354   Article in La Lucha (Madrid), 17 de febrero, 1934.
       S. "ataca a los anarquistas pues repudian a los soviets
como órganos de poder alegando que Rusia es un país lejano
y que España tiene formas propias de organización" (Nonoyama, 1357).

355   "La cultura española en la ilegalidad," Tensor (Madrid),
       8 (agosto, 1935), 3-21. (According to Nonoyama
       [1357], the "grupo Tensor" of Marxist persuasion was
       formed in 1935 and directed by S.)
       "Sender polariza la cultura española en legítima e
ilegítima o sea la oficial y la no-oficial. Defiende la última,
continuadora de la tradición popular, contra la primera
representada por la clase feudal y clerical o el Estado y la
Inquisición. Va trazando la contribución del pueblo desde la
Edad Media para mantener la unidad y la continuidad"
(Nonoyama, 1357, p. 73).

356   Article in Juventud (¿Madrid?), 15 de enero, 1936.
       A lyrical defense of the Frente Popular. "El hombre
lucha en nuestro campo por mantener su eterna fidelidad,
su identificación con la naturaleza" (quoted by Nonoyama,
1357).

357   "El novelista y las masas," Leviatán (Madrid), 1, 1
       (mayo, 1936), 31-41. (Only three numbers of this
       journal were issued--May-October, 1936; microfilm
       copies are available in the Yale University Library.)
       S. accuses bourgeois literature of a lack of "princi-
pio vital"; such principle can be found only in literature
identified with the needs and aspirations of the masses.

358   Speech by Sender, El Sol (Madrid), 11 de noviembre,
       1936.
       El Sol publishes a speech delivered by S. on the Com-
munist radio station. S. declares that he favors neither the
Communists nor the Anarchists but that he applauds the
unity of the Frente Popular against Fascism (Nonoyama,
1357, p. 40).

359   "The People's Front in Spain," New Masses, 23, 5
       (April 20, 1937), 3-4.
       S. praises the Popular Front in Spain. Members of

the petty bourgeoisie who up until now had opposed proletari-
an policies have, he writes, changed their minds and "now
take their places with us to obtain the most advanced solution possible within the framework of a democracy." The
Civil War is between Fascism and Democracy.

360   "The Peasant's War," Nation, 145 (October 30, 1937),
       475-77.
       An excerpt from Counter-Attack in Spain (63), praising
the fighting spirit of the peasants against Fascism.

361   "On a Really Austere Aesthetic," Books Abroad, 16, 2
       (April, 1942), 119-23.
       An important statement on the author's view of lite-
rary creation, and the subconscious as the primary source
of such creation.

362   "My Grandfather Was a Mountaineer," Harper's Maga-
       zine, 186, 1114 (March, 1943), 377-79.
       S. relates a conversation that he, as a young writer,
had with his aged rural grandfather.

363   "My Grandfather Was a Mountaineer," Scholastic, 49
       (December 6, 1943), 19-20.
       A reprint of 362.

364   "Speaking of Epitaphs," Books Abroad, 19, 2 (April,
       1945), 222-27.
       A negative view of James Joyce.

365   "A Rhapsodic Age," tr. by Dudley Fitts, Partisan
       Review, 12, 1 (Winter 1945), 107-11.
       An optimistic view on the creation of poetry in Spanish
America. "May it not be that America, the whole of America, north and south, is living in the very age of the rhapso-
dists?"

366   "The Parabola of Poetry," View--The Modern Maga-
       zine, Series 5, 5 (December, 1945), 10.
       The place of poetry is where the conscious and the
subconscious intersect to create a kind of "transcendental
consciousness."

367   "The Spanish Autobiography of Arturo Barea," tr. by
       Leslie C. Schwartz, The New Leader, 30, 2 (January
       11, 1947), 12.
       A review of Barea's book, The Forging of a Rebel.

368 "Unamuno: The Statue and the Crime," The New Leader, 30, 10 (March 8, 1947), 12.
A rectification of a report of an interview with Unamuno in the French newspaper, Carrefour.

369 "Hace cuatro siglos que nació Cervantes," Las Españas (México), 2, 4 (19 de marzo, 1947), 3.
The most noble monument of the Renaissance "es el Quijote." The humanism of the Quijote stands in direct opposition to "la España Fascista," writes S. in this essay commemorating the 400th anniversary of the birth of Cervantes.

370 "1947's Biggest Literary Anniversary," Saturday Review of Literature, 30 (August 9, 1947), 7.
An article on the occasion of the fourth centenary of the birth of Cervantes and observations on the moral-political situation in Spain today (1947).

371 "D. H. Lawrence: 'The Fatalities of Light and Shadow'," The New Leader, 30, 35 (August 30, 1947), 10.
A review of The Portable D. H. Lawrence (edited by Diana Trilling) and observations on Lawrence's biography.

372 "The Fourth Sally of Don Quixote," The New Leader, 31, 20 (May 15, 1948), p. 8.

373 "Valéry: The Parabolic Road of Narcissism," The New Leader, 31, 26 (June 26, 1948), 10.
A review of Paul Valéry's Reflections on the World Today.

374 "Camus and Panic," The New Leader, 31, 41 (October 9, 1948), 11.
Comments on The Plague.

375 "Humility and Heroism: Guitérrez Arrived First," The New Leader, 31, 48 (November 27, 1948), 9.
An American soldier of Hispanic background distinguished himself in battle during World War II.

376 "The Impossible Bridge: Literature Under Franco," The New Leader, 31, 52 (December 25, 1948), 10.
Comments on the conditions of culture and literature in Spain at the time (1948).

377 "Proust--Man of Genius?," The New Leader, 32, 20

(May 14, 1949), 11.
S. reviews Letters of Marcel Proust, edited by Mina
Curtiss.

378   "Culture and T. S. Eliot," The New Leader, 32, 25
       (June 18, 1949), 10.
       A review of Eliot's book, Notes Toward the Definition
of Culture.

379   "Faustian Germany and Thomas Mann," New Mexico
       Quarterly Review, 19, 2 (Summer 1949), 193-206.
       A discussion of the Germanic mentality as seen by S.
in Mann's Doctor Faustus.

380   "Three Centuries of Don Juan," Books Abroad, 23, 3
       (Summer 1949), 227-32.
       A general discussion of the vitality of the Don Juan
theme through three centuries of European literature.

381   "Celine Again," The New Leader, 32, 40 (October 1,
       1949), 8.
       A review of Celine's Journey to the End of the Night.

382   "The Wrong Side of the Tapestry," The New Leader,
       32, 46 (November 12, 1949), 11.
       A laudatory review of Samuel Putnam's translation of
Don Quijote.

383   "Celine Anti-everyone, Still Great Writer," The New
       Leader, 32, 48 (November 26, 1949), 11.
       A defense of Celine's works on the basis of their
esthetic values, and not on Celine's political and anti-Semitic views.

384   "Literature in the Middle of This Century," Phi Kappa
       Phi Journal, 29, 4 (December, 1949), 15-25.
       Reflections on the tendency of man to believe somehow
or other in his superiority simply because of his advanced
technology. Literature must counter the growing superfici-
ality by a new "essential action" which regards life and
death as two sides of "the same equation." Poets may have
their "heads in the clouds" but technological man should not
forget that "lightning comes from the clouds."

385   "Lorca, Poet of the People," The New York Times
       Book Review, January 1, 1950, 3.
       A favorable review of Arturo Barea's book, Lorca:

The Poet and His People.

386   "Latin American Literary Criticism, " The New Leader,
      33, 13 (April 1, 1950), 11.
      Comments on a book by the critic and professor A.
Torres Ríoseco, New World Literature.

387   "La doncella y el doncel de Avila o los castellanos
      interiores, " Las Españas (México), 5, 15-18 (edición
      especial de 4 números) (abril, 1950), 81-85.
      St. Theresa and St. John of the Cross have, says S. ,
forever endowed the Spanish "soul" with a mystical dimension, a dimension which gives life a sense of totality and
plenitude.   "... [S]eamos, en la medida que le sea posible
a cada cual, alcaides más del castillo interior que de las
Castillas" (p. 85).

388   "Complicity and Propitious Error, " The New Leader,
      33, 43 (October 30, 1950), 11.
      S. accuses the Communists of seeking accomplices
throughout the world with whom to share their guilty acts.
He also criticizes "imprudent statements" made by certain
unnamed U. S. Government officials.

389   "The Crisis of Naturalism, " The New Leader, 33, 49
      (December 11, 1950), 23.
      Movies can now do better what hitherto has been done
by naturalistic and realistic literature.

390   "Freedom and Constraint in André Gide, " New Mexico
      Quarterly, 20, 4 (Winter 1950-51), 405-19.
      Commentary on the tension between "freedom" and
"constraint" (inhibitions stemming from Christianity, etc.)
in the work of the French author.   (See 391.)

391   "Libertad y 'contrainte' en André Gide, " Atenea, año
      28, 100, 309 (marzo, 1951).
      Originally appeared in English.   (See 390.)

392   "Sobre la novela rapsódica y la urbe, " Revista Ibero-
      americana, 17, 34 (enero, 1952), 269-83.
      A discussion of four examples of the Iberoamerican
rhapsodic novel: Don Segundo Sombra, Doña Bárbara, Hijo
de ladrón, and Lanchas en la bahía.   The last two of the
four--by Manuel Rojas--define "la ciudad chilena y tal vez
la suramericana" just as, for S. , Don Segundo Sombra de-
fines the pampas or Rivera's La vorágine, the jungle.

393   "La gestación literaria de Valle-Inclán," Cuadernos
       Americanos (México), 62, 2 (marzo-abril, 1952), 270-
       81.
       The essence of this article is in S.'s book, Valle-
Inclán y la dificultad de la tragedia (66). The Galician writer originally conceived his works as masses of colors.

394   "Manuel de Falla and His Essential City," New Mexico
       Quarterly, 22, 2 (Summer 1952), 131-41.
       An essay on the motivating factors and purposes in
Falla's musical creation. He lived in his own imaginary
city, his "essential city" and wrote for its residents. A
comparison of Stravinsky and Falla is included.

395   "Valle-Inclán y la dificultad de la tragedia," Cuadernos
       Americanos, 68, 5 (septiembre-octubre, 1952), 241-54.
       Republished in the chapters on Valle-Inclán in items
64 (p. 69-83) and 65 of this bibliography as well as in Valle-
Inclán y la dificultad de la tragedia (66).

396   "Canciones lúgubres," New Mexico Quarterly, 23, 4
       (Winter 1953), 474-76.
       Review of a book on the Spanish Conquistador, Cristó-
bal de Oñate, by F. Murcia de la Llana.

397   "Algo más sobre Valle-Inclán," Cuadernos Americanos,
       68, 2 (marzo-abril, 1953), 275-83.
       Discussion of the qualities of Valle-Inclán's work which
are incompatible with the theater. Valleinclanesque drama
is only for reading, not for staging.

398   "Santayana, español del 98," Las Españas (México),
       núms. 23-25 (abril, 1953), 3-5.
       Laudatory comments on George Santayana whom S.
sees as being a man on the margin, a skeptic who most
clearly incarnated the ideals of the "Generation of 1898."

399   "Farrell and the Invading Emptiness," The New Leader,
       36, 50 (December 14, 1953), 17.
       A review of The Face of Time, a novel by James T.
Farrell. Spanish version (517) published later.

400   "Después del año catorce," Ibérica (ed. española), 2,
       1 (15 de enero, 1954), 7.
       After more than fourteen years in exile S. reflects
upon the sense of Spanish nationalism still alive and active
in him and in his fellow-exiles.

401   "After Fourteen Years," Ibérica (English ed.), 2, 1
      (January 15, 1954), 7.
      English version of 400.

402   "El puente imposible," Cuadernos (París), 4 (enero-
      febrero, 1954), 65-72.
      A discussion of Spanish writers in and out of Spain:
      Baroja, Eugene d'Ors, Benavente, Menéndez Pidal, Ortega
      y Gasset, Azorín, Cela, and Laforet. S. finds the construc-
      tion of a bridge or means of vital communication between the
      exiled writers and those still in Spain impossible under exist-
      ing conditions.   Of Cela and Laforet he writes that they are
      "los dos casos de escritores nuevos y con talento original
      surgidos en la España de los últimos diez años."

403   "Ayer, hoy y pasado mañana," Ibérica (ed. española),
      2, 5 (15 de mayo, 1954), 3-4.
      Discussion of the present-day "backwardness" of Spain
      in which S. accuses the generals and bishops of impeding a
      natural synthesis of the two "Spains": the castrense (mili-
      tary) and the colonial (agricultural).

404   "Yesterday, Today and Day after Tomorrow," Ibérica
      (English ed.), 2, 5 (May 15, 1954), 3-4.
      English version of 403.

405   " 'Official Truth' on Civil War Spain," The New Lead-
      er, 37, 27 (July 5, 1954), 18-19.
      A review of Claude G. Bowers' book, My Mission to
Spain.

406   "Dos estrategias en pugna," Ibérica (ed. española), 2
      10 (15 de octubre, 1954), 3-4 y 11.
      S. criticizes the American diplomatic strategy in Eu-
      rope, especially the policy of aiding Franco's government.

407   "Two Opposed Strategies," Ibérica (English ed.) 2, 10
      (October 15, 1954), 3-4, 11.
      English version of 406.

408   "Sobre lo colonial y lo castrense," Ibérica (ed. espa-
      ñola), 2, 11 (15 de noviembre, 1954), 10-11.
      A reply to an article by Salvador de Madariaga that
criticized S. for his tendency to delimit in space the two
"Spains" ("la castrense y la colonial") in his article, "Ayer,
hoy, y pasado mañana" (403).

409   "On the Colonial and Castrense," Ibérica (English ed.),
       2, 11 (November 15, 1954), 9-10.
       English version of 408.

410   "La miseria y la 'virtud obligatoria,' " Ibérica (ed.
       española), 3, 5 (15 de mayo, 1955), 5 y 7.
       Comments on the side-by-side existence of the Catholic
Church and dire poverty in Spain and in other "países muy
católicos."

411   "Poverty and the 'Obligatory Virtue'," Ibérica (English
       ed.), 3, 5 (May 15, 1955), 5, 7.
       English version of 410.

412   The New York Times, July 10, 1955 (Section 7, p. 6).
       A review of the English translation of La Celestina, by
Lesley B. Simpson.

413   "Nuevas salidas de don Quijote," Cuadernos (París),
       núm. 13 (julio-agosto, 1955), 54-58.
       Whenever a new edition--in English or German trans-
lation, for example--appears we get the impression that Don
Quijote himself has once again sallied forth. A beautiful
essay on the necessity of having an "ideal self" and of the
intimate identification of Cervantes and Don Quijote, of author and creation. "Seguiremos todos viviendo el sueño de
nosotros mismos, pero quizá seremos dignos del yo ideal
cada vez que sepamos--como hizo Cervantes--sacrificar ese
ideal sin amargura."

414   "El dibujo, la sátira y la perplejidad lírica hacia 1850,"
       Cuadernos Americanos, 73, 5 (septiembre-octubre,
       1955), 197-210.
       Discussion of the drawings and lyrical and satirical
elements found in the Mexican weekly magazine, El Tío
Nonilla (published in 1850).

415   "Hacia un nuevo período clásico," Ibérica (ed. españo-
       la), 3, 11 (15 de noviembre, 1955), 3-5.
       S. opines that, both in and out of Spain, Spanish lite-
rary and intellectual life is richer and better today than ever
before. "... [L]os españoles estamos entrando sin darnos
cuenta en un nuevo período clásico en lo que se refiere a
las artes y más concretamente a la literatura" (p. 3).

416   "The Dawn of a New Classicism," Ibérica (English ed.),
       3, 11 (November 15, 1955), 3-5.

English version of 415.

417   "Inside African Jewry," The New Leader, 38, 50 (December 19, 1955), 18.
       A review of The Pillar of Salt, by Albert Memmi.

418   "La dificultad del maquiavelismo," Ibérica (ed. española), 4, 4 (15 de abril, 1956), 3 y 10.
Comments on Franco's maneuvers in Africa to counter an unexpected action by France: the granting of independence to French Morocco.

419   "The Trouble with Machiavellianism," Ibérica (English ed.), 4, 4 (April 15, 1956), 3, 11.
       English version of 418.

420   "Collected Essays by Herbert Read," The New Leader, 39, 24 (June 11, 1956), 24.
       A review of A Coat of Many Colors.

421   "Contradicciones y tristes espejismos," Ibérica (ed. española), 4, 6 (15 de junio, 1956), 6-7.
Comments on Spain's efforts to enter the North Atlantic Treaty Alliance upon the failure of Spanish policies in Morocco and Ifni.

422   "Contradictions and Sad Mirages," Ibérica (English ed.), 4, 6 (June 15, 1956), 6-7.
       English version of 421.

423   "Menéndez Pelayo, la confusión y la conspiración," Ibérica (ed. española), 5, 1 (15 de enero, 1957), 10-11.
Though M. P. was a liberal and a master of clarity, some of his present "promoters" demonstrate neither liberalism nor clarity in their writings. In a specific instance to which S. refers this lack is perhaps to be credited to official censorship at the last moment before publication.

424   "Menéndez Pelayo: Confusion and Conspiracy," Ibérica (English ed.), 5, 1 (January 15, 1957), 10-11.
       English version of 423.

425   "Pió Baroja a través de su obra," Cuadernos (París), núm. 22 (enero-febrero, 1957), 70-73.
A discussion of lyricism in Baroja's novels as well as the anti-bourgeois attitude of the novelist who at the same

time "un esclavo de las convenciones. " Reprinted in the
book Baroja y su mundo (91), edited by Fernando Baeza.

426   "Myth and Poetry," The New Leader, 40, 15 (April 15,
       1957), 23-24.
       A review of The Nature of Literature, by Herbert Read.

427   "Prólogo de 'Los cinco libros de Ariadna'," Ibérica (ed.
       española), 5, 7-8 (15 de julio, 1957), 8-9 y 12.
       A reprinting of the important (revealing) prologue to
       Los cinco libros de Ariadna (20, 95, 428).

428   "Prologue to 'Los cinco libros de Ariadna': A New
       Novel of Ramón Sender," Ibérica (English ed.), 5, 7-
       8 (July 15, 1957), 6-8.
       English version of 427.

429   "¿Qué clase de 'Commonwealth?'," Ibérica (ed. espa-
       ñola), 6, 1 (15 de enero, 1958), 9.
       Commenting on a recent proposal to create a "common-
       wealth" of Hispanic countries, S. demonstrates that the con-
       ditions indispensable for the creation of a "commonwealth"
       are absent both within Spain and without.

430   "What Kind of Commonwealth?" Ibérica (English ed.),
       6, 1 (January 15, 1958), 9.
       English version of 429.

431   "And the Bell Still Tolls," Saturday Review, 41, 23
       (June 7, 1958), 13-14.
       Reflections on contemporary Spain and the book by Sal-
       vador de Madariaga, Spain: A Modern History.

432   "Roma y la monarquía en puerto," Ibérica (ed. espa-
       ñola), 6, 10 (15 de octubre, 1958), 4-7.
       S. criticizes a new book by Calvo Serer, La fuerza
       creadora de la libertad.

433   "Rome and the Monarchy," Ibérica (English ed.), 6,
       10 (October 15, 1958), 4-7.
       English version of 432.

434   "Los pequeños monstruos de Baroja," Cuadernos
       (París), núm. 35 (marzo-abril, 1959), 43-50.
       In his literary creation Baroja upon making a "selec-
       ción de su memoria sensitiva" tended to choose "románti-
       camente lo más agrio y amargo," hence, the "pequeños

monstruos" in his work.

435   "Posthumous Baroja," New Mexico Quarterly, 30, 1
       (Spring 1960), 6-10.
       An essay on the life, personality and beliefs of Pío
Baroja with comments upon the publication in English trans-
lation, of a book by the Basque author, The Restlessness of
Shanti Andía and Other Writings (University of Michigan
Press, 1959).

436   "The Man of Blood, by José Villalonga; The Fell of
       Dark, by James Norman; Fiestas, by Juan Goytisolo,"
       Saturday Review, 43 (June 11, 1960), 23, 35.
       A review of the three novels named above. S. calls
Goytisolo "the best of the young Spanish writers."

437   "Man and Angel in Our Apocalyptic Age," Américas
       (English ed.), 14, 2 (February, 1962), 23-27.
       A fanciful essay on the possibilities of man's having
angelic experiences through scientific developments, e.g.,
weightlessness and a new time dimension experienced by as-
tronauts--both "angel-like" experiences. S., in his unique
and humorous manner, selects certain aspects of the artistic, literary and religious history of angelology to illuminate
his points. Essentially reprinted in 458, Spanish version
(438).

438   "El hombre y el ángel en nuestra era apocalíptica,"
       Américas (ed. española), 14, 3 (marzo, 1962), 23-27.
       The original, Spanish version of 437. See also
"Actualidad de los ángeles" (458).

439   "Sobre localismo y federación," Combate (San José,
       C.R.), 4, 25 (noviembre-diciembre, 1962), 17-26.
       S. predicts that the Iberian Peninsula (Portugal and
Spain) will become a Federation. "El día de la comunidad
federal ibérica, Aragón ofrecerá su núcleo cultural bien
definido histórica, jurídica, etnológica y antropológicamente."

440   "La migratoria cruz," Cuadernos (París), núm. 68
       (enero, 1963), 14-25.
       A study of the symbolism of the cross in different
ages and in diverse religions. The cross is "el árbol
cósmico." Republished in Ensayos sobre el infringimiento
cristiano (67).

441   "Un reino efímero en el Amazonas," Américas (Wash-

ington, D. C. , ed. española), 15, 6 (junio, 1963), 28-
32.

A narrative-essay on the Spanish expedition down the
Amazon in 1561 during which the expeditionaries assassinated
their commander, Pedro de Ursúa, and declared themselves
independent from the Spanish throne under the leadership of
the infamous Lope de Aguirre. The historical matter here
discussed forms the basis of Sender's novel, La aventura
equinoccial de Lope de Aguirre (29).

442   "Ephemeral Amazon Kingdom, " Américas (English ed.),
       15, 6 (May 1963), 28-32.
       English version of 441.

443   "La ecuación libertad: Dios en la política, " Política
       (Caracas), 3, 33 (abril, 1964), 41-59.
       An exposition of the absolute necessity to maintain the
ideal of personal liberty if we want to preserve civilization.
God or the idea of Him is the source of human liberty.

444   "Notas sobre lo real absoluto, " Cuadernos (París),
       núm. 94 (marzo, 1965), 67-74.
       Science today finds "lo real absoluto" beyond the speed
of light, a realm accessible to poetry and/or religion. Important and original speculations on the conjuncture of modern
physics, poetry and religion.

445   "Saints and Sinner, " Times Literary Supplement (Lon-
       don), 3, 418 (August 31, 1967), 781.
       A letter to the editor critical of a review of Tres
novelas teresianas, published in the TLS (August 3, 1967),
followed by a rebuttal by the anonymous reviewer.

446   "Los escritores frente a Vietnam, " España Libre
       (N. Y.), 28, 6 (noviembre-diciembre, 1967), 5. Also
       in Comunidad Ibérica (México, D. F.), núm. 33 (marzo-
       abril, 1968), 20-22.
       The American effort in Vietnam is seen as a political
strategy to contain the spread of imperialism, and as such
"el esfuerzo americano en Vietnam merece respeto. "

447   "Caducidad de la tragedia, " Norte (Amsterdam), 9, 5
       (septiembre-octubre, 1968), 97-99.
       Tragedy (as a work of art) is dead today because there
is no common ground of firm beliefs, no unity but rather
"una clase de caos que en tiempos clásicos no existía. "

448   "Miserias y grandezas del viajar," Destino, núm. 1625
       (23 de noviembre, 1968), 71-73, 75.
       Discussion of traveling and travelers in general followed
by observations on A View of All the Russias, by Laurens van
der Post. Traveling helps destroy stereotyped images of
foreign peoples.

449   "Probabilidades lunares," Destino, núm. 1628 (14 de
       diciembre, 1968), 42-43.
       Speculations on possibilities of exploiting the moon (as
a source of industrial energy, e.g.) supported by data from
specialized scientific journals.

450   "Las golfos de Buda y otros inocentes excesos," Des-
       tino, núm. 1632 (11 de enero, 1969), 53-55.
       Discussion of Voodoo in Haití by Alfredo Métraux, and
of "hippies" ("golfos de Buda"), "inquietantes como heraldos
de un tiempo caótico que todos querríamos evitar.... "

451   "Chaplin a propósito de Upton Sinclair," Destino, núm.
       1635 (1 de febrero, 1969), 8-9.
       Reflections on Charles Chaplin, his life and art, and
on his socialism, "el idealismo generoso de un humanista, "
to which he was influenced by Upton Sinclair.

452   "Los centauros, los hombres, los ángeles y el infi-
       nito," Destino, núm. 1638 (22 de febrero, 1969), 24-
       26.
       Reflections inspired by William Howell's new book, La
humanidad en formación. The origin of man, life on other
planets, angels, God, etc. are discussed by S.

453   "Sobre mexicanos, mayas e incas," Destino, núm.
       1641 (15 de marzo, 1969), 19-21.
       A discussion of Bernal Díaz del Castillo's history of
the Spanish conquest of Mexico, also of a book on Mayan
civilization by Eric S. Thompson and the Incan drama,
Ollantay.

454   "Martirilogio de las letras rusas," Comunidad Ibérica
       (México), núms. 39-40 (marzo-junio, 1969), 15-16.
       S. "lamenta la degradación del realismo socialista en
Rusia. ... Pero afirma Sender que la mejor literatura
existe en Rusia en forma clandestina por su 'realismo
veraz, directo, sencillo, sin la menor sombra de retorcis-
mo' " (Nonoyama, 1357).

455   "Ese gran hombre casi centenario," Destino, núm.
      1644 (5 de abril, 1969), 24-27.
      Praises Bertrand Russell and briefly reviews two of his
books of fiction: El suplicio de Miss X and Satanas en el
suburbio.

456   "Un coleccionista de cabezas," Destino, núm. 1647 (26
      de abril, 1969), 21, 24-25.
      Commentary vaguely based on a reading of Vincent
Brome's biography, Frank Harris; The Life and Loves of a
Rascal.

457   "Las ciudades, los años y las gentes," Destino, núm.
      1650 (17 de mayo, 1969), 36-39.
      Comments inspired by the reading of La ciudad en la
historia, by Lewis Mumford, on cities, the future, and population growth.

458   "Actualidad de los ángeles," Destino, núm. 1654 (14
      de junio, 1969), 29-31.
      Essentially a reprinting of an earlier article (437, 438),
"Los hombres podemos flotar," i. e., overcome gravity
("mal")--as do the angels.   "Pero ¿existen los ángeles?"

459   "Los atlantes y el binomio Cortés-Quetzalcoatl,"
      Destino, núm. 1658 (12 de julio, 1969), 24-25, 27.
      Inspired by the reading of Atlantis, a book first pub-
lished by Ignatius Donnelly, S. supports his belief that both
European and American peoples and cultures had a common
origin in the submerged continent of Atlantis.

460   "¿Vale la pena la luna?," Destino, núm. 1660 (26 de
      julio, 1969), 24-25.
      S. says "yes," the exploration of the moon is worth
the cost.

461   "Sobre los mitos," El Urogallo, 2, 7 (enero-febrero,
      1971), 11-15.
      Man needs "una realidad superior inmanente y eterna
para que existan los accidentes del tiempo.... En ese nivel y dimensión de lo permanente del cual sacamos nosotros
la raíz de la aventura de la vida diaria--o de la desventura
y fracaso de nuestra fe--es donde prospera y se establece
el mito." The artists are in large part the creators of the
new myths of their times.

462   "Chessman," Destino, núm. 1749 (10 de abril, 1971),
      11-13.

S. discusses the convicted California murderer, Caryl Chessman, who on death row wrote three books and who is the protagonist of one of Sender's short stories, "Las rosas de Pasadena," in the book, Cabrerizas Atlas (48).

463   "Trotski," Destino, núm. 1827 (7 de octubre, 1972), 30-33.
A discussion of Trotsky and his role in the Soviet revolution and of his relationships with Stalin and Lenin. S. tells his impressions of Trotsky when invited to visit him in Coyoacán, Mexico. Trotsky "daba la impresión de un profesor de liceo francés."

464   "Baroja, paradojal," Destino, núm. 1837 (16 de diciembre, 1972), 37.
An appreciative evaluation of Pío Baroja's novelistic work, especially of his autobiographical series, Memorias de un hombre de acción (though not mentioned by title), of El laberinto de las sirenas and Los visionarios. S. especially praises Baroja's communicative power. "Una frase de Baroja está más cargada de sentido que de cualquier otro novelista de su tiempo."

465   "Túpac Amaru," Destino, núm. 1845 (10 de febrero, 1973), 19.
This one-page article is the author's preface to his novel, Túpac Amaru (39), published later in 1973. S. hopes to re-establish the truth concerning the laws the Spanish Consejo de Indias passed during the colonial period granting the same rights to the Indians as held by the Spaniards, laws or royal decrees, however, which were not in general upheld by the underpaid Spanish colonial administrators, and were, therefore, rendered inoperative.

466   "En un futuro próximo," Norte (Amsterdam), núms. 2-4 (marzo-agosto, 1973), 26-28.
Reflections on the need for the creation soon of one World in which national boundaries disappear but at the same time a World which preserves "natural" cultural groups (such as the Basques, et al.). The article then reproduces a typewritten draft of a page (chosen at random) from Sender's then unpublished Nancy, doctora en gitanería (41) (and requested for inclusion in this issue of Norte dedicated exclusively to S.; see 1141).

467   "G. B. S.," Destino, núm. 1875 (8 de septiembre, 1973), 8-11.
Commentary on George Bernard Shaw inspired by Sen-

der's reading two books: a collection of letters, Shaw and
Molly Tompkins, compiled and edited by Stanley Weintraub,
and Bernard Shaw: A Reconsideration, by Colin Wilson.

468   "Divagación mosaica," Destino, núm. 1905 (6 de abril,
      1974), 26-28.
Observations about Jews and Arabs and anecdotal ac-
counts of Sender's friendship with Max Jacob, the Jewish
writer who became a Catholic. "Max Jacob era un escritor
de talento. Fue de él y de Jules Renard de quienes nacieron las greguerías de Gómez de la Serna."

469   "Texto íntegro de la conferencia pronunciada por Ramón
      José Sender en el Ateneo de Zaragoza el día 3 de junio
      de 1974," Aragón Exprés, 4 de junio, 1974.
      The text of an address given by S. in Zaragoza during
his visit (of about two weeks' duration) late in May and early
in June of 1974. Though the Bibliographer has not read this
entry he is including it here because of its possible special
significance to Senderian scholars.

F.   SYNDICATED COLUMN, "LOS LIBROS Y LOS DIAS"

         Listed in this section are 663 articles which have ap-
peared in Sender's syndicated column, "Los libros y los
días," in Spanish-language newspapers throughout the Western
Hemisphere during the period, 1953-1974 inclusive. Since
the beginning Sender's column has been distributed by the
American Literary Agency (11 Riverside Drive, New York
10023), managed until his death in 1974 by Joaquín Maurín,
the Spanish writer, and since then until her retirement on
June 30, 1975, by Maurín's widow, Jeanne M. de Juliá.   It
is to Mrs. Jeanne M. de Juliá that I wish to express my
most sincere gratitude.   Without her help this Senderian
Bibliography would never have been completed; she provided
me with copies of over 300 of the 663 articles annotated in
this section, together with the date on which each article
was released by the American Literary Agency to the newspapers subscribing to the Senderian column.   In all entries
below, the date which follows the title of each article or
"column" is that of its release by the Agency; in a few in-
stances the exact date has been unobtainable.
         Although there have obviously been numerous changes
in the list of those newspapers which have through the
twenty-two years covered by this bibliography subscribed to

Sender's column, the following newspapers have published the column more or less regularly, at least in recent years:

La Opinión (Los Angeles, Cal.)
Diario de Nuevo Laredo (Laredo, México)
Diario de Torreón (Torreón, México)
Diario de Yucatán (Yucatán, México)
Siglo de Torreón (Torreón, México)
Tribuna (Campeche, México)
El Porvenir (Monterrey, México)
El Dictamen (Veracruz, México)
El Imparcial (Guatemala)
La Estrella de Panamá (Panamá)
La Prensa (San Pedro Sula, Honduras)
El Caribe (Santo Domingo, República Dominicana)
El Diario de Hoy (San Salvador, El Salvador)
El Universal (Caracas, Venezuela)
Panorama (Maracaibo, Venezuela)
El Universo (Guayaquil, Ecuador)
Presencia (La Paz, Bolivia)
El Mercurio (Valparaiso, Chile)
El Sur (Concepción, Chile)

In addition to the above newspapers a chain of about thirty-five newspapers in Mexico, Periódicos Unidos de los Estados, is a regular subscriber to Sender's column.

I have already acknowledged the valuable collaboration of Dr. Rafael Pérez Sandoval (of Los Angeles, Cal.) in the compilation and annotation of this section. Of the articles that follow, 246 have been annotated by Pérez Sandoval, and are marked with an asterisk; 412 have been annotated by me; five were unavailable from either the American Literary Agency or Pérez Sandoval's private collection of copies of about 500 of Sender's "Los libros y los días" articles.

Whenever known, the places and dates of publication of an article are given right after the release date; e.g., in item 765, " 'España vista desde el Canadá,' 6 de mayo, 1959; Lectura, 129, 4 (15 de junio, 1959), 109-12," the article was released on May 6 and was published in Lectura (a bimonthly journal published in Mexico City) in its issue of June 15, 1959 (vol. 129, no. 4, pp. 109-12).

1953

470   "Santayana o el gran hombre del margen," 3 de enero, 1953.

A poet of sublimated mysticism, a keenly speculative essayist and a novelist of transcendent realism, Santayana represented a synthesis of the estheticist and philosophical tendencies of the group of '98, but in his essence eluded definition or classification. *

471   "Hemingway y el culto de la hombría," 5 de enero, 1953.
Comments on Hemingway's The Old Man and the Sea and Hemingway's fascination with Spanish life and character, once evinced in his remark, "Yo querría haber nacido en España."

472   "Mauriac y la definición del mal," 10 de enero, 1953.
S. sees Mauriac, Nobel Prize Winner, as more convincing than the other two major French religious novelists of today, Bernanos and Claudel.   To define evil Mauriac explores the dark labyrinths of the human soul, analyzing the bitter setbacks of bourgeois attempts at goodness. *

473   "Dioses, sepulcros y sabios," 11 de enero, 1953.
S. reviews favorably C. W. Ceram's book, Gods, Graves, and Scholars, an enthusiastic (non-academic) account of recent archeological discoveries.

474   [No entry]

475   "Toreros y escritores en América," 2 de febrero, 1953.
Out of the plethora of recent books on the subject of bullfighting, S. focuses on Sidney Franklin's sincere and intelligent autobiography Torero de Brooklyn and discusses various lyrical and symbolic aspects of the fiesta brava, an "auto sacramental" uncomprehended by most Americans. *

476   "La ballena blanca," 2 de febrero, 1953.
S. views Melville's Moby Dick as the national novel of the U. S. A. --a collective epic battle against the monster of despair.

477   "Héroes del norte y del sur," 2 de febrero, 1953.
Alison William Bunkley's posthumous book, The Life of Sarmiento, is an important contribution to the humanistic current flowing against the tide of overspecialization and technology in the American universities.   Sarmiento offers to U. S. culture a noble example of practical idealism and

peaceful understanding among peoples. *

478   "Unamuno o el vasco transcendental, " 28 de febrero,
1953; El Diario de Hoy (San Salvador), 29 de marzo,
1953.
Unamuno discreetly appears again on the American
scene in a volume of poetry translated by Eleanor Turnbull.
The ability of Unamuno to "mantener en el alma los frescos
registros de la infancia, lo mismo en el entusiasmo que en
la desesperación, y en la glosa sabia que en el anatema" is
one of the secrets of the virginity of lo español, says S. *

479   "Fumadores en el 'bunker', " febrero, 1953.
Georges Blond, in his thoroughly documented L'Agonie
de l'Allemagne, recounts many incidents of the Nazis' last
months before the defeat of Germany, adding a richness of
small details to the stark panorama of well-known historical
events.   S. says that this will be a chilling lesson-book for
future generations. *

480   "Eluard ha muerto en Francia, " 3 de marzo, 1953.
S. discusses the surrealistic school (including André
Breton and Max Jacob), of whose writers Paul Eluard was
the most faithful to the world of pure poetic mystery.   S.
says that surrealism has won its battle, in the sense that
modern writers now dare occasionally to disarticulate reality. *

481   "Carl Sandburg o el poeta entre la gente, " 20 de marzo, 1953.
Upon reading Sandburg's fervent autobiography, Always
the Young Strangers, S. observes that the poet, as always,
uses the simple language of the common people, distilled
from his experience as vagabond and worker, extracting the
true essence from apparent vulgarity and triviality.   Sandburg is the spiritual son of Walt Whitman, S. says. *

482   "Las utopías en las letras de hoy, " 4 de abril, 1953.
Reflections on man's tendency to dream of utopias,
with special attention to Aldous Huxley's Brave New World,
Orwell's 1984, Kurt Vonnegut's Player Piano, and Robert
Ardrey's The Brotherhood of Fear.   Current "utopian" writers are pessimistic and "se burlan del porvenir, "
though formerly utopian literature was considered "esca-
pista. "

483   " 'Stalingrado' y 'Moscú,' de Plievier," 4 de abril,
       1953.
       Teodoro Plievier, German "documental" novelist who
spent years in Russia, has written Stalingrado (an epic of
World War II) and Moscú ("una visión grandiosa de la descom-
posición de un régimen monolítico"), masterful testimonies
that digest the raw facts of history and expose the secretly
horrified conscience of both the winners and the losers in
war. *

484   "Stalin y la literatura rusa," 4 de abril, 1953.
       S. gloomily surveys the effects of Stalin's reign of
terror on the Soviet literature of his time and since: Russia's most promising writers faced with censorship, exile,
death or the worst torture of all--'la de la imaginación
creadora ... consumiéndose en su propia impotencia. '"*

485   "Cómo murió el Marqúes de Bradomín," 4 de abril,
       1953.
       S. gives a lyrical account of how the gallant literary
character born of Valle-Inclán's imagination lived secretly
within the depths of the poet's own personality, "asomándose
a veces a los mirajes de las gafas de Don Ramón," and of
how the noble and romantic Bradomín received his mortal
blow.   He was not survived long by his creator, faithful to
the high ideals of the dream he had known how to live. *

486   'Baroja, el inefable hombre del saco," 4 de abril,
       1953.
       Contradictions abound in every 'hombre natural," and
Pío Baroja's nine autobiographical volumes, with their affected carelessness and gruff tendency to reveal his imper-
fections, make him a sympathetic figure to the enlightened
and a bogeyman to the small-minded, says S. *

487   "Lawrence, solitario animal de Dios," abril, 1953.
       D. H. Lawrence, whose work improves with time, was
an uncompromising dissenter perpetually defending the indi-
vidual--creator of culture--against civilization's obsession
to devour: to devour the magic in everyday reality, the pur-
ity in man's animality, the mystic trance of solitude.   But
the fierce humorlessness of Lawrence's nonconformity se-
verely impeded his making those concessions that link one
to his fellow beings.

488   "La primera Elisabeth de Inglaterra," 5 de mayo, 1953.
       Jacques Chastenet's biography, Elizabeth I, occasions

Sender's commentary on the political genius of the monarch who established the power of the British empire while consolidating democracy as its perpetuating force. S. is reminded that the medieval Aragonese courts set the precedent for the democratic principles of the Magna Carta. *

489   "Wright y su última novela negra," mayo, 1953.
Richard Wright's The Outsider, a novel of "devilish beauty," gives perspectives on the apparent "inferiority" of the Blacks, an "inferiority" that has produced outstanding compensating aptitudes, and which in reality is just one aspect of human weakness.

490   "La voz póstuma de George Orwell," mayo, 1953.
A tribute to Orwell the man and the writer, "hombre de cabeza fría y conciencia ardiente," who faced a hard life with moral strength, physical heroism and a sense of humor. Orwell's disillusionment implies a positive world-view, unlike the nihilism of the skeptic. His sincerity survives him in his last book, ironically entitled Such, Such Were the Joys.

491   "Faulkner y el prestigio de lo que muere," junio, 1953.
S. says that as Thomas Wolfe is the novelist of the future and Sinclair Lewis of the established present, William Faulkner is the poet of America's dying past, of that almost European atmosphere of eccentricity that is rotting away in the post-colonial, post-bellum rural South without ever really having ripened. *

492   "Sobre los gitanos cantores," 4 de julio, 1953.
If music came before speech, then the Andalusian "modulación enharmónica" and the gypsy "cante hondo" are a natural inheritance from the primitive language of the cavemen, says S. The music of Falla and the poetry of Lorca, both based on "la materia de los sueños," strike a hidden chord in the collective unconscious that is still latent in the modern world as it has been since the origins of humanity. *

493   "La novela póstuma de Marcel Proust," 5 de julio, 1953.
S. finds Jean Santeuil, Proust's unrevised last manuscript, to be less narcissistic and intellectually coquettish than his polished "contraepopeya de nuestro tiempo," A la recherche du temps perdu. Being more spontaneous, this novel is more human. *

494 "Azorín y su curiosa renuncia, " 30 de julio, 1953.
     Upon Azorín's announcement that he will write no more,
S. comments that "en España la literatura es una vocación
religiosa, o al menos, una dramática superstición. " In
normal times, a writer could live well, economically and
above all morally, in Spain. But under Franco that reverent atmosphere is shattered by noise and inattention, ab-
surdity and irresponsibility. Azorín's reality is gone and
his public is gone. And the inexorable development of today's reality goes forward everywhere but in Spain. *

495 "Machado y la cifra de Castilla, " julio, 1953.
     Antonio Machado, despite his Andalusian origin, "ha
quedado incorporado al mito castellano: la mesura estoica,
la grave sencillez ... y esa noción del mundo según la cual
el momento que vivimos es eterno en su esencia. " His poetry was distilled essence. *

496 "Thomas Wolfe o el idilio americano, " 3 de agosto,
     1953.
     Richard Walser's The Enigma of Thomas Wolfe leads
S. to reflect on Wolfe's idealistic longings and his poetic
wisdom in which he charted the fields of the future for
American literature.

497 "Galdós en los Estados Unidos, " agosto, 1953.
     The publication in English of Pérez Galdós' Tormento
leads S. to remark on the novelist's genius for description
of the physical world, harmony of composition, and his
more generous than keen gift for interpretation. The weaknesses of Galdós are those of his period: "garulería, verbo-
sidad y elocuencia polémica. " S. adds that Galdós' novels
were not as popular in the U.S. as his theater. *

498 "Vercors y las fronteras de lo humano, " agosto, 1953.
     The French novelist Vercors, in You Shall Know Them,
in a satirical attempt at a legal-moral definition of man,
suggests that humanity is an exclusive club in which mem-
bership is determined by arbitrary rules, but by means of
complex lyrical dimensions he leaves the problem open. *

499 "Tres irlandeses, entre ellos Joyce, " 1 de septiembre,
     1953.
     Arland Ussher, in Three Great Irishmen, gives another
Irishman's view of Joyce, Shaw and Yeats. S. dubs them
innocent devil, entertaining devil's advocate and dangerous
angel respectively. *

500   "La sátira benévola de Sinclair Lewis," 3 de septiembre, 1953.
      Lewis' novels of 1920-1935 faithfully reflect, according to S., American life of that same period. In his later production graver tones prevail over his earlier satirical manner.

501   "Noticia general de John dos Passos," 3 de septiembre, 1953.
      High praise for Dos Passos "quien es al mismo tiempo un estilista, un riguroso esteta, y un hombre de inspiración combativa," and comments on his attraction for Hispanic life and culture, his "cultura adoptiva."

502   "Un nuevo clásico: Henry James," 4 de septiembre, 1953.
      Adding his voice to the current re-evaluation of James, S. reviews the author's production, with its atmosphere of psychological mystery and contained fire, and declares James a classic--one who has crystallized indisputable evidence. *

503   "García Lorca en Norteamérica," septiembre, 1953.
      Lorca's Romancero Gitano, called Gypsy Ballads in the English translation, was the work that established his reputation, embodying the tradition of "la hermandad inefable de la luz con la sangre y la sangre con la voluptuosidad." Lorca represents a return to the essential, the permanent and the eternally virginal--a new classic period, says S. *

504   "El magisterio de Ortega y Gasset," 2 de octubre, 1953.
      The idealistic liberalism of Ortega belongs to the highest Spanish tradition, says S., and the extraordinary influence of his essays raised the dignity of literary journalism to the level where Larra had left it. Ortega dared, like Socrates, to organize his thought within the undefined and unforeseen zones of his own intellectual sensibility; thus the poetic quality of his analysis and its frequent divergence from the well-worn paths of the immediately obvious. *

505   "Churchill y el Premio Nóbel," 4 de octubre, 1953.
      Churchill is more of a historian and a man of action than a man of letters, according to S. Yet, though political interest may have influenced the decision to award Churchill the Nobel Prize, S. concedes that the Britisher was "un escritor de talento ... y eficacia" who has shown himself

worthy of the history that he has lived. *

506   "Bertrand Russell, autor de novelas," 10 de octubre,
       1953.
       At 81, Russell published a volume of short novels,
Satan in the Suburbs, in which the emotions are those of the
intellect, says S. That is why Russell's novels "serán espe-
cialmente gustadas por los escritores más que por los lectores usuales."*

507   "Una antología de Rudyard Kipling," 1 de noviembre,
       1953.
       Maugham's collection, The Best of Kipling, with its
extensive and rhapsodic preface on the Anglo-Indian author,
sparks S.'s own appraisal. Master of the surest road to
originality, that of being true to one's unique self, Kipling
generated the lyrical spontaneity of his novels and poetry in
a seemingly effortless flow.

508   "Paton en la tierra de los 'mau-mau'," 2 de noviembre,
       1953.
       Alan Paton, author of Cry, the Beloved Country, por-
trays in his second novel, Too Late the Phalarope, the unfortunate reality of racial relations in South Africa today: a
deep current of enmity between blacks and whites. The time
of the phalarope, a rare or extinct jungle bird symbolizing
a primitive, idyllic goodness and well-being, is past. *

509   "Resumen literario de 1953 en EE. UU.," 4 de novi-
       embre, 1953.
       Though producing "nada realmente nuevo" literary life
in the U.S.A. in 1953 has had "una diversidad rica y sub-
stanciosa dentro de lo que nos es ya familiar." S. comments rapidly on many books which appeared during the
year, including Simone de Beauvoir's book of travel impressions, America Day by Day (which, S. asserts, reveals the
author's false view of the United States), Farrell's The Face
of Time, etc.

510   [no entry]

511   "Martín du Gard opina sobre Gide," 15 de noviembre,
       1953.
       Du Gard and Gide were friends who viewed both life
and the novel from opposite poles. In his objective evaluation, "Remembranzas de André Gide," du Gard contrasts
his own rectilinear "temporal" approach with the lyrical

vagueness and "spatial" radiation of Gide.*

512   "Eugenia Clark con un venablo en la mano," 29 de
       noviembre, 1953.
       S. reviews two recent books by women writers, The
Lady with a Spear, by Eugenia Clark, and Icebound Summer,
by Sally Carrighar. Both books "tienen las cualidades ne-
cesarias para apasionarnos," though S. regards Carrighar's
book as superior in literary quality to Clark's.

513   "Recuerdo y devoción de Eugenio O'Neill," 7 de dici-
       embre, 1953.
       On the death of O'Neill, S. sums up the restless
dramatist's life and work. "En general, se podría decir
que O'Neill dió al teatro moral y filosófico de Ibsen el vigor de la naturaleza americana y también la delicadeza y
la brillante aptitud para los sueños que tienen las culturas jóvenes. "*

514   "Ha sido otorgado el Premio Goncourt," 28 de dici-
       embre, 1953.
       General commentary on the history and function of the
Goncourt Prize in French letters and a discussion of El
Tiempo de los muertos, by Pierre Lascar, awarded the
prize for 1953.

1954

515   "Gaceta y elegía de Dylan Thomas," 1 de enero, 1954.
       On the death of the Welsh poet Dylan Thomas at the
age of 38, S. comments on his life, his poetry and his
"sentido luminoso de las palabras" that produces at times an
almost delirious lyricism.*

516   "José Martí en los Estados Unidos," 17 de enero, 1954.
       The 1953 centennial of Martí's birth produced a num-
ber of good books and articles on the Cuban poet, hero and
martyr. According to S., "Sólo los hombres de acción quedan, y sobre todo los hombres cuya acción va guiada por el
amor. Sólo el amor penetra y permanece.... Sólo el amor
edifica. "*

517   "James Farrell y el vacío invasor," 31 de enero, 1954.
       Farrell's The Face of Time portrays the animal inno-
cence of a family of poor Irish immigrants, victims of industrial civilization. In the U.S., says S., that same inno-

cence when corrupted by the possession of affluence becomes
an aggressive intellectual vacuum--"el vacío invasor. "

518   "Albert Camus o la voz de Francia, " 3 de febrero,
       1954.
       In his long moral and political essay, The Rebel, Ca-
mus takes the trouble to think clearly for the rest of France.
After L'Etranger, he outgrew the existentialist school and is
now the "Anti-Sartre" of French society. He mourns the
decadence of a generation of lazy intellectuals who prefer
conformity to responsibility, and seeks instead "el camino
que satisfaga al mismo tiempo nuestra necesidad de protesta
y nuestra conciencia y nuestra mente. "*

519   "La conciencia sensitiva de Waldo Frank, " 7 de febre-
       ro, 1954.
       Frank, esteemed in the Hispanic world for his works
of social philosophy and historical interpretation, is under-
appreciated in the U. S. for his lyrical novels. His last
novel, Not Heaven, shows the bitter reality of our time but
forges hope out of faith, imagination and love of life. *

520   "Valle-Inclán y el sentido común, " 21 de febrero, 1954.
       S. expounds on the practicality of poets (defining prac-
ticality as the aptitude for living tranquilly and pleasantly)
and especially on the simplicity and common sense of Valle-
Inclán, unjustly maligned as a megalomaniac. S. movingly
remembers the poet's noble serenity and good nature in
stressful and difficult times. *

521   "Papini o el abogado del diablo, " 28 de febrero, 1954.
       G. Papini, a passionate rebel against philosophy and
dogma in his youth, entered the Catholic mainstream with
his Life of Christ (1921) and left it again in his old age with
The Devil (1954). As Orígenes suggested in the third century, Papini emotionally claims that Satan has a right to
God's forgiveness someday. S. adds that if His mercy is
truly infinite, ¿why not?*

522   "Giono o el jinete en el tejado, " 7 de marzo, 1954.
       Jean Giono, who has lived with his back turned on
Progress, urban technological civilization and the perver-
sions of politics, shares the almost mystical pantheism of
the Catalonians. In his novel, Le hussard sur le toit, he
only halfway reaches his goal of trying to re-establish man's
faith in generosity and in moral and physical courage, says
S. *

523   "White y el ensayo moderno," 14 de marzo, 1954.

524   "Ben-Gurion y el estado de Israel," 21 de marzo, 1954.
      In discussing Renaissance and Destiny of Israel by Ben
Gurion, S. remarks that the novelty of Israel's democratic-
theocratic "mosaic" represents a return full circle to its
ancient traditions. *

525   "Lucrecia Borgia cuatro siglos después," 29 de marzo,
      1954.
      S. sees María Bellonci's The Life and Time of Lucre-
zia Borgia as a sympathetic but rigorously documented historical study of the life of Lucrezia Borgia. *

526   "Emmanuel Roblès y el honor hispánico," 2 de abril,
      1954; "Emmanuel Roblès et l'honneur hispanique" in
      Pour saluer Roblès, published as special number (30)
      (in new series volume 8) of journal, Simoun (Oran, 1959),
      p. 25-28.
      Roblès, a French author of Spanish parentage, has an
inside perception of the Hispanic sense of honor, which S.
differentiates from the social, hierarchical Germanic code.
The indigenous Iberian loyalty, he says, is not to the group
but to the individual's transcendent idea of himself and his
destiny. *

527   "Starkie y los gitanos de España," 18 de abril, 1954.
      S. observes that Walter Starkie's book Sara's Tents,
though short on the imagination necessary for a work of art,
has an extraliterary value as an informative reference document that holds up a mirror to gypsy life. *

528   "Robert Frost y las cosas silvestres," 3 de mayo,
      1954.
      Frost, who found freedom "en la servidumbre a la
naturaleza y a la poesía," defined poetry as the place where
wild things live. On Frost's 80th birthday, S. remarks that
his poetry is more discreet than wild, for today's tastes. *

529   "Ivan Bunin, testigo del esplendor," 9 de mayo, 1954.
      Bunin (now deceased), the last witness of "la última
generación de titanes en las letras humanas," writes discreetly about them in Memoirs and Portraits (e. g. , Tolstoy
the epicure, Dostoyevsky the stoic, Chekhov the cynic). S.
comments on the great "don del olvido de sí mismos" of the
Russians, for whom "la sociedad no suele ser ... más que
el páramo por el cual hay que pasar."*

530   "Sobre una novela 'esperimental' inglesa," 16 de mayo, 1954.
       Walter Baxter's The Image and the Search overflows the standard mold of naturalism cultivated to such perfection by English and, especially, by American novelists. Withdrawn from distribution soon after publication (presumably because of its raw erotic realism) the book nevertheless conveys an intuition of mysticism through its merging of the world of the instincts with that of the highest cravings of the soul. *

531   "Carroll y los ángeles domésticos," 24 de mayo, 1954.
       The diary of Lewis Carroll (Charles Dodgson) sheds some light on the enigmatic Protestant pastor and professor of mathematics who wrote Alice in Wonderland and Through the Looking Glass. S. reflects on the relation between fantasy (the playful dreamlike incongruities we invent) and imagination. *

532   "La sonrisa de Eça de Queiroz," 31 de mayo, 1954.
       S. observes that the work of Eça de Queiroz "está en un plano equidistante de los dos extremos naturalista y realista," and adds that "la ponderación y la medida es siempre lo mejor de Eça de Queiroz. "*

533   "Trotsky en su reducto de Coyoacán," 2 de junio, 1954.
       S. takes issue with certain aspects of Isaac Deutscher's book on Trotsky, The Prophet Armed, and recalls his own visit to Trotsky's well-guarded enclave in Mexico and his impressions of the man's weakness, vulnerability and reciprocal influence from his enemy Stalin. *

534   "El Victor Hugo de André Maurois," 4 de junio, 1954.
       Maurois' biography depicts Hugo's poetic genius and titanic personality. By descent German, by choice Spanish, by nature French (the French miracle making all madnesses assimilable), Hugo in all good faith believed himself an agent of God and was in fact "para la Francia liberal un especie de nuevo e inspirado Carlomagno. "*

535   "Castro y la medalla española," 13 de junio, 1954.
       Américo Castro, in his most important book to date, La realidad histórica de España, explores with inspiration and emotion the Eastern and Western influences on Spanish culture (Iberian, Jewish, Arabic, Celtic, Visigoth, Roman, etc.) and their integration into a whole. *

536   "El círculo vicioso de Sartre," 1 de julio, 1954.
The vicious circle, in Sartre's existentialism, is the
chaotic vacuum of life: man is born needing freedom and
struggles constantly for it, but can only be free in death.
Another vicious circle is Sartre's Communism, which appears to offer through action a deliverance from metaphysical obsession, but in reality robs man of what little freedom he has. *

537   "Don Jacinto en la hora de la verdad," 2 de julio,
1954.
Upon the death of Benavente, S. discusses the dramatist's admirable production.   Los intereses creados made
his reputation, but by 1925 Don Jacinto had little popularity
in the literary world of Madrid.   Having dared to invent an
arbitrary reality Benavente should have dared to go farther
and create a valiant and convincing unreality, as did Valle-
Inclán. *

538   "Los terribles muñecos de Celine," 3 de julio, 1954.
The French author Celine, in Guignol's Band, grapples
once more with "el más alto problema de la cultura: la
definición del mal. " S. points out the exasperated love behind his bitter satire, the savage but pure religious senti-
ment behind his apparent blasphemies, and calls him a modern Jeremiah "con sus toques líricos y sus tremendas impre-
caciones. "*

539   "Kafka y el monstruo," 25 de julio, 1954.
S. discovers that Kafka's angustia and intellectual essence situate him within the world of Dostoyevsky's imagination, and makes some revealing comparisons between the
former's Metamorphosis and the latter's The Idiot. *

540   "Machado y la cifra de Castilla," julio, 1954.
Antonio Machado, despite his Andalusian origin, "ha
quedado incorporado al mito castellano: la mesura estoica,
la grave sencillez ... y esa noción del mundo según la cual
el momento que vivimos es eterno en su esencia. "*

541   "Traducciones y ediciones del Quijote," 2 de agosto,
1954.
According to Cervantes, a translation is "el reverso
de un tapiz. " According to S. , Samuel Putnam's English
version of Don Quijote is "el mejor reverso que conozco. "
S. expounds on some of the inherent limitations of the complex art of translation, deplores Walter Starkie's mutilated

edition, and rejoices in the miracle of imagination by which
the accumulated disasters of the Knight of the Woeful Counte-
nance are converted into greatness and final victory. *

542   "Un libro 'infausto' de Tomás ·Mann, " 8 de agosto,
      1954.
      Mann's The Black Swan is "una novela torpe, " "una
obra fallida, " which, like his Doctor Faustus, is weakened
by the author's "preocupación del prestigio nacional, personal, profesional. " Fortunately, however, it is not for these
two books that the author of The Magic Mountain and Death
in Venice will be remembered. *

543   "El difícil y exacto Paul Valéry, " 15 de agosto, 1954.
      Norman Suckling's book on the work of Valéry elicits
Sender's own appraisal.   Valéry's lyric poetry paradoxically
sought to express intellectual "emotions" through exact logical stimuli, cultivating a pleasurable though sterile perplex-
ity in place of human truth. *

544   "Un oasis en la novela española.   Tres novelas bajo
      una misma luz, " 22 de agosto, 1954.
      Luisa Forellad, in her novel Siempre en Capilla, side-
steps the problem of censorship by choosing a theme without
political, moral or religious implications: the human hor-
rors of an epidemic.   This genre, cultivated with distinction
in France by Camus (La peste) and Giono (Le hussard sur
le toit), is basically optimistic in its premise that man's
instinctive faith in man enables him to rise above catastroph-
ic circumstances.   Luisa Forellad's austere "interior" style,
all bone and sinew, shows the new Spanish trend away from
the decorative contours of the generation of '98. *

545   "Noticia póstuma de Colette, " 3 de septiembre, 1954.
      Colette was a harmonious and controlled spirit gifted
with natural intelligence, morality and understanding.   Her
creative imagination instinctively expressed love as simple,
natural and "propicio como la luz de cada día. "*

546   "Gorki, protagonista de novela, " 10 de septiembre,
      1954.
      S., while waiting to receive Igor Gouzenko's just-
published novel The Fall of a Titan (on the life and death
of Maxim Gorki) writes about Gorki's two personalities:
rough and violent in public (cultivating his own legend),
modest and amiable with his friends. *

547   "Alarcón en la sierra de Taos," 18 de septiembre,
      1954.
      S. tells of his encounter, in an isolated mountain com-
munity of New Mexico, with a patriarchal family living self-
sufficiently outside the flow of time and money and conserving
a heritage of archaic Spanish speech and customs as well as
a copy of Alarcón's first novel (1855), El Final de Norma,
which S. finds engagingly innocent and better than most of
the romantic narratives of the period.*

548   "Frida y el recuerdo de Lawrence," 25 de septiembre,
      1954.
      D. H. Lawrence's widow Frieda, author of Not I, But
the Wind, remains a discreet guardian angel to her husband's
posthumous aura.   S. speaks of the sense of harmonious
plentitude that she radiates and of her reciprocal influence
with Lawrence, for whom her delicate intuition could always
open new windows and horizons.*

549   "La novela de Igor Gouzenko," 2 de octubre, 1954.
      The Fall of a Titan explores the scandalous tragedy of
Gorki's assassination.   Gouzenko writes, like a good re-
porter, "con más convicción que arte," but his passionate
sincerity and the inspiring example of Gorki's heroism and
moral energy give the book a transcendent eloquence.*

550   "En la semana de don Juan," 4 de octubre, 1954.
      Comments on Armand Edwards Singer's bibliography of
more than 500 publications inspired by the blasphemous anarchist Don Juan Tenorio.   Don Juan, cynical libertine,
represents the antithesis of the idealistic Don Quixote, says
S., and both extremes excite the public's admiration.*

551   "Manuel de Jesús Galván en inglés," 9 de octubre,
      1954.
      The UNESCO translation by Robert Graves of Galván's
classic, Enriquillo (1879), does justice to this vivid and
profound evocation of the vain struggle of the Antilles Indians, confronted with the depredations of the conquistadores,
to salvage what they could of the harmonious dignity of
their lives.   S. remarks that Galván enriches historical
truth by his imaginative incorporation of legends.*

552   "La grandeza y la decadencia de los mayas," 16 de
      octubre, 1954.
      Eric Thompson writes with "emoción religiosa" of
2000 years of Mayan culture.   S. reflects on the Mayas'

harmonious moral sense and poetic cosmogony, and comments on how often the violence of civilization comes to destroy
the peacefulness of culture. *

553   "Hemingway, Premio Nóbel de 1954, " 31 de octubre,
      1954.
      S. looks at the life and works of Hemingway, the man
always "dissatisfied with life" which he viewed as combat--
as a cruel and meaningless game of chance. His sternly
sporting attitude resulted in a spare, brutal lyricism and
produced the most strongly "American" novels since Melville. *

554   "Sobre las memorias de Arthur Koestler, " 9 de novi-
      embre, 1954.
      In the two volumes of his memoirs, Arrow in the Blue
and The Invisible Writing, Koestler combines "el encanto de
la novela y la energía discursiva del ensayo. " The autobiography, S. believes, is really unnecessary in that it reveals
a weaker side of Koestler's personality than seen in his excellent novels--a certain Nietzschean intoxication with his
own self-importance--but in a Jewish intellectual who survived the Nazi holocaust, that "alegría de ser" is understand-
able and a source of vital experience for his readers.

555   "Sobre los santos de Mauriac, " 14 de noviembre, 1954.
      François Mauriac, in L'Agneau, concerns himself as
always not with the obvious ancient human vices but with the
ambiguous evils that are often unconscious or disguised as
virtues in today's society: decorous abjection. He presents
modern saints within, but not of, this world, who by love
and faith leap the barriers of law and dogma to discover the
original moral sense: the conscience before God. *

556   "Lorca, balcón abierto de España, " 20 de noviembre,
      1954.
      The publication by Aguilar of García Lorca's complete
works leads S. to comment on the poet's quality of living
tradition. The people adopted his verses as their own, like
the medieval romancillos, finding in them 'las cosas inefa-
bles que todo el mundo ha sentido desde hace más de 20
siglos en Andalucía. '*

557   "Adios a la Generación del 98, " 11 de diciembre, 1954.
      S. sums up the virtues, defects and influences of the
generation of '98 (Baroja, Valle-Inclán, Azorín, Unamuno,
Maeztu and--although he wrote neither in Spanish nor in

Spain--Santayana). Their unanimous atmosphere of skepti-
cism and protest may be said to have engendered the Republic, and the Republic's failure left them mired in frustration.
Aesthetically, Baroja and Valle-Inclán will survive. *

558   "Aga Khan en sus mil y una noches, " 14 de diciembre,
       1954.
       Aga Khan reveals himself in his memoirs as a man
whose Moslem liberalism has gained him the sympathy and
friendship of the Western world and who "dice que en toda
su vida no ha tenido un solo minuto de perplejidad ni de
aburrimiento. "*

559   "Resumen literario de 1954--Faulkner, " 21 de diciem-
       bre, 1954.
       In literature 1954 has not been "muy brillante, pero
tampoco ha sido tan pobre y sórdida como algunos comen-
taristas dicen. " After citing at length contradictory critical
opinions about Faulkner's A Fable, S. expresses his own
very high esteem for it, a novel in which the author has
achieved his purpose in writing it.

                              1955

560   "Steinbeck y otros autores, " 2 de enero, 1955.
       Reviewing the novelistic production of 1954, S. places
Steinbeck's Sweet Thursday and Dos Passos' Most Likely to
Succeed in the "escuadra avanzada de la novela norteamericana, " together with Faulkner, Hemingway, Farrell, and
Waldo Frank. He equates sincerity with originality and
hopes that 1955 will be more propitious for the heroism of
sincerity. *

561   "Más libros sobre Pablo Picasso, " 8 de enero, 1955.
       Picasso and the Human Comedy, a book of 180 draw-
ings accompanied by French and English critical studies, inspires Sender's commentaries on the genius and artistic integrity of Picasso, "cuyo sincero vigor le pone a salvo de
las definiciones de la crítica. "*

562   "La Dama de Elche, abuela de España, " 16 de enero,
       1955.
       S. , enamored of the superhuman calm and "dulce hier-
atismo" of the Dama de Elche, is disappointed in the prosaic
treatment accorded her by García Bellido in the section of
España Prerromana dedicated to Iberian sculpture. Her

aristocratic perfection of form, her mystery, her almost
mythical significance as genuine indigenous religious art, de-
serve a more poetic approach. *

563   "Tres poetas de hoy y uno de ayer," 23 de enero, 1955.
        S. discusses two new books: Jean Casson's Trois
poètes: Rilke, Milosz, Machado (Paris, Plon, 1954) and B.
Clariana's translation into Spanish of Catullus' poems, Odio y
amo (N. Y., Las Américas, 1954). The German Rilke (a mystic
of aesthetic emotion) and the Lithuanian Milosz (a mystic of human love) almost seem more Spanish than the Spaniard Machado
(a stoic in the non-decadent Senecan tradition of serenely fatalistic hombría), S. says. *

564   "El hombre del profesor Snow," 31 de enero, 1955.
        C. P. Snow's novel, The New Man, is a rich reflec-
tion of the conflict between his two inner faces: "la del
hombre y la del sabio." It is an intelligent exploration--too
intelligent to be satisfying, says S. --of the "plano moral
virgen" of our time, in which technology seeks independence
from human morality and establishes its own laws without
trying to legitimize them. *

565   "Schweitzer o la reverencia por la vida," 5 de febrero,
        1955.
        Inspired by the book of photographs with commentaries
by Erica Anderson, The World of Albert Schweitzer, S. discusses the struggle we all have between our egoistic and
altruistic inclinations, briefly reviews the life and accom-
plishments of Schweitzer, and concludes that the famous
doctor "es un hombre de genio que se ha inclinado del lado
altruísta," but whose "egoísmos" from a certain level of his
personality provide him with a sense of "utilidad y de plenti-
tud."

566   "¿Era Dumas un escritor 'considerable'?" 13 de
        febrero, 1955.
        S. finds, in Voyage en Russie by A. Dumas (pere),
true genius, and comments on the respectful biography by
André Maurois, just published, Alexandre Dumas (1954). *

567   "Cuentos de hadas y asesinos," 19 de febrero, 1955.
        S. considers marginal literary genres such as fairy
tales and crime or horror stories. Among the best writers
of the former he places Carroll, Andersen, Stevenson and
Kipling. Of the second, Poe, Balzac, de Maupassant, Mary
Shelley, Simenón and Chesterton, with Conan Doyle and

Ellery Queen receiving a kind of honorable mention.

568   "En la muerte del poeta Paul Claudel," 27 de febrero,
      1955.
      Of Claudel's poetry the best is religious. Of his
theater, the best has the qualities of classical tragedy ("la
invocación lírica a la fatalidad cruel que nos invita a ser
víctimas y verdugos de nosotros mismos"). S. contrasts,
not too complimentarily, Claudel's "clamor jeremíaco" with
the "repertorio mágico" of Rimbaud, whom Claudel envied. *

569   "¿Es la nuestra una era de creación?," 5 de marzo,
      1955.
      Having read New Horizons in Creative Thinking: A
Survey and Forecast (1954), edited by Robert M. MacIver,
S. laments the lack of imaginative exploration of new terrain
in contemporary literature. World War I was "un movimi-
ento revulsivo que estimuló la imaginación," but World War
II "no era novedad alguna. Fué la repetición de la primera
con una ligera diferencia: más máquinas que hombres.
Más técnica que inspiración," etc.

570   "Hablemos otra vez de Valle-Inclán," 12 de marzo,
      1955; El Diario de Hoy (San Salvador), 27 de marzo,
      1955.
      In the two-volume edition of the complete works of
Valle-Inclán, a fragmentary preface by Azorín and a mediocre one by Benavente move S. to lament the continuing sub-
stitution of picturesque anecdote for serious biography and
enthusiastic eulogy for critical analysis. Valle-Inclán, whose
hungry-minded admirers devoured him in his lifetime, deserves a better posthumous recompense, says S. *

571   "La obra de Whitman cien años después," 14 de marzo,
      1955.
      Upon the centenary of the publication of the first edi-
tion of Walt Whitman's Leaves of Grass, "se celebra en
América el primer siglo de la independencia cultural de los
Estados Unidos. Según la crítica moderna, es hacia 1855
cuando los Estados Unidos se dan cuenta de que poseen una
personalidad definida en el mundo de las letras." Discusses
Whitman as "el hombre 'adánico' en una sociedad compleja
y naciente como la América de 1855."

572   "Un raro análisis del 'Ulises'," 26 de marzo, 1955.
      A discussion of Stuart Gilbert's book, James Joyce's
Ulysses, which S. finds "más chispeante y luminoso que el

'Ulises' mismo, como suele pasar con los estudios claros
sobre libros oscuros. "

573   "Sobre la sonriente y sangrienta China, " 4 de abril,
1955.
      S. discusses American policy with respect to China
and Alice Tisdale Hobart's second novel on China, Venture
into Darkness. Hobart's novel "no es mala. Tampoco
podemos decir que sea una buena novela. "

574   "Crónica real de la ideal Greta Garbo, " 16 de abril,
1955.
      S. says that Greta Garbo, whose acting was an exten-
sion of her feminine temperament, was always the same in
her films and in her private life. Thus John Bainbridge's
non-adulatory biography leaves her unscathed, since there is
nothing invented or artificial in Garbo. *

575   "El último libro de Albert Einstein, " 30 de abril, 1955.
      Einstein's Ideas and Opinions causes S. to remind us
of the philosopher-physicist's religiosity (science and pantheism transcending to the metaphysical realm), his innocent
humor, and his warnings to modern society on the danger of
producing "trained dogs" and on the arrogance of the man of
applied science. *

576   "Una novela francesa muy reveladora, " 4 de mayo,
1955.
      Simone de Beauvoir's Les mandarins depicts, like a
historical fresco, the left-wing intellectual life of Paris in
the postwar years. The novel is contradictory in its political aspects, but is saved from banality by its extraordinary
portrayal of "una pasión de mujer sin falsos pudores, terri-
blemente emocional y lúcidamente intelectual. "*

577   "Diez ensayos del 'distraído' Maugham, " 7 de mayo,
1955.
      In The Art of Fiction Maugham comments on ten great
novelists: Fielding, Austen, Stendhal, Balzac, Dickens,
Flaubert, Melville, Emily Brontë, Dostoyevski and Tolstoi.
Maugham's idea of the aim of a novelist is to entertain,
i. e. , to "distract" his readers. But in our time, writes S. ,
people are already distracted and frequently seek the opposite, to be "abstracted"--precisely what Maugham's ten
novelists accomplish.

578   "Los alemanes y la difícil lección, " 15 de mayo, 1955.

Upon reading Ernst von Salomón's book, Fragebogen, S. comments upon the character of the German people--admirable as individuals but as a people lacking in good political sense. "Excelentes soldados, los alemanes han ganado muchas batallas en la historia, pero son los únicos europeos que no han tenido nunca un imperio. Ni lo tendrán. "

579   "Orden del día: Rusia," 21 de mayo, 1955.
S. reviews two new books on Russia: N. Sukhanov's The Russian Revolution of 1917 (history by an eye-witness of prodigious memory) and M. Soloviev's My Nine Lives in the Red Army (which portrays Russia as an immense madhouse). S. adds that the abusive Soviet opportunists hiding behind Marx's doctrines have bungled their chance and may have some nasty surprises in store for them. *

580   "Madrid, castillo famoso," 28 de mayo, 1955.
Madrid, by Juan Antonio Cabezas, is a brilliant historical, literary, graphic, social, demographic compendium of that noble, cultured and enchanting city whose antiquity may extend back 300,000 years.   S. says that Madrid is more stoic than baroque, and that in its graceful style of "vigor contenido" it represents the Spanish national character better than any other city. *

581   " 'La Celestina' en los Estados Unidos," 5 de junio, 1955; El Universal (Caracas), 18 de junio, 1955 ("Indice literario," p. 1).
Fernando de Rojas' La Celestina, the first European novel (Don Quijote a century later was the second), in spite of the excellence of its English translation by Lesley Byrd Simpson, will not be widely read in the U.S. where the imagination is enslaved to civilized values and prejudiced against the violence of absolute ones, says S. *

582   "Thomas Mann en sus ochenta años," 12 de junio, 1955.
S. disagrees with Mann's descriptions of himself as a humorist, perceiving rather 'la sensación de solemnidad y grandeza decorativa ... presente siempre en su obra. '*

583   "¿Es el teatro un género en decadencia?," 19 de junio, 1955.
The drama critic Walter Kerr, in How Not to Write a Play, concludes that the theater is on the road to its own total extinction.   S. is not so pessimistic, saying that if dramatists can avoid the decadent trap of speaking only to

an élite and remember how to kindle the rich imagination of
ordinary people, then the apparently paralytic effects of con-
servative financing and "competition" from semi-infantile
cinema may turn out to be beneficial stimuli in disguise. *

584   "La mitológica antigüedad de Andalucía," 25 de junio,
       1955.
    Adolf Schulten, in Tartessos, identifies that ancient
Andalusian city with the legendary Atlantis of Plato.   S.
comments that the heritage of that old culture is still alive
today in the area's graceful schools of dance, painting, poetry and the cult of the bull, to say nothing of those Atlantean
descendants Picasso, Lorca and Falla. *

585   "El caso turbador de Simone Weil," 3 de julio, 1955.
    Simone Weil, says S., combines the qualities of hero-
ism, poetic genius and saintliness, serenely reconciling soul
and intellect.   All her writings (S. mentions Gravity and
Grace, The Need for Roots and Waiting for God) were published after her death in 1943 at the age of 34.   'Buscando
'su realidad' ... encontró la 'realidad absoluta'. '*

586   "Sobre el maestro Domenico," 10 de julio, 1955.
    Antonina Valentín's biography of El Greco (Domenico
Theotocopuli) stimulates more curiosity than it satisfies.   S.
speaks of Spain's ancient cultural links with Crete; the Hispanic fusion of Western mind and Eastern spirit; the Byzantine impressionism shared by El Greco, Goya and Picasso;
and the "notable dosis de literatura (de tendencia conceptual)"
in the work of all great painters. *

587   "Sobre los grupos culturales 'de color'," 27 de julio,
       1955.
    Observations on the place of Blacks in American life
with reference to recent books on the subject, including
Samuel R. Spencer's Booker T. Washington and the Negro's
Place in American Life, Comer Vann Woodward's The
Strange Career of Jim Crow (1955, revised in 1957), and
Robert Ruark's Someting of Value (though the last deals pri-
marily, of course, with the Mau-Maus of Africa).

588   "El libro de Arciniegas sobre Vespucci," 30 de julio,
       1955.
    Amérigo y el Nuevo Mundo, by the Colombian author
Germán Arciniegas, sympathetically presents the Florentine
navigator and cartographer as a man of intellectual curiosity
in the liberal stoic tradition.   S. adds that Spain's contribu-

tion to the Renaissance was the dimension of action. *

589   "Vida y letras de Saint-Exupéry," 7 de agosto, 1955.
The Winged Life is the biography by Stewart and Rum-
bold of Antoine de Saint-Exupéry, French author and pilot.
A man of action with a dose of quijotismo, "es decir, de
idealismo feudal militante," he converted his moral experience and metaphysical curiosity into simple writings of
subtle and poetic wisdom. *

590   "La heroica tierra del mestizaje," 15 de agosto, 1955.
The Grand Canyon's powerful and magical indifference
contrasts with the human sadness of the mestizo's plight in
America today, distorted through the "corny" romantic lens
of a Canyon tour guide's book. *

591   "De Bogotá la bien hablada," 20 de agosto, 1955.
S. deplores the closing down of El Tiempo, Colombia's
most prestigious newspaper, because its director refused to
print a government communiqué that he considered unjust.
S. says that the closure is even more stupid than unjust. *

592   "California y sus visitantes famosos," 27 de agosto,
1955.
Commenting on California's attraction for visiting writers, S. mentions Gabriela Mistral (the last great poet of innocence), Aldous Huxley (perhaps the most intelligent man
of letters today), and Thomas Mann (who prefers prestige to
the convincing madness that is the secret of the modern
novel). *

593   "Miró y los problemas del estilo," 4 de septiembre,
1955; El Universal (Caracas), 17 de septiembre, 1955.
Gabriel Miró's decorative modernist rhetoric and Le-
vantine Pantheism are too preoccupied with style to qualify
as great literature, but Miró's refined sensibility has left
us an evocative vision of the Spanish countryside and traditions. *

594   "El pícaro español en EE. UU.," 10 de septiembre,
1955; El Universal (Caracas), 1 de octubre, 1955.
The Spanish pícaro is too antisocial to be popular in
the U.S., says S. Yet Lazarillo de Tormes and Rinconete
y Cortadillo, "los únicos libros de picardías que tienen el
acento estoico, sereno, entre resignado y cínico que define
el género," imply a certain natural affability and sympathy
in the pícaro. La Celestina disqualifies as picaresque be-

cause of its tragic solution; Guzmán de Alfarache and Peri-
quillo Sarniento are more in the tearful and moralizing tone
of a Christian confession; and Buscón is more sarcastic and
impudent than picaresque. *

595   "Lorca y su 'Poeta en Nueva York'," 17 de septiembre,
      1955; El Universal (Caracas), 24 de septiembre, 1955.
      On the publication in English of García Lorca's Poet in
New York, S. observes that some of the poems in the collection are "versos de una vulgaridad literaturizante que no
parece digna de él" although others are master strokes, such
as the poem to the King of Harlem and the one to Walt Whitman. *

596   "Tres libros sobre un pasado reciente," 24 de septiem-
      bre, 1955.
      S. discusses Thomas Mann's posthumously published
novel, Confessions of Felix Krull (calling it excellent and in
general terms classifying it as "una novela picaresca. A la
manera alemana, esto es, con solemnidad, transcendencia y
preocupación metafísica"), the second volume of the biography
of Freud by Ernest Jones, and Our Samoan Adventure by
Fanny and Robert Louis Stevenson (which includes Mrs.
Stevenson's diary that had formerly remained unpublished).

597   "Sobre los judíos de Túnez," 2 de octubre, 1955.
      The Pillar of Salt, written in French by Memmi, is an
autobiographical novel of the author's youth in the Jewish
ghetto of Túnez.   Memmi records the daily fears and frus-
trations that S. feels are perhaps worse than the major ca-
tastrophes. *

598   "Una dama extraña y genial," 8 de octubre, 1955.
      Comments on Virginia Woolf and on her biography by
Aileen Pippett, The Moth and the Star.

599   "El maestro Ortega y Gasset ha muerto," 22 de octu-
      bre, 1955.
      On the death of Ortega "cuando tanto se podía esperar
aún de su maduro intelecto y de su limpia y sensitiva conciencia," S. says he brought dignity, decorum and responsibility to the modern Spanish essay, as well as a poetic
sense of truth concerned with man's total essence.   The
last great liberal, Ortega "llenó la vida española de preguntas nuevas."*

600   "Halldor K. Laxness, Premio Nóbel, 1955," 4 de

noviembre, 1955.

S. observes that Laxness is an unusual novelist who writes "no dentro de la sociedad, sino al margen de ella." Though Independent People is an excellent book and Laxness a first-rate author, the author's moral sense is that of an "anti-puritano sectario--es decir, puritano a su vez."*

601   "En Francia se ocupan de los Incas," 13 de noviembre, 1955.

Louis Baudin's La vie quotidienne dans les temps des derniers Incas occasions Sender's remarks on the ingenuity of Inca medicine, architecture, social and economic organization, and the complex, modern and sophisticated imagination of their oral literature. *

602   "Una nueva traducción de Turguenev," 20 de noviembre, 1955.

A volume in English containing long novels (On the Eve, Fathers and Sons, Smoke and Rudin) and short ones (A Quiet Backwater, First Love and Diary of a Superfluous Man) illustrates the results of Turgenev's cold intelligence put to the service of elemental passions. S. calls him "el genio redentor" of everyday vulgarity. *

603   "Este universo en que vivimos," 26 de noviembre, 1955.

Fred Hoyle's Frontiers of Astronomy reminds S. that in addition to telescopes and mathematics, imagination is necessary in order to conceive of the universe. He adds that the expanding universe is like an exploring and conquering universe, paralleling on a grand scale our own heroic human task of combatting la nada, i. e., non-being, with our daily action and hope and our nightly dreams. *

604   "La presencia del hombre prehistórico," 2 de diciembre, 1955.

Upon reading Herbert Kuhn's On the Track of Prehistoric Man, S. reflects on anthropology's advances "hacia atrás" in tracking down the development of the human mind. Viewing the power and exquisite sensibility of Stone Age art, S. concludes that primitive man was richer in imagination than today's "civilized" man. *

605   "El nuevo libro de Madariaga," 10 de diciembre, 1955.

Salvador de Madariaga's Retrato de Europa (a keen intuitive appraisal of its spiritual reality, not its political actuality) stimulates the imagination and inspires the reader to

extend the author's line of thought into other areas.   The
idea of a unified Europe acting as a cultural link between
Russia and the U.S. suggests that a unified Latin America
might create a comparable harmony of forces in the Pacific. *

606   "Don Miguel o el castellano universal," 17 de diciem-
       bre, 1955.
       Sebastián Arbó's life of Cervantes is a reverent and
well-documented narration capable of holding the interest of
the common man as well as the scholar.   Don Miguel and
his alter ego Don Quijote managed to win the battle against
their time, and left us this lesson: "nuestra imaginación
asistida por la fe puede cambiar las condiciones de la realidad, no sólo idealmente, sino prácticamente, también. "*

607   "A propósito del libro del doctor Eduardo Santos," 25
       de diciembre, 1955.
       Santos, in La crisis de la democracia en Colombia y
"El Tiempo," recalls the respect for democratic institutions
that existed during his presidency, and contrasts it with the
dictator's mentality that led Gen. Rojas Pinilla to cut off
publication of the Newspaper El Tiempo.   That exasperated
act of the General, says S. , is a gesture of rabid impotence
and fear in the face of a power greater than his own: that
of intelligence. *

                              1956

608   "Balance y divagación de fin de año, " 1 de enero,
       1956.
       Were the Spanish-American countries to join together
to allow free circulation of books from one country to another, authors from those countries would have an abundance
of readers since, all together, Spanish-American readers
outnumber those in the United States (where an edition of
100,000 copies is not at all uncommon).   But an effective
continent-wide circulation of books in Spanish America would
require a continental monetary unit and an organized distri-
bution.

609   "Dos libros sobre Santayana, " 9 de enero, 1956.
       S. reviews two books on Santayana.   The Mind of Santa-
yana, by Richard Butler, a Catholic priest, fails to be convincing in its dogmatic attack on the philosopher as a materi-

alistic corrupter without talent. Daniel Cory's Cartas de
Jorge Santayana sheds new light on the personality, complex
thought and esthetic faith of the transplanted Spaniard (a
stoic, skeptic, ascetic, fundamentally Platonic thinker possessed by doubt). *

610   "En el centenario de Bernard Shaw," 13 de enero, 1956
      Only five or six years after Shaw died (1950), bequeath-
ing his fortune to the orthographic reform of the English
language, the centennial of his birth (in 1856) is being celebrated in England. Shaw, whose best joke and most confus-
ing disguise was that of the naked truth, also left a great
psychological, ethical and logical legacy in the extravagant
sincerity of his work. *

611   "Kazantzakis, novelista de Creta," 14 de enero, 1956.
      In Kazantzakis' Freedom or Death the historical content
is "sólo un pretexto para el trabajo libre de la imaginación,"
which makes use of "un realismo directo y a veces brutal"
and "una implacable desnudez en lo sentimental y pasional. "*

612   "Sobre el teatro español de ahora," 27 de enero, 1956.
      S. surveys the Spanish theatrical scene, finding in the
work of Grau, Lorca, Casona, Buero Vallejo and Sastre
reason for the most exalted optimism. He discusses their
disparate styles and strengths, and credits them with a common virtue: that of not sacrificing art for the sake of popularity. *

613   "A propósito de Ferrater Mora," 4 de febrero, 1956.
      José Ferrater Mora, in his Cuestiones disputadas, de-
fends and practices, says S. , the concept of philosophy as
art (vs. philosophy as science) and that of the unity of creation (vs. fragmented specialization in knowledge). S. holds
that the Greek atom was an integrative, philosophical atom,
and that the disintegration inherent in today's specialized
technology is what weakens our moral base and creates our
anxiety. *

614   "El honesto talento de Orwell," 11 de febrero, 1956.
      Orwell, though possessing artistic and moral strengths,
revealed in his works some bourgeois weaknesses. His Keep
the Aspidistra Flying, 1936, constitutes a powerful accusation
of the evils of bourgeois vulgarity. The poor are the only
ones beyond the reach of satire.

615   "Novelas francesas en Canadá," 17 de febrero, 1956.
       Dostaler O'Leary's Le roman canadien-français reminds
S. of the dismal contrast between the lack of literary production among the large Spanish-speaking population of the U. S.
and the rich abundance of literature written by the smaller
French-Canadian community.   O'Leary reviews this heritage
from early adventure stories through backwoods narratives
to the modern novel of psychological analysis and transcendent dimensions. *

616   "Más sobre el teatro contemporáneo," 26 de febrero,
       1956.
       To supplement his article "Sobre el teatro español de
ahora," S. comments on two "pequeñas obras maestras"
from the Aguilar anthology, Teatro español: Edgar Neville's
"El baile" and Miguel Mihura's "Tres sombreros de copa. "*

617   "Una obra póstuma de Eugenio O'Neill," 4 de marzo,
       1956.
       O'Neill, his country's greatest dramatist, bequeaths an
autobiographical tragedy: Long Day's Journey Into Night,
which succinctly expresses "la secreta fruición con la cual
el genio descubre la misteriosa armonía que hay en los fon-
dos más infaustos de la realidad. " In this work, adds S. ,
the love of death is not decadent but lyrical. *

618   "Dostoyevski y el espejo infausto," 9 de marzo, 1956.
       On the 75th anniversary of Dostoyevsky's death, S.
says that the Soviets could not tolerate the great novelist because he held up too faithful a mirror to the tortuous ambi-
valence and natural idealism of the Russian people, and that
Stalin himself seemed to be one of Dostoyevsky's "personajes
satánicos. "*

619   "La noche de Veríssimo en inglés," 17 de marzo,
       1956.
       The Night, by Erico Veríssimo, does not refer to an
ordinary night but rather, S. says, to a universal and time-
less night that descends upon the amnesiac protagonist of
this novel, in which Veríssimo finds "planos de armonía en
lo violento, lo feo, lo innoble y lo delirante. "*

620   "Una biografía sobre Rachmaninoff," 31 de marzo, 1956.
       In the biography of Rachmaninoff by Bertensson and
Leyda, "el hombre domina su propia obra como un gigante. "
S. Speaks of Rachmaninoff's Russian monumentalist tendency,
of his "superación de Tchaikovsky," and compares the pure

lyricism of music to the occasional "doble plano" of literature, where "ideas" may add another dimension to the ineffable. *

621   "Cocteau, en su verde vejez," 7 de abril, 1956.
       S. says that he has never been fascinated by Cocteau's
avant-garde qualities but rather by the seriousness of his
dedication and his secret veneration of the literary profession.   S. paraphrases for his Spanish-speaking readers the
chapter on Cocteau in Cristina Garnier's Confidences d'Ecri-
vains. *

622   "El arte difícil del ensayo," 14 de abril, 1956.

623   "Hace cien años que murió Heine," 21 de abril, 1956.
       The centennial of the Jewish-German poet reminds S.
of the unconscious assimilation of Heine into the poetic sensibility and style of today (Bécquer, Housman, sometimes Verlaine).   S. calls attention to the exact and inevitable quality
of Heine's prose, the mark of a genuine poet who instinctively chooses ineffable forms of expression. *

624   "Fuentes galaicas de Valle-Inclán," 28 de abril, 1956;
       El Diario de Nueva York, 13 de mayo, 1956.
       Professor José Barcia's erudite study, Valle-Inclán y
la literatura gallega, offers valuable insights into the thematic
and stylistic influences of his own region on the work of the
great Galician, especially strong in the four Sonatas, in
Flor de Santidad and in the novels of the Carlist wars.
Valle-Inclán's lyrical fusion of the harmony of nature with
the turbid chaos of human violence has a long tradition in
the literature of the terra meiga, including the work of the
author's own father. *

625   "Bernal Díaz del Castillo estuvo allí," 5 de mayo, 1956.
       On the publication of Maudlay's English translation of
La historia verdadera de la conquista de la Nueva España,
S. says that among the many marvels of this singular book
the most impressive is its naturalness of expression, the
same fresh and vigorous style to be found in the prose of
Santa Teresa and San Juan de la Cruz. *

626   "Sobre La yegua verde de Aymé," 12 de mayo, 1956.
       Aymé's novel, La jument verte, follows in the French
tradition of Rabelais, in which medieval liberties of expression become an advanced form of art.   In the genre of rural realism, he explores the contrast between the perfection

of nature and the "perfection" of society's dictates of virtue: anarchy vs. order.*

627   "El increíble Mr. Sickles," 21 de mayo, 1956.
The eloquence of facts, basis of the U.S. culture, makes for American expertise in the historical novel. W. A. Swenberg's The Incredible Mr. Sickles absorbingly demonstrates the 19th-century U.S. physical bravado, innocent irregularity of actions, and challenge to fatality.*

628   "La rebelión de los adolescentes," 27 de mayo, 1956.
The book Youth, by Gesell, Ilg and Ames, causes S. to reflect that today's adolescents have as much need to rebel as ever, but that instead of concerned parental tyranny they encounter indifferent parental liberalism. Thus their rebellion tries to forge negative bonds rather than break positive ones.*

629   "Erotismo en primera persona," 2 de junio, 1956.
Françoise Sagan, whose first novel, Bonjour tristesse, revealed a slightly perverse innocence (less masterful than that of Colette), in her second novel, Un certain sourire, tries but fails to achieve distinction through sensationalism and vulgarity.*

630   "La tragicomedia 'Esperando a Godot'," ¿10? de junio, 1956.
"Es el mejor ejemplo que existe en lengua francesa o inglesa de teatro poético en prosa. Como el teatro es acción, la poesía de 'Esperando a Godot' está en la estructura y en los hechos."

631   "Viladrich y las doncellas cimbreantes," 21 de junio, 1956.
The recently deceased Catalonian painter Viladrich, "como muchos primitivos, interpretaba el paisaje a través de los tipos humanos," just as S. prefers to do in his writings. Viladrich's campesinas radiate a transcendent simplicity and grace and represent "siglos de estilo depurado."*

632   "Casals, el viejo patriarca de Prades," 30 de junio, 1956.
José María Carredor's Conversaciones con Pablo Ca-

sals is an insightful study of the life, art and complex personality of the great Catalonian musician.   Says S. , "a
Casals su arte impregnado de sentido moral lo ha hecho
venerable como un santo. "*

633   "Victor Serge y los cuidados de Stalin, " 7 de julio,
      1956.
      S. recalls the part he played, by helping to manipulate
Stalin's fear of the "intellectual" community, in the early release from prison of Victor Serge, who left Russia and wrote,
among other memorable novels, The Case of Comrade Tula-
yev, which contains a "penetrating portrait of Stalin. "*

634   "O'Flaherty, el narrador irlandés, " 21 de julio, 1956.
      Although The Informer and The Puritan do not reinvent
nature with the imagination, S. recognizes O'Flaherty's
classic virtues of dramatic narration.   In The Short Stories
of Liam O'Flaherty the reader can find complex moral and
prophetic dimensions if he orients his mind in that direction. *

635   "Mrs. Holiday, Coleridge y la 'tontería' lírica, " 6
      de agosto, 1956.
      Recognizing the underlying affinity of two apparently un-
related books (Billie Holiday's Lady Sings the Blues and E.
L. Griggs' Letters of Coleridge), S. comments that only
great artists dare to show themselves whole, with the lyrical abandon of "esa sublime tontería" that reveals our unconscious world and becomes the basis of originality. *

636   "Héroes y monstruous del pasado americano, " 8 de
      agosto, 1956.
      S. praises the interpretive skill and insight of Rosa
Arcinega in her two historical chronicles: Dos rebeldes en
el Perú and Pedro Sarmiento de Gamboa, el Ulíses de
América. *

637   "Mark Twain y la risa de los yanquis, " 12 de agosto,
      1956.
      Samuel Clemens' most effective weapon as a humorist
was his devastating sincerity, says S.   Avoiding the pitfalls
of scepticism, farce, rancor or over-intellectualism, Mark
Twain through his sympathy and poetic grace made his country laugh as no one else could. *

638   "De la Mare, o la belleza terrible," 1 de septiembre,
      1956.
      On the death of Walter De la Mare at the age of 83,
S. comments on the English poet's unique qualities of fresh
fantasy, melancholy, romantic nobility, daring imagination
and precision. His work is characterized, says S., by "el
terror de la belleza," that is, the tremor of fatality that the
poet's sensibility encounters in any expressible form of
beauty. *

639   "Goya entrevisto por Malraux," 7 de septiembre, 1956.
      S. finds André Malraux's book, Saturn; An Essay on
Goya, pedantic and deficient in its appreciation of the great
Aragonese painter.

640   "Las cenizas de Frida Lawrence," 10 de septiembre,
      1956.
      Reflections (soon after the death of Frieda Lawrence)
upon the role Frieda played in the life and work of her
famous husband, D. H. Lawrence.

641   "Sobre 'España en la encrucijada'," 18 de septiembre,
      1956.
      Semprún Gurrea, in Spain at the Crossroads, studies
the complicated realities of the economic, political and moral life of the Franco regime. S. brings up another dimension of Spain's dilemma: that of the succession. *

642   "Otra vez Hugo, el abuelo proceloso," 24 de septiem-
      bre, 1956.
      Victor Hugo's Quatre-vingt-treize balances romantic
vigor and classic discipline. "Huto fue el abuelo proceloso
... que nos dió a todos una segunda nacionalidad," and his
work continues as meaningful as ever to humanity today. *

643   "En las orillas verdes del Amazonas," 6 de octubre,
      1956.
      In Pasión y crónica del Amazonas, E. Rodríguez
Fabregat writes about that fabulous river combining "la investigación histórica, la exploración geográfica y la sociología con la poesía." He sheds new light on the suggestive
legend of the Amazons and convinces S. that they really
existed. *

644   "Thomas Wolfe, escritor de cartas," 13 de octubre,
      1956.
      Wolfe's letters speak of himself with a sacred egoism,

an innocent narcissism that generously seeks--and finds--in others his own exaltation of life. *

645   "Colin Wilson y el miedo al caos, " 22 de octubre, 1956.

S. praises the vision, if not the style of Wilson's The Outsiders, a sort of encyclopedia of philosophical and moral nonconformism, of explanations for the rejection by some people of reality, discussion of the conflict between anarchy and order, and of society's fear of chaos.

646   "El Premio Nóbel a Juan Ramón Jiménez, " 26 de octubre, 1956.

The "matriz sonora" of Jiménez' idyllic poetry is the lyrical orientalism of Andalucía, together with the Christian-Moslem mysticism of San Juan de la Cruz, says S. who calls Juan Ramón "el abuelo de los poetas modernos en España, y de no pocos de este continente. "*

647   "El 'hombre malo de Itzea' se ha marchado, " 6 de noviembre, 1956.

On the death of Baroja, S. quotes many of the disdain-ful and bitter opinions of the frustrated genius about his con-temporaries and predecessors, fellow inhabitants of "un universo estúpido. " But Baroja's hates, says S. , are the other sides of "un amor imposible, que fermenta y da aquí y allá, ocasionalmente, flores exquisitas. "*

648   "Los escritores 'culpables' de los EE. UU. , " 10 de noviembre, 1956.

To the question, "Why do writers give a false im-pression of life in the U. S. ?, " S. replies on two levels: first, it is characteristic of novelists to satirize or ignore the virtues of their nations, and, second, the U. S. lives for the present, an illusory reality vanishing at every mo-ment as the future becomes the concrete past--a dream dreamed with hands and machines: slippery ground for writers. *

649   "Aquel Antonov Ovsenko de Barcelona, " 18 de no-viembre, 1956.

S. reminisces about his friendship with the "intellectu-al aristocrat" Ovsenko in Barcelona before he was denounced and sent back to his death in Moscow by the same Gero who was the Communist party leader in charge of quelling the current Hungarian uprising. *

650   "Read y la definición de la poesía," 3 de diciembre,
       1956.
       A thoughtful and important review of Herbert Read's
book, The Nature of Literature. In some points S. disagrees
with Read, e.g., in the relationship of poetry and myth.
"Todos los grandes mitos fueron antes poesía," asserts S.,
"nacieron en la poesía, como Penélope, Prometeo, Pygmali-
ón y, más recientemente, Don Juan." S. does not share
Read's veneration for Freud.

651   "Tres libros de gran actualidad," 12 de diciembre,
       1956.
       Three books on Russia (Wolfe's Khrushchev and
Stalin's Ghost; Gorkin's Marx and the Russia of Yesterday
and Today; and How the Soviet System Works by Bauer,
Inkeles and Kluckhohn) confirm S.'s impression that the Soviet Union's strength is its use of terror, its weakness is
also its use of terror, and that the neutralization of strength
and weakness cancels out the possibility of progress and
leads to a dead end. *

652   "Escritores franceses en los Estados Unidos," 18 de
       diciembre, 1956.
       Comments on four French novelists recently translated
into English (Sagan, de Beauvoir, Giono--the best--and
Aymé) and one yet untranslated novel, La chute, by Camus,
which illustrates the tendency towards a "secularización de
Dios"--a direct and humanized religion without dogmas,
church or priests. *

653   "Brujerío en los libros y en la realidad," 24 de
       diciembre, 1956.

654   "Gary, Premio Goncourt, y su mensaje," 29 de di-
       ciembre, 1956.
       Romain Gary, French consul, wins the Goncourt Prize
for Las raíces del cielo (Les racines du ciel), a novel whose
protagonist identifies freedom with jungle animals and becomes a "cazador de cazadores," destroyer of destruction.
Gary's message, according to S., is a plea for the primitive candor of natural man, and for the elimination of frivolous values. *

<u>1957</u>

655   "Admiración y rencor por Lord Byron," 7 de enero,
       1957.
       Eileen Bigland's biography of Lord Byron offers noth-
ing substantial that has not already been said in other biographies of the poet (e.g., Maurois'). Some of her observations, says S., are abusive, but he is not surprised that
women are still offended and enchanted by the shadow of
Byron. *

656   "El último 'Lawrence of Arabia'," 15 de enero, 1957.
       Aldington's Lawrence of Arabia: A Biographical Investi-
gation seeks to debunk the myth jointly created by a worship-
ful public, enthusiastic biographers and the willing hero's
own bag of tricks. Too late, says S.: "tales son ahora las
proporciones del mito Lawrence, que este libro, demoledor
y todo, no le hará daño ostensible. "*

657   "Ensayos sobre Gabriela Mistral," 19 de enero, 1957.
       Having read Benjamín Carrión's Santa Gabriela Mistral,
S. takes the opportunity to express his enthusiasm for the
poet whom the Spaniards have long considered to be "ni más
ni menos la voz de este continente. "*

658   "Los conquistadores y la historia 'romántica'," 27 de
       enero, 1957.
       The Frenchman Jean Descola writes a flattering, im-
aginative account of the Spanish conquest of the New World
in his book, The Conquistadors. An Englishman would have
treated the subject with less romanticism and a colder,
more critical admiration. S. remarks on the instinctive
"espíritu civil" of those uncultured men whose respect for
their own improvised legality was "la fuerza principal de la
conquista. "*

659   "Conrad, el soñador de los mares," 10 de febrero,
       1957.
       Comments on Joseph Conrad (and possible explanation
for the lack of commercial success of his "complete works"
when published in the United States thirty years earlier)
upon the centennial of the Polish novelist's birth.

660   "Arte nuevo de vivir y de morir," 18 de febrero,
       1957.
       Leslie Shepherd's essay, "Vuelo Interestelar" (pub-
lished in Outer Space), ignites Sender's imagination with its

revelations about the effects of antigravitational space travel on the span of human life measured in earth years. S. is reminded once more of Simone Weil's metaphysical proposition that the force of gravity is the force of evil, of sin, of ignorance, of ruin, and thus by extension to the physical realm, says S. , perhaps the cause of sickness, aging and death. *

661   "Las sombras de Lenín, Trotsky y Stalin," 3 de marzo 1957.
      Bertram Wolfe's penetrating study Three Who Made a Revolution; A Biographical History (1956), read by S. in the Spanish translation, is a "voluminosa historia del socialismo despótico" that gives dramatic evidence of the sterility of the Revolution of 1917. The error in Lenin's philosophy, says S. , was to consider politics a science with absolute rights when it is really an art with moral responsibilities. *

662   "El primer libro sobre Hungría," 19 de marzo, 1957.
      Víctor Alba's book Hungría, 1956 reveals its author's alert sensibility and historical sense of everyday reality, and reflects the progressive and dynamic atmosphere of international concern in Mexico today. S. agrees with Alba's conclusion that the eventual downfall of Russian Communist imperialism will come from within; and the Hungarian revolution is a symptom of the inevitable consequences of the assumption that the proletariat doesn't know what it wants and thus will tolerate any amount of abuse imposed from above. *

663   "Frost y la diversidad en lo bello," 21 de marzo, 1957.
      The most revealing aspects of Sidney Cox's biography of Robert Frost, A Swinger of Birches, refer to his years as professor of literature at Amherst, teaching, if not poetry-writing, at least poetry-reading. Conscious of his limitations but rich within them, Frost in his definition of beauty avoided the sublime extremes and intensively cultivated the middle ground. *

664   "Las drogas, la calma y la cordura," 1 de abril, 1957.
      A discussion of the use of tranquilizers in today's society (in the U.S.), and the difference between tranquility and sanity and between the Latin and the Anglo-Saxon worlds, inspired by reading A Man Against Insanity, a biography of a psychiatrist written by Paul de Kruif.

665   "En los próximos veinte años," 6 de abril, 1957.
An optimistic view of possible changes to occur during
the next two decades (1957-1977). "Empujados por la economía, la técnica, la sociología y la antropología ... vamos
a un nuevo clasicismo de proprociones sorprendentemente
nuevas y originales. "*

666   "Valéry, el caos y la geometría," 13 de abril, 1957.
Valéry's book of essays, Dialogues, stirs S. to reflect
on the two tasks of the novelist: to identify the chaos of his
microcosm (or continent), and to emerge from that chaos and
from the prison of words by heroically inventing his own secret geometry and imposing it upon the free space of his
chaos--something the Hispanic American writers have not yet
dared to do. *

667   "Los incas y otros mitos de América," 23 de abril,
1957.
The World of the Incas, by Bertrand Flornoy, leads S.
to ponder the significance of "aquel imperio monolítico, teo-
crático, con extrañas formas socialistas. " The Incas, Mayas and Aztecs represent the three great myths of the American continent whose mystery by far overshadows what facts
have survived about them. *

668   "Madame Bovary ha cumplido cien años," 26 de abril,
1957.
Flaubert's Madame Bovary was a sensation in 1857.
S. , however, agrees with the contemporary criticism of
Baudelaire, who called the novel vulgar, commonplace and
unimaginative. Les liaisons dangereuses by Laclos and Le
rouge et le noir by Stendhal are the classics of libertinism
in French literature; by comparison the hysterical but tepid
Madame Bovary pales. *

669   "Belloc no era lo que parecía," 4 de mayo, 1957.
Hilaire Belloc, the eccentric Catholic essayist-poet,
historian-novelist, represented "una mezcla de buen sentido
francés y de violenta originalidad inglesa. " Though he con-
fused his contemporaries, Belloc will illumine and make
verisimilar for future readers the rich and agitated reality
of his time. *

670   "Valle-Inclán y la mentira inspirada," 11 de mayo,
1957.
S. reminisces about the intervention of the imagination
in his conversations with his friend Valle-Inclán. "Yo leía

entonces cosas extrañas ... para documentar mi imaginación
y alimentar mejor el fuego sagrado de nuestras confidencias.
S. says that humanity, always composed of fools and inspired
lunatics, owes everything to the latter. *

671   "La última novela de Faulkner," 17 de mayo, 1957.
      A review of Faulkner's novel, The Town, and comments
on the dangers and difficulties in the novelist's new fame (as
a result of his having received the Nobel Prize).

672   "Bertrand Russell 'dibuja' a sus amigos," 1 de junio,
      1957.
      In Portraits from Memory, and Other Essays (1956),
Russell shows himself to be, at 85, a generous man, an ex-
ceptional teacher and a writer of selective mind, imagination
and depth. *

673   "Las cartas del diabólico Joyce," 8 de junio, 1957.
      The letters of James Joyce reveal certain vulgar or
ordinary aspects of the man, but also the tortured sensibilities of the artist who, in Ulysses, "se entretiene en esa
tarea [mefistofélica] de la desintegración de la realidad. "*

674   "Paréntesis del recuerdo trivial," 15 de junio, 1957.
      S. recalls two separate but parallel anecdotes in which
Unamuno and the king of Spain reacted with misgivings to
his reluctance to offer adulation to anyone he did not know
personally. S. defends the dispassionate professional nature
of his criticism of Unamuno and says that the Basque writer's wounded vanity was simply that of a "niño prodigio"
grown old. *

675   "Colette, su marido y sus gatos," 22 de junio, 1957.
      Colette's third husband, Maurice Goudeket, seventeen
years her junior, publishes a memoir Auprès de Colette,
adding a lover's perspective to what we knew of her feline,
feminine grace from the tender lyricism, sensuality and unaffected simplicity in her novels. *

676   "La carcajada y la sonrisa," 27 de junio, 1957.
      Taking Kingsley Amis' That Uncertain Feeling as a
point of departure, S. reflects on the nature of modern humor, more sophisticated and difficult than satire, its opposite. In addition to the classical 'burla contra sí mismo,"
today's sense of humor is directed against all of reality,
"con un fondo poético o filosófico" that is obsessed with originality (i. e. , fruitful liberty). *

677   "España en los libros más recientes, " 29 de junio,
1957.
S. reviews three American books on Spain that merit
special attention: Herbert Matthews' The Yoke and the Ar-
rows (about the Falange party), Rex Smith's Biography of the
Bulls (an anthology of paintings and stories of the "fiesta
brava"), and Walter Starkie's The Road to Santiago (the picturesque narrative of a pilgrimage from Arles to Santiago de
Compostela). *

678   "Folk-lore a lo largo del continente, " 6 de julio, 1957.
John Englekirk's thorough study, El teatro folklórico
hispanoamericano, casts doubt on the authenticity of any sur-
viving versions of pre-Columbian theater.   But S.   says that
the genius of the mestizos even today for "danza-mimo-drama"
is irrefutable evidence of the richness that Indian oral tradition must have represented before the conquest. *

679   "Schoenberner conserva su cabeza, " 14 de julio, 1957.
Taking as his point of departure Franz Schoenberner's
new book, You Still Have Your Head, S. discusses the violence that sleeps beneath the surface of modern civilization,
and the crisis of confidence in today's world. *

680   "La esclava literatura rusa, " 21 de julio, 1957.
S. comments on the recent letters, published in the
European press, between the Italian writer Ignazio Silone
and the director of Inostrannaya Literatura, Ivan Anissimov,
in which Silone is rabidly denounced for raising a series of
questions about the most glaring contradictions of Russian
intellectual life. *

681   "Tiberio dos mil años después, " 10 de agosto, 1957.
Gregorio Marañón's biographical, almost clinical analysis of Tiberius attempts to establish rational and biological
bases for the depravity of the Roman emperor.   S. says,
however, that Tiberius' excesses are so far out of bounds
morally that it would take a poet, rather than a scholar, to
shed any real light on the aberrations of that intelligent
monster. *

682   "Los autores españoles de teatro, " 18 de agosto, 1957.
Though S. laments the "bárbara y cerril" Spanish censorship he finds that it stimulates the imagination and the
resourcefulness of the best Spanish playwrights of today in
evading the censor.   "En todo caso, Mihura con 'A media
media luz los tres' y 'Sublime decisión, ' López Rubio con

'La otra orilla', Edgar Neville con 'El Baile' y 'Adelita' han
puesto la comedia española al nivel de los mejores tiempos
de nuestro teatro. "

683   "Platero en la Quinta Avenida, " 1 de septiembre,
       1957.
       Upon publication of Platero y yo in English translation
by the University of Texas, S. doubts that this poetic prose
of Juan Ramón Jiménez will be much read in the U.S. because without a sense of essentiality and without quiet pools
of time in which contemplation is possible, Platero's small
dose of eternity will go unappreciated. *

684   "Retrato del artista como enemigo, " 14 de septiembre,
       1957.
       Geoffrey Wagner's Wyndham Lewis: Portrait of the
Artist as Enemy shows Lewis as the model of negative genius, the "natural enemy. " In addition to the instinct of self-
destruction, he was infected with the sickness of our time:
a sort of spiritual shell-shock from the excess of contradictions buffeting our sensibilities, an intellectual desperation
that became the very source of his talent.

685   "Biografías o memorias de millonarios, " 22 de septi-
       embre, 1957.
       A new edition of Carnegie's autobiography, the first
volume of Baruch's memoirs, and a biography of Ford lead
S. to comment on the New World sport of making millions.
Only the Americans can, after dedicating their lives to the
acquisition of wealth, philanthropically redistribute their
riches back to society whence they came. *

686   "El último drama de O'Neill, " 29 de septiembre, 1957.
       Another posthumous drama, A Touch of the Poet, leads
S. to observe that O'Neill's communicative genius shares the
passion of Shakespeare, but is more controlled; the keen
analysis of Shaw, but is more humanistic; and the transcendent philosophical and poetic direction of Ibsen and Strind-
berg. *

687   "Un libro monumental de Trotsky, " 5 de octubre,
       1957.
       The excellence of the collected writings of Trotsky,
published by the University of Michigan under the title History of the Russian Revolution, cannot make S. forget that
Trotsky was only a more civilized, cultivated and intelligent
version of Stalin ("pero con todos los defectos sectarios y

las obsesiones maquiavélicas de Stalin"), and that a twist of
fate in Trotsky's favor would not have greatly changed the
basic nature of the Russian "revolution."*

688   "Cosmogonías y riesgos latentes," 11 de octubre,
       1957.
Two books of Milton Munitz, one a historical study of
theories of the universe and the other an exploration of the
philosophical aspects of scientific cosmology, lead S. to remark that at certain levels, poetry, philosophy and physical
science are one and the same.*

689   "Un millón de ejemplares," 21 de octubre, 1957.
       S. discusses The Prophet, a book by Kahlil Gibran
which sold in its English translation a million copies in the
United States. "Esa curiosidad inocente y sincera [de los
norteamericanos] y ese deseo de entrar en el conocimiento
moral y religioso de las iglesias ha sido la base del éxito
de 'El Profeta'."

690   "Pasternak ha escrito una novela," 2 de noviembre,
       1957.
The inimitable Pasternak, who confuses the political
bureaucrats with his "formalist" poetry, also fails to charm
them with his first novel (rejected by the Union of Soviet
Writers). S. eagerly awaits its publication in the West,
with the promise of originality and depth suggested by the
poet's complex and inspired sensibility.*

691   "Calderón con un pretexto mínimo," 16 de noviembre,
       1957.
There is a military Spain and a colonial Spain (colonial, from a Latin word meaning to cultivate the land). Calderón de la Barca is, according to S., "el único gran poeta
de mentalidad castrense" (military) of the 17th century. His
central concern was honor: the personal (Arabic), the
family (the Iberian tribe), the class (Visigoth) and the clan
honor (Castilian). *

692   "La primavera en el polo norte," 19 de noviembre,
       1957.
Comments on travel literature in general and on
Katherine Scherman's book, Spring on an Arctic Island, in
particular.

693   "Camus y la difícil inocencia," 26 de noviembre, 1957.
       Camus, Nobel Prize winner, approaches the irrational

complexity of life with an extreme lucidity in spite of his
intellectual intoxication with freedom.   In the novel, the
drama and the essay, the French author maintains "una inocencia límpida ... unida a la más aguda aptitud de análisis
crítico. "*

694   "Agee y el sol de los muertos, " 1 de diciembre, 1957.
       James Agee, unsatisfied with his success in writing
for movies and TV, left A Death in the Family as his true
work of art--posthumously.   More poetic than narrative, the
novel is densely lyrical, with a solidity and resonance of
language at once ancient and modern. *

695   "Sátira rusa de ayer y de hoy, " 6 de diciembre, 1957.
       S. contrasts V. Dudintsev's satirical novel Not by
Bread Alone with the work of Gogol, Russia's first great
satirist.   Although the former represents a valiant and able
attack on the bureaucratic mass that suffocates thought and
authorizes the atrocities of its leaders, its tone of resigna-
tion cannot compare with the essence of contained joy and ten-
derness that underlies even the most destructive and corro-
sive works of Gogol. *

696   "El año hispánico en Norteamérica, " 16 de diciembre,
       1957.
       A survey of the most noteworthy books in English
translation by Hispanic writers and other books in English
(such as Mexico Today by John Crow) which were published
in the United States in 1957.

697   "La vida como una orgía peligrosa, " 21 de diciembre,
       1957.
       After reading Dylan Thomas in America, by John
Brinnin, and Leftover Life to Kill, by Thomas' wife Caitlin,
S. marvels at the self-destructiveness of the poet's wild
and wanton life, which must be understood as an integral
part of his poetry. *

                              1958

698   "Las letras y los excéntricos, " 5 de enero, 1958.
       Comments inspired by a new edition of Edith Sitwell's
book, Eccentric Englishmen (originally published in England
in 1933).

699   "El mejor o el peor de los mundos, " 12 de enero,
1958.
    Aldous Huxley's Brave New World Revisited reminds
us that the cold dominion of technology over spirit and the
imposition of state norms of behavior, may be as much of
an invitation to chaos as are the atrocities of dictatorships.
But a minority of active heroes, says S. , will always exist
to fight for freedom. *

700   "Los odios póstumos y la guitarra, " 12 de enero,
1958.
    Upon the publication of The Collected Poems of Roy
Campbell S. reveals his dislike for both Campbell (who ex-
pired a few months earlier) and for his poetry.

701   "El diario de Helena Morley en inglés, " 18 de enero,
1958.
    An enthusiastic and laudatory review of The Diary of
Helena Morley (translated into English from the original
Portuguese by Elizabeth Bishop).

702   "El diario romano de Stendhal, " 1 de febrero, 1958.
    S. reviews a new illustrated edition of Stendhal's book,
Roman Diary.

703   "En el centenario de 'Las flores del mal, '" 8 de febrero, 1958.
    Reflections on Baudelaire, the man and the poet. Al-
though in his poetry "sigue siendo el maestro inconfundible,
en sus actitudes y opiniones Baudelaire ha sido superado. "

704   "Los tres mosqueteros eran cuatro, " 15 de febrero,
1958.
    André Maurois' Les titans, biography of the three
Dumas (grandfather Alexandre, father and son) shows how
an infusion of Negro blood brought to French literature "la
excrecencia o el retoño tropical del romanticismo" in the
overwhelming vitality of Dumas père, creator of myths that
today have become truisms. *

705   "Crítica de autores de ayer y hoy, " 19 de febrero,
1958.
    Reading some of the works of Spain's young novelists
(Goytisolo, Sánchez Ferlosio, Miguel del Castillo, Aldecoa)
causes S. to caution today's critics against the mistakes
made by the generation of '98. With the exception of Valle-
Inclán and Machado, there was in all of them a humorous

contradiction between Nietzschean haughtiness and gross errors of judgment. *

706   "Sherwood Anderson en Broadway," 22 de febrero,
      1958.
      Comments on Sherwood Anderson, the man and the
artist (including his great influence among American novelists), upon the Broadway production of his play, "Winesburg,
Ohio. "

707   "Escritores ingleses fugitivos," 1 de marzo, 1958.
      Inspired by Monica Sterling's biography of the English
writer Louise de la Ramée (known by her pseudonym Ouida),
The Fine and the Wicked, S. comments on Ouida and other
English writers who preferred (and prefer) living outside
Great Britain.

708   "Un libro sobre los judíos españoles," 8 de marzo,
      1958.
      José María Estrugo offers a lively and erudite study
of Los sefardíes (the Spanish Jews), today the aristocracy
of the world's dispersed Jewry.   He describes the role played
by Sephardim in the politics of Western Europe and in the
discovery of America (including the possibility that Columbus
himself was a Jew). *

709   "Escritores viajeros en España," 15 de marzo, 1958.
      Upon reading Gerald Brenan's South of Granada, Rich-
ard Wright's Pagan Spain, and Somerset Maugham's Don
Fernando (published some years earlier), S. comments on
the difficulties foreigners have in properly understanding the
Spanish character.   Of the three authors "el más enterado
es Maugham. "

710   "Balzac como héroe de novela," 22 de marzo, 1958.
      A discussion of Balzac and of a novel with the French
author as the protagonist, Wine of Life, by Charles Gorham.

711   "Desde la ventana de la embajada," 28 de marzo, 1958.
      Laudatory comments on Ambassador Claude G. Bowers
and on his book, Chile Through Embassy Windows, 1939-
1953.

712   "Malentendidos en torno de Lawrence," 6 de abril,
      1958.
      A discussion of some misunderstandings of D. H. Law-
rence that have arisen from his biographies (that the atmos-

phere around him was decadent and that he was a mystic--
"no es un místico, sino un asceta--todo lo contrario").

713   "Ideas de Ortega sobre el amor," 12 de abril, 1958.
        A discussion of some of the ideas in Ortega y Gasset's
latest book to be published (posthumously) in English translation, On Love.

714   "Van Doren y Don Quijote," 18 de abril, 1958.
        A review of Mark Van Doren's book, Don Quixote's
Profession, and reflections on Cervantes the man, "un genio
afable y conciliador." "Casi todo el mundo ha sido injusto
con Cervantes."

715   "La generación del 98 y el regreso de Juan Ramón,"
        3 de mayo, 1958.
        Another spirited defense of the originality of Valle-
Inclán as an artist, and comments on Juan Ramón Jiménez
(whose decision to remain in Puerto Rico rather than return
to Spain at this time, S. applauds).

716   "Dos novelas norteamericanas," 12 de mayo, 1958.
        S. comments on two recent novels, Cozzens' By Love
Possessed and Frederick Buechner's The Return of Ansel
Gibbs, as examples of "las normas y patrones norteameri-
canos que las masas de lectores aceptan como tales." The
first S. judges to be a poor and sordid novel; the second, a
good one, "inteligente e inspirada."

717   "Un mal libro de un buen cineasta," 18 de mayo, 1958.
        S. finds Marcel Pagnol's book, La gloire de mon père,
to be deficient in substance and art.

718   "Nuevas luces sobre Andrés Bello," 24 de mayo, 1958;
        Lectura, 123, 3 (1 de junio, 1958), 87-91.
        Favorable review of a new book on Bello, by the
Chilean historian, Guillermo Feliú Cruz.

719   "El 'para qué' de Ansaldo," 31 de mayo, 1958.
        On the death of Col. Juan Antonio Ansaldo, S. looks
back on the life and only book (¿ Para qué?) of the disen-
chanted hero and voluntary exile. Ansaldo's memoirs, a
sage blend of the historic and the personal, ask what was
gained by all the anguish of the Civil War, and elicit Sender's own comments on the monarchy and the predicament
of Spain. *

720   "Las novelas de Snow sobre Inglaterra," 6 de junio,
1958.
      Comments on C. P. Snow's series of novels, "Strangers
and Brothers," and a review of its latest addition, The Conscience of the Rich.

721   "La pobre varonía yanqui," 14 de junio, 1958.
      Comments on the "war of the sexes" in the United
States. "El macho americano ha aceptado su derrota hace
tiempo." The result of female domination "tiene que ser
funesto y lo señalan los psiquiatras en la forma de una tendencia a la homosexualidad."

722   "El mensaje optimista de Jung," 20 de junio, 1958.
      Upon the publication of a revised and enlarged version
of Jung's Psychology and Religion, S. points out essential
differences between Freud and Jung, and finds in Jung's passionate defense of liberty and the integrity of the individual
an optimistic message.

723   "El hombre ingrávido y los ángeles," 27 de junio,
1958.
      Imaginative speculations on the possible effects or
benefits man may experience by "overcoming" gravity. "El
hombre puede flotar hoy en el aire por algunos segundos
(experiencias de neutralización de la gravedad) y mañana
flotará en el espacio, como dicen que flotan los ángeles."

724   "La novela del minotauro," 7 de julio, 1958.
      A review of Mary Renault's novel, The King Must Die,
and general comments on the art of writing historical novels.

725   "Rusia y las curiosidades legítimas," 12 de julio,
1958.
      Discusses the immense curiosity of Americans about
Soviet life, history, politics, literature, and science; an
alert but dispassionate curiosity, devoid of hate and analo-
gous to the American attitude towards war (not as a vital
act of glory but as a hard job to be done). Has special
praise for John Gunther's Inside Russia Today.*

726   "El gran diccionario de Ferrater Mora," 21 de julio,
1958.
      A review of José Ferrater Mora's Diccionario de
Filosofía along with biographical notes on its author.

727   "¿Es de veras la edad de los dragones?," 28 de julio,

1958.

From a novelistic viewpoint, Alice Eker-Rotholz in The Time of the Dragons tries to resolve the problems of the difficulties of understanding between the West and the East. To S. the dragons represent Lucifer, symbol of the atomic destruction which only the miracle of love can forestall.

728 "El hombre, las estrellas, y el tiempo," 4 de agosto, 1958.

Astronomer Harlow Shapley, in his book Of Stars and Men, finds "highly probable" the existence of millions of other intelligent worlds, and, agreeing with the conclusions of other scientists, predicts man's eventual victory over time. S. asks: when the day comes that we have conquered gravity, space and time, can't we say that we have conquered the kingdom promised by the religions?*

729 "Ingleses y cazadores de cabezas," 9 de agosto, 1958.

A discussion of The People of Borneo, by Malcolm MacDonald (son of the former British Premier) which relates the author's unusual experiences in Borneo during the years 1946-1949. The book "recuerda, por el idioma desnudo y directo y por el carácter colonial, los de Bernal Díaz del Castillo, Solís y Las Casas en los tiempos de la América virgen."

730 "Turguenev y sus últimas 'reminiscencias'," 17 de agosto, 1958.

Turgenev's Literary Reminiscences (translated into English by David Magarshack), a collection of stories, fragments and sketches from the latter part of his life, reveal the novelist's noble humility, generous stoicism and clearsightedness. S. says that Turgenev's serene and penetrating psychological mastery, eclipsed by the violent heyday of Communism and Fascism, is now regaining the esteem it deserves. *

731 "En la muerte de Martin du Gard," 30 de agosto, 1958.

Roger Martin du Gard continued the tradition of French realism from the previous century, but imposed upon it his agile imagination. "A pesar de su positivismo ... tenía ese espíritu encendido de los que un día han visto la dimensión milagrosa de la realidad y no pueden olvidarlo ya nunca."*

732 "Baroja y las mujeres," 5 de septiembre, 1958.

S. observes that Pío Baroja "describe mucho mejor lo

que odia que lo que ama. " That is why every woman in his novels is a vague, timid romantic shadow in search of a male to dominate her (yet secretly superior to him). In general, Baroja's characters, male and female, never outshine the omnipresent author. *

733   "Retoques al retrato de Joyce," 15 de septiembre, 1958.

Mary and Padraic Colum, in Our Friend James Joyce, shed new light on the incongruous figure of their lifelong comrade: on his extremisms, his years of poverty and artistic rejection, his exemplarity as a transcendent, if heretic, Catholic spirit. *

734   "Paréntesis en los altos bosques, " 20 de septiembre, 1958.

S. writes of his vacation experiences in a log cabin in a remote area high in the mountains along the state line between New Mexico and Colorado--his walks, the rain, the animals, an old book he finds in his cabin and reads (Antic Hay by Aldous Huxley), etc.

735   "El 'Doctor Zhivago' de Boris Pasternak, " 27 de septiembre, 1958.

S. writes of Pasternak, poet of luminous inner vision, who adjusts to political reality without "losing his soul, " and whose first novel was prohibited in Russia, precisely for being "a lyrical explanation of one man's destiny. "*

736   "Upton Sinclair tiene ochenta años, " 6 de octubre, 1958; Lectura, 126, 1 (1 de noviembre, 1958), 23-27.

A general discussion of Sinclair with special attention to his cycle of ten novels, "The End of the World, " which S. compares to a collection of tapestries or mural paintings.

737   "En la gloria póstuma de Schubert, " 13 de octubre, 1958.

In Otto Deutsch's Schubert: Memories of his Friends and Maurice Brown's Schubert: A Critical Biography, the composer is "una época histórica y un lugar geográfico del planeta. También una zona secreta del alma de cada cual. " S. adds that Schubert's communicative lyricism is "un ejemplo preclaro de integración de los planos sensual, afectivo e intelectual. "*

738   "La 'ninfeta' y el viejo enamorado, " 20 de octubre, 1958.

S. recognizes the literary ability of Nabokov, but criticizes the decadence of <u>Lolita</u>: "habríamos preferido ver su talento empleado en otro tema."*

739   "Aquel buen Stephen V. Benét," 30 de octubre, 1958.
       Upon publication of Charles Fenton's biography, S. reminisces about his friend Benét, novelist and poet with pantheistic tendencies of luminous mystery, who wore his literary honors as naturally as he won them.*

740   "Obras ligeras sobre temas profundos," 10 de noviembre, 1958.
       H. Allen Smith writes humorously of the light side of Mexico in <u>The Pig in the Barber Shop</u>. Rafaello Busoni presents the life of Cervantes as if it were a "novela de caballerías" in <u>The Man Who Was Don Quixote</u>. Both are lightweight <u>treatments</u>, says S., of profound and ambivalent themes.*

741   "O'Neill y la dificultad del teatro," 10 de noviembre, 1958.
       S. quotes from and comments on a collection of letters and anecdotal reminiscences of Eugene O'Neill, who sees man's tragic sense as perhaps the only significant aspect of his reality, as something that can be neither influenced nor affected by destiny and thus holds out some possibility of victory even in defeat.* (Note: has the same title as another column, dated November 24, 1961 [822].)

742   "Los hombrecitos de Van der Post," 17 de noviembre, 1958.
       <u>The World of the Kalahari</u>, an informative and poetic study of the Hottentots by Col. Laurens Van der Post, who lived among them, fascinates S. with its evocation of the inspired instincts and natural intelligence of a people who serve as a mysterious link to our own pre-history.*

743   "El lugar del hombre en el universo," 24 de noviembre, 1958.
       Norman Berrill, in <u>You and the Universe</u>, says that mind, spirit, energy and matter are one. S. adds that, at the highest levels of thought, art, science, poetry, philosophy, metaphysics and religion are also one. The transcendent task, then, is "la objetivación del ente pensante y sensitivo ... [estableciendo] sus relaciones con la materia de donde procede y con la ilusión de sí mismo a donde va."*

744   "Rimbaud como héroe de novela," noviembre, 1958;
      Lectura (México), 126, 3 (1 de diciembre, 1958), 90-
      94.
      A discussion of the French poet's incapacity for enjoy-
ing a bourgeois life and of the keen sensitiveness that caused
him to see in all of God's creation a strange perfection,
Satanic or angelic.

745   "El libro atlántico de los poetas," 8 de diciembre,
      1958; Lectura, 78, 4 (15 de abril, 1959), 121-25.
      A review of The Atlantic Book of British and American
Poetry, an anthology compiled by Edith Sitwell.   For S. ,
poetry is accent and tone.   "Nada más y nada menos.   En
Inglaterra, aquí o en China. "

746   "Grecia o el despertar de los héroes," 15 de diciem-
      bre, 1958.
      S. reviews two books: Leonard Cottrell's The Bull of
Minos and Nikos Kazantzakis' La Odisea: una continuación.
In the former an archeologist extends the history of Greece
backward to 3000 B.C. ; in the latter, a poet extends the adventures of Ulysses forward. *

747   "Los autores, los lectores y la Navidad, " 23 de
      diciembre, 1958.
      Reflections on the increased popularity during the
Christmas season of books of the classical literature of
Greece and Rome.   "La gente prefiere regalar aquellos libros que dan la impresión de ser más duraderos que el
hombre y de poder vencer tal vez al tiempo. "   A good book
can defend one against a crushing soledad or "aloneness. "

                              1959

748   [No entry]

749   "Las distracciones de Ortega y Gasset," 2 de enero,
      1959.
      S. , citing some inexactitudes of Ortega that show his
distracted poetic side, says that "esa salud de lo espontáneo"
was perhaps the philosopher's best characteristic.   To Ortega
it is as lyrically satisfying to travel the road leading to
truth as to reach its goal. *

750   "Arciniegas y la magia americana," 8 de enero, 1959.
      Germán Arciniegas, in the title of his book América
mágica, alludes to the heroes (Juárez and Sarmiento predomi-
nate), poets or saints of this continent who seem to reflect
in their life and their work "la grandeza alucinante de la
naturaleza." As always, Arciniegas has a lyrical touch and
is "ligero y profundo a un tiempo. "*

751   "Los granujas y el 'dharma'," 15 de enero, 1959.
      Jack Kerouac's novel, The Dharma Bums, elicits Sen-
der's comment that today's rebellious youth are the product
of the protest literature of the past 50 years, as they
follow docilely in the tracks of yesterday's non-conform-
ists. *

752   "Novedades sobre los 'muertos vivos'," 16 de enero,
      1959; Lectura, 135, 1 (1 de mayo, 1960), 27-31.
      A condemnation of irresponsible writing about drug ad-
dicts ("muertos vivos") in the United States.

753   "Un retrato cándido de Maugham," 24 de enero, 1959.
      Karl Pfeiffer's Candid Portrait of his friend, Somerset
Maugham, is the occasion for Sender's comments on
Maugham's talent in being able to transport the reader pleasantly and absorbingly to a reality more prestigious than the
reader's own reality.

754   "El caso notable de Edgar A. Poe," 30 de enero,
      1959; Lectura, 128, 2 (15 de marzo, 1959), 53-57.
      "Digerir la muerte y nutrirse de ella provechosamente
es lo que hace el poeta y quiere enseñar a los demás.   Es
lo que hizo Poe."

755   "Recuerdos e ideas de Pasternak," ¿enero?, 1959;
      Lectura, 127, 3 (1 de febrero, 1959), 84-88.
      Commentary on the English translation of Pasternak's
autobiographical book, I Remember.

756   "Togo y los singulares japoneses," 4 de febrero, 1959;
      Lectura, 128, 1 (1 de marzo, 1959), 23-27.
      A discussion of Japan and the Japanese provoked by
the publication of a biography of the Japanese admiral, Hei-
hachico Togo, in French by George Blond.

757   "Lawrence y la confusión poética," 13 de febrero,

1959; Lectura, 128, 4 (15 de abril, 1959), 121-25.
Commenting on the third and final volume of a biography of D. H. Lawrence by Edward Nehls, S. studies the problem of obscurity (in meaning) in modern poetry.

758   "John Gates: excomunista yanqui," febrero, 1959; Lectura, 128, 4 (15 de febrero, 1959), 117-21.
A review of Sol Regenstreif's The History of an American Communist, in which Gates (Regenstreif) explains his desertion of the Communist Party.

759   "Vida y muerte del autor de 'Carmen'," 6 de marzo, 1959; Lectura, 136, 2 (15 de junio, 1960), 55-59.
Commentary on Bizet's life and work, inspired by the appearance of a biography of the composer (in English) by Mina Curtiss, Bizet and His World (1958).

760   "Pedro el Grande fue un hombre que...," 13 de marzo, 1959.
Henri Ballotton's biography of Peter the Great treats revealingly the crucial moments in the life of that despotic political genius who was born in 1672 "en un país caótico sin personalidad y sin unidad, pero dejaba al morir [1725] una nación constituida, una cultura cristalizada, un pueblo organizado y en marcha."*

761   "El caballero Casanova en Venecia," 20 de marzo, 1959; Lectura, 148, 1 (1 de julio, 1962), 23-27.
A new translation of the Venetian Years from Jacques Casanova's memoirs confirms that "cuando un libro tiene genuino valor literario no puede ser pornográfico." S. mentions the importance for understanding history of "la manera de entender lo erótico en los diferentes pueblos" and comments on the undercurrent of sadness in the picaresque victories of Casanova.*

762   "La madurez de la señora Eliot," 27 de marzo, 1959; Lectura, 131, 1 (1 de septiembre, 1959), 24-28.
Reviews The Middle Age of Mrs. Eliot, a new novel by the English writer, Angus Wilson.

763   "Alejandro Dumas y el perro pequinés," 3 de abril, 1959.
Dumas was ecstatic over his 1846 visit to Spain but it failed to fire his powerful imagination. Adventures in Spain, the worst travel chronicles of his career, skimmed the surface but did not capture the Spanish essence, avers S.*

764 "La estrella de Trotsky vuelve a lucir," 13 de abril, 1959; Lectura, 131, 2 (15 de septiembre, 1959), 55-59.
On the occasion of the reprinting of a book on Trotsky, Great Companions, by Max Eastman, S. relates some interviews he had with the Communist leader in Mexico.

765 "España vista desde el Canadá," 6 de mayo, 1959; Lectura, 129, 4 (15 de junio, 1959), 109-12.
A review of A History of Spain by Harold Livermore, which S. calls "la mejor aportación académica de los últimos cincuenta años al conocimiento histórico de España y de los españoles."

766 "Aquel extraño Mauricio Utrillo," 16 de mayo, 1959.
The strange life of the painter Utrillo is chronicled by John Storm in The Valadon Drama. "Sus cuadros estaban iluminados por la luz de una secreta gracia" which eventually led him out of the poverty, alcoholism, rejection and tormented insanity of his youth into a later life of opulence and a more serene and enlightened madness. *

767 "O'Neill y las alturas sombrías," 3 de junio, 1959; Lectura, 130, 2 (15 de julio, 1959), 60-64.
Commenting on the latest biography of Eugene O'Neill, The Curse of the Misbegotten, by Croswell Bowen and Shane O'Neill, S. asserts that all of O'Neill's dramas are colored by a dark melancholy--stemming from the playwright's sad, solitary, and tragic life.

768 "Los gangsteres y los 'gatos fríos'," 15 de junio, 1959; Lectura, 136, 1 (1 de junio, 1960), 28-32.
In a comparison of the qualities of gangsters and hippies ("gatos fríos") the latter appear inferior.

769 "Thurber y los neoyorkinos amables," 1 de julio, 1959; Lectura, 133, 2 (15 de enero, 1960), 54-58.
An essay on Thurber's humor and of The New Yorker, with quotations of varied examples.

770 "Ney y los crímenes colectivos," 2 de agosto, 1959.
Harold Kurtz's historical reconstruction, The Trial of Marshal Ney, protests the unjust execution of Napoleon's most popular general, an almost mythological figure in the novels of Hugo and Stendahl. S. points out that such "collective crimes" are not new to the 20th century and that the true verdict given by the future helps compensate the heavy hand of fate. *

771   "Rilke escribía a una princesa bohemia," 18 de agosto,
       1959.
       The letters of Rainer María Rilke and Princess María
von Thurn, translated into English by Nora Wedenbouch,
have one very grave defect: more than 100 of them have
been mutilated by the censorship of the translator in the du-
bious editorial interest of amenity or brevity.   Of Rilke, S.
says that he is an elegiac poet "enamorado de las sombras"
who lived his poetry with passion. *

772   " 'La caverna' de Penn Warren," 3 de septiembre,
       1959.
       A discussion of Robert Penn Warren's novel, The Cave.

773   "Baroja póstumo en Norteamérica," 1 de octubre,
       1959.
       Upon the University of Michigan's publication in one
volume of several works of Baroja, with a preface offering
information new to America (if not to Spain), S. gives further insights into the essential nature of Pío Baroja's life,
work, personality and opinions by means of a series of revealing anecdotes. *

774   "Quasimodo, Premio Nóbel de literature," 25 de octu-
       bre, 1959.
       S. discusses the work of Nobel poet Salvatore Quasi-
modo, little known outside of Italy.   Quasimodo is an im-
pressionist, but a passive one, content to preserve in puri-
fied form and unaltered content the lyrical images of the unconscious. *

775   "Los niños yanquis también escriben," 18 de noviem-
       bre, 1959; Lectura, 138, 3 (1 de diciembre, 1960),
       91-95.
       Comments on H. Allen Smith's Write Me a Poem,
Baby, and several quotations of ingenuous and charming writing by several American children--from Smith's book.

776   "El obseso Joyce sale al proscenio," 1 de diciembre,
       1959.
       Ulysses the novel, says S. , contains a drama: the
drama, complete with Destiny as narrator (like a Greek
chorus), ends at midnight; the novel goes on till dawn.   The
predominance of fantasy puts certain limitations on the theatrical adaptation (by Marjorie Barkentin) but might make a
magnificent impressionist-expressionist film. *

1960

778   "En la carrera de los bestsellers," 7 de enero, 1960.
      Compares the commercial-documentary-opportunist
"novels" of the U.S. editorial industry--such as those ex-
ploiting popular interest in the statehood of Hawaii--to the
mediocre, popular films of Hollywood: a way to kill time
and make money but completely unrelated to the fine arts. *

778   "Magia, esquizofrenia y ascensores," 15 de enero,
      1960.
      Geza Roheim's Magic and Schizophrenia is the occasion
for S.'s observations on schizophrenia from the artistic point
of view.   The difference, says S., between the use by the
poet of words in their magic sense, and the use by the men-
tally ill, is that the former is conscious while the latter is
not. *

779   "Voodoo o la imaginación 'functional'," 17 de enero,
      1960.
      Alfred Métraux's Voodoo en Haiti, a good academic
work, leads S. to observe that Negro music and dance, with
or without "voodoo," are "poesía práctica," the result of a
functional imagination that maintains a closeness to the mystery of origins. *

780   "Viñeta de Chekhov en su centenario," 2 de febrero,
      1960; Lectura, 135, 2 (15 de mayo, 1960), 49-53
      (title changed to "Meta de Chekhov...").
      Some biographical data and anecdotes on Chekhov, in-
cluding his conversations with Iván Bunín, previously unpublished in Spanish.

781   "Chessman y las rosas de Pasadena," 2 de marzo,
      1960.
      Caryl Chessman, victim of technology, unrepentant
rapist, arrogantly irrational "sportsman of vice" and "engineer of sin," author of three books in his twelve years on
Death Row, is brought out of his solitary cell to watch the
Rose Bowl Parade on television with five other condemned
men (they destroy the TV set and nearly each other).   Absurd and pathetic, says S. *   (In substance reprinted as a
short story, "Las rosas de Pasadena," in Cabrerizas Altas
[48].)

782   "Nueva York recuerda a Ben Gabirol," 17 de marzo,
      1960.

Reflections upon the celebration of the 900th anniversary of the death of the Spanish Jewish philosopher and poet, Ben Gabirol, author of La fuente de la vida (written in Arabic). Mayor Wagner proclaimed 1960 as the year of Ben Gabirol in New York City.

783   "El extraño caso de Søren Quist" 1 de abril, 1960.
The Trial of Søren Qvist, by Janet Lewis, is the historical account of a seventeenth-century Protestant minister who let himself be hanged for a murder he did not commit. S. ponders his motives: guilt for insufficient generosity to his servant? A voluntary expiation for too saintly a reputation? etc. *

784   "Los que se van y los que se quedan," 18 de abril, 1960.
S. discusses the differences between the Latin World and the Northern European countries and the United States in the attention paid in the press to the dying of great writers. "El culto de la muerte que hay entre nosotros se puede defender de mil maneras y se puede atacar de otras mil.... Pero no deja de ser notable esta diferencia radical entre los pueblos del norte y nosotros."

785   "Mark Twain tenía un amigo," 4 de mayo, 1960.
Clemens' letters, with himself as subject, give the highest measure of the author's delicious humor. Mark Twain's irony at himself--as archetype of the human essence --shows us the only way to tolerate others' laughing at us. *

786   "Harris coleccionista de gárgolas," 20 de mayo, 1960.
Vincent Brome's biography Frank Harris: Life and Loves of a Rascal presents the double aspects of violence and innocence in the outrageous adventurer and former cowboy whose literary talent as a biographer and editor went hand in hand with his "manía transcendente" of chopping off gargoyles from high on cathedral facades and adding them to his magnificent collection. *

787   "El color local y la cara del público," 3 de junio, 1960.
The use of local color, says S., is a minor literary trick unless it forms part of the author's interior reality, as in Faulkner or in some of the Hispanic American writers. Now, in the U.S. where people are made uniform by the mass media, local color is giving way to a worse commonplace: colorless cosmopolitanism written for a faceless

public. *

788   "Nombre y dirección de Matthews, " 23 de junio, 1960.
     T. S. Matthews, for 25 years editor of Time magazine,
gives free rein to the imagination in his rich autobiography,
Name and Address, confronting "la complejísima perspectiva
social, intelectual y moral de América" in a way that the
journalism industry never permitted: as a potential novelist
and poet. *

789   "El fantasma de Thomas Wolf, " 20 de julio, 1960.
     Elizabeth Nowell's biography of Wolfe is rich in facts
but avoids analysis. S. comments that Wolfe's combination
of monumentalism and subtlety portrayed the complexity of
modern American life with a lyricism comparable to that
with which Dostoyevski, Turgenev, Chekhov and Gogol sur-
veyed the vastness of Russia. *

790   "El poeta cazador de ballenas, " 3 de agosto, 1960.
     Melville's letters confirm the immense solitude of
genius. S. says that the deliberate primitivism of Melville's
writings differs from that of Gauguin or Rousseau: "en Melville el vigor de lo pintoresco sostiene el peso moral y filosófico. "*

791   "El teatro de O'Casey, " 17 de agosto, 1960.
     David Krause, in Sean O'Casey: The Man and His
Work, speaks more of the work than of the man (perhaps in
view of the dramatist's six-volume autobiography). In his
tragicomedies O'Casey combines violent realism with lyrical
fantasy, the tragic with the grotesque, and conceives his
work according to the expressionist school that corresponds
with the best of Shakespeare. *

792   "El inolvidable Axel Munthe, " 5 de septiembre, 1960.
     Axel Munthe, the Swedish physician whose Libro de
San Michele reveals him as "un prodigio de armonía, delicadeza y profundidad, " is the subject of a biography by his
son Gustaf. Through the universal lens of Munthe's own
affirmative generosity, man is a noble creature and death is
a reverent adviser to life. *

793   "El señor de la colina de las fresas, " 22 de septiem-
       bre, 1960.
     The prolific letters of Sir Horace Walpole, more
memorable than his Gothic novels or other works, present
with passionate subjectivity and colorful anecdotes a pano-

rama of turbulent eighteenth-century life and thought. *

794   "Berenson en el mundo de las imágenes," ¿septiembre?,
       1960; Lectura, 137, 3 (1 de octubre, 1960), 92-96.
       Reflections on the life and ideas of Bernard Berenson,
author of the famous book, Aesthetics and History in the
Visual Arts.

795   "Eichman o la estupidez dañina," 2 de octubre, 1960.
       The journalist Quentin Reynolds, with the collabora-
tion of two Israeli secret service agents, has written Minister of Death: The Story of Adolf Eichmann, a revealing
and eloquent human document that enters deeply into the
true reality of ignominy. S. says that stupidity is more
criminally dangerous than intelligent malevolence. *

796   "Un río nace y otro muere," 19 de octubre, 1960.
       A lyrical description of the small Brazos river in
Northern New Mexico (where S. was vacationing), and its
sharp differentiation from the Brazos river in Texas. John
Graves' book, Goodbye to a River, "una mezcla hábil de
geografía, historia, poesía y novela en la que dominan ...
los dos elementos primeros," is the story of the Texas
river and its "death" in the service of humanity and, writes
S. , "la técnica industrial que nos amenaza de muerte cada
día. "

797   "St. John Perse o el príncipe de Léger," 29 de octu-
       bre, 1960; Lectura, 138, 2 (15 de noviembre, 1960),
       60-64; Estilo (San Luis Potosí, Mex.) núm. 57 (enero-
       marzo, 1961), 5-8.
       A discussion of the life and work of Saint-John Perse
(Alexis Saint-Léger Léger) who had just won the Nobel Prize
for literature.

798   "Cartas de amor del sabio 'obsceno'," 18 de noviem-
       bre, 1960.
       The most interesting of Sigmund Freud's letters (col-
lected by his son Ernest) are his love letters to Martha
Bernays, who became his wife. They reveal a woman "re-
spetable y adorable" who undoubtedly contributed much to
his insights into the curative and reintegrating nature of the
sexual instinct. *

799   "Importancia de la frivolidad," 1 de diciembre, 1960.
       Maurice Zolotow's biography, Marilyn Monroe, leads
S. to remark on the value of the inspired and intelligent

frivolity of this actress, a "sex symbol" in the sense that she symbolizes the erotic nature of today's man who, beset with fatalities on all sides, does not want the seriousness of a femme fatale but rather a graceful and spontaneously frivolous voluptuosity that does not add to his burdens. *

800   "Dos libros," Lectura, 138, 4 (15 de diciembre, 1960), 117-25.
Commentary on Vincent Brome's Frank Harris: Life and Loves of a Rascal and Robert Penn Warren's The Cave, both new books.

801   "El hombre de hoy y Pallas Atenea," 22 de diciembre, 1960.
A discussion of German writers and of Gottfried Benn's book Primal Vision, the first of the recently deceased (1956) German author's books to be translated into English (though its contents first appeared--for the most part--in the 1920s).

1961

802   "Una novela multitudinaria," 9 de enero, 1961.
A review of the first novel by a young Russian-American, Alexander Fedoroff, The Side of the Angels.

803   "Albert Einstein, el último profeta," 19 de enero, 1961.
A discussion of the possibilities of world peace based on a recently published book, Einstein on Peace, by Otto Nathan and Einz Norden (with a preface by Bertrand Russell).

804   "Un escritor original ha muerto," 2 de febrero, 1961.
The French novelist and poet Blaise Cendrars, polyglot and restless adventurer, was an unforgettable man of powerful and inspired instincts who lived life with the same "fuerte y cáustica originalidad" that saturated his writings. *

805   "Una posada en el Japón," 20 de febrero, 1961.
Reflections on Japan and the Japanese, their history and their culture, which S. finds expressed in the story of a Japanese inn, the Minaguchi-ya, told by an American soldier, Oliver Statler, in his book, Japanese Inn.

806   "Canciones de cuna y de parque," 2 de marzo, 1961.
A discussion of nursery rhymes in England, Spain, France, and America inspired by the publication of the

Oxford Dictionary of Nursery Rhymes, edited by Iona and Peter Opie.

807   "Dos Passos y la verdad de America," 20 de marzo, 1961.
        Favorable comments on Dos Passos' latest novel, Midcentury--"un documento vivo de la vida de esta gran nación [the U.S.A.] en lo que va de siglo, con un énfasis mayor en los años últimos."

808   "La crítica como una de las bellas artes," 4 de abril 1961; Lectura, 147, 2 (15 de mayo, 1962), 61-64.
        A discussion of Bernard Shaw and his literary work, especially his 1960 book, How to Become a Musical Critic.

809   "Las lunas de afuera y las de dentro," 24 de abril, 1961.
        Ralph Lapp's book Man in Space leads S. to speculate on how the imagination might follow the lead of science and arrive at a new metaphysics to go with the new physics, il·luminating man's inner space as he conquers outer space. S. also remarks on the irony of the Russians' efforts to unbind humanity's shackles to the earth while still tyrannizing their own people.*

810   "Los megalopolimaníacos," 3 de mayo, 1961.
        Some reflections on modern city life inspired by Lewi; Mumford's study, The City in History. "Ya no es civilizad la ciudad en la que se ha inmiscuído el caos de la selva virgen."

811   "Toynbee y el entender del mundo," 17 de mayo, 1961
        Comments on the present threat to freedom in the world inspired by A. J. Toynbee's "obra monumental," A Study of History, and a book about the famous historian, The Intent of Toynbee's History; A Cooperative Appraisal, by Edward T. Gargan.

812   "Stegner y los pobres ricos," 7 de junio, 1961.
        Comments on Wallace E. Stegner's novel, A Shooting Star, and on a theme implicit in it, the "poor rich" and, bɔ inference, the "rich poor."

813   "Dos libros y un paisaje polar," 26 de junio, 1961.
        Reflections on the Arctic inspired by two new books: Adventures in the Arctic, edited by Peter Freuchen's widow, Dagmar, and Ordeal by Ice, written by Farley Mowat. The

first book relates the experiences of Peter Freuchen in the Arctic (written by Freuchen before his death).

814 "Miller, el amor y la risa," 7 de julio, 1961.
Reflections on Henry Miller as a writer (whom S. knows personally) and on his novel, Noches de amor y de risa--Spanish translation of Nights of Love and Laughter.

815 "Baza lúgubre de ases y reyes," 17 de julio, 1961; Lectura, 152, 3 (1 de abril, 1963), 93-96.
On the occasion of the death of Enrique Larreta, Hemingway, and Celine--aces and kings from today's pack of cards (authors)--S. briefly evaluates their contributions.

816 "Las esposas y los hijos de Young," 2 de agosto, 1961.
Upon reading Irving Wallace's life of Ana Eliza, Brigham Young's twenty-seventh wife who left him to campaign for monogamy, S. reflects on certain aspects of feminine "liberation," Mormonism and polygamy. *

817 "El escándalo de Motherlant," 11 de septiembre, 1961.
Comments on Henry de Montherlant and two of his books, The Bachelors (in its first English translation) and Selected Essays (in its second English translation).

818 "México, la verdad y la antropología," 17 de septiembre, 1961.
S. says that a "machine-written" book (by tape recorder), like Oscar Lewis' The Children of Sanchez can give only half-truths. The recorder favors decadent self-consciousness over imaginative insight, and the "autobiografía de una familia mexicana" degenerates into a surprisingly uninteresting and commonplace version of their sordid reality. *

819 "La experiencia de lo divino," 9 de octubre, 1961.
Reflections inspired by Max Scheler's book, On the Eternal in Man. The atheist "al privarse de la experiencia de lo divino se priva también de lo mejor de la experiencia humana."

820 "Lo hispánico y la eterna actualidad," 24 de octubre, 1961.
Brief comments on four recent books of interest to Hispanic scholars: The Spanish Civil War by Hugh Thomas, The Modern Spanish Novel by Sherman H. Eoff, Nueva his-

toria de la literatura española by Richard E. Chandler and Kessel Schwartz, and an English translation by Edwin Honig of four Calderonian plays.

821   "Ivo Andric, Premio Nóbel," 2 de noviembre, 1961; Armas y Letras, 4, 4 (octubre-noviembre, 1961), 99-102.
Comments on the life and work of the latest winner of the Nobel Prize for literature, Andric of Yugoslavia.

822   "O'Neill y la dificultad del teatro," 24 de noviembre, 1961.
Comments on Eugene O'Neill upon the eighth anniversary of his death (November 27, 1953). (The title is the same as another in "Los libros y los días," dated November 10, 1958 [741].)

823   "Un ordinario ser excepcional," 6 de diciembre, 1961.
Reflections inspired by Philip Thody's book, Albert Camus, 1913-1960. "Era Camus el más 'ordinario' de los hombres extraordinarios de nuestro tiempo."

824   "Crónica ligera sobre un tema grave," 18 de diciembre, 1961.
S. discusses the humility and greatness of the philosopher Ludwig Wittgenstein (as a contrasting example to a self-satisfied, affected, and empty, academic philosophical lecturer whose lecture S. had attended the day before).

1962

825   "Opinión, costumbres y sátira yanqui," 4 de enero, 1962.
Reflections on life in the United States inspired by three books: The Joiners, by Murray Hausknecht, A Nation of Sheep, by William J. Lederer, and Image of America, by Raymond L. Bruckberger (translated from the French).

826   "Cartas indiscretas sobre D. H. Lawrence," 22 de enero, 1962.
Comments on the English author and his marital life upon the reading of a book of letters by Frieda Lawrence. The Memoirs of Correspondence, compiled and prefaced by E. W. Tedlock.

827   "La ligereza de lo terrible," 19 de febrero, 1962;
Lectura, 145, 4 (15 de febrero, 1962), 124-27. Reprinted in Lectura, 149, 3 (1 octubre, 1962), 90-93.
Some observations on "suspense" novels in general and
on Alfred Hitchcock's My Favorites in Suspense in particular.

828   "Las profecías de Dostoiewsky," 5 de febrero, 1962.
Comments on the accurate predictions of Dostoyevsky
as to the course of the Soviet revolution and its subsequent
developments as seen by C. M. Woodhouse in his book,
Dostoiewsky.

829   "El primer día en Los Angeles," 3 de marzo, 1962.
Upon his arrival in Los Angeles, S. visits the Spanish-language newspaper, La Opinión, and views the film, El Cid.
The film as a spectacle "es de veras glorioso. Como reconstrucción histórica y obra de arte, objecionable."

830   "Hace cuatro siglos que nació Lope de Vega," 19 de
marzo, 1962.
Comments on Emilio González López's new book, Historia de la literatura española; Edad media y siglo de oro,
and on aspects of Lope de Vega's theatrical art.

831   "La zorra en el ático," 3 de abril, 1962.
A laudatory review of the novel, The Fox in the Attic
(1961, 1962), by the Welsh author Richard Hughes. "He aquí
una obra con todas las cualidades de la gran literatura...."

832   "La guerra de los sexos," 16 de abril, 1962; Lectura,
146, 1 (1 de marzo, 1962), 24-27.

833   [No entry]

834   "El genio y la niña hermosa," 2 de mayo, 1962.
Comments on Bernard Shaw's longstanding affection for
Molly [Mary] Tomkins upon the publication of the book, Shaw
and Molly Tomkins, by Peter Tomkins.

835   "La nave de los locos," 17 de mayo, 1962.
A favorable review of the novel, Ship of Fools, by
Katherine Anne Porter.

836   "Un 'Guernica' rapsódico," 4 de junio, 1962.

Reflections on Picasso's painting, "Guernica," and a poem on the same subject by the Brazilian writer Geraldo Ferraz--both speak "en ese idioma siempre vivo de la verdad y de la belleza" at this crucial moment in history.

837   "Grandeza y miseria de Hollywood," 19 de junio, 1962.
"Hollywood ... está en decadencia." But S. sees hope that organizations such as the newly opened Lytton Center of Visual Arts might lead to a better future for the film capital.

838   "Libros de versos para niños," 3 de julio, 1962.
Comments on the relative abundance of poetry for children in the English-speaking world and the scarcity of such poetry in Spanish letters.

839   "Los que se van y los que vienen," 17 de julio, 1962.
"Después de la muerte de esas grandes figuras [T. Wolfe, Hemingway, Faulkner] se ha hecho un silencio grave y en él se oyen aquí y allá voces aisladas. Se puede suponer quiénes van a sucederles, pero no se trata de grupos ni rebaños y ni siquiera de una generación que trae tal o cual color." An important article.

840   "América y el prodigio de la unidad," 3 de agosto, 1962.
Salvador Madariaga proposes, in Latinoamérica entre el águila y el oso, a unified political and economic federation of Latin American states. S. applauds this proposal, saying that such a bloc would heavily influence the world's destiny with the weight of its humanistic traditions and that "la unidad es el factor determinante del prodigio."*

841   "El Greco y el 'desnacer'," 17 de agosto, 1962.
The inner "return" to one's adolescence, childhood, and to the womb itself--desnacer--is illustrated in El Greco's famous painting in Toledo, "Entierro del Conde de Orgaz." "La trinidad Greco-Goya-Picasso es la clave del orbe de la sensibilidad hispánica--incluído el mundo iberoamericano."

842   "Un sabio en las artes visuales," 3 de septiembre, 1962.
Reflections upon the deceased art critic Bernard Berenson's judgment of El Greco as being a genius but unconvincing and melodramatic. "Berenson y el Greco se rechazan como se han rechazado siempre el genuino creador

y el genuino crítico. "

843   "Un maestro del periodismo literario, " 17 de septiem-
       bre, 1962.
       Praise for the director of El Diario de Hoy of San Sal-
vador, N. Viera Altamirano. S. commends Latin American
newspapers in general for providing intellectual nourishment
(in contrast to most newspapers in the United States which
fear offending the ignorance of the ignorant).

844   "Gabriela, clavo y canela, " 1 de octubre, 1962.
       A review of the English translation of the novel Gabriel,
by the Brazilian Jorge Amado. S. praises both the work
and its faithful translation.

845   "Personalismos en las letras de hoy, " 22 de octubre,
       1962.
       A discussion of the Spanish writer Luis Araquistáin,
"autor de genio discreto, congenial y suasorio, " and of the
impersonality in most of today's writing.

846   "Don Marcelino y el mandarinismo, " 31 de octubre,
       1962.
       Inspired by a chapter in Luis Araquistáin's book, El
pensamiento español contemporáneo ("el mejor ensayo escrito en los últimos años sobre Menéndez y Pelayo"), S.
praises Don Marcelino very highly as a man and as an author.

847   "Rothschild y la almohada de los sueños, " 19 de no-
       viembre, 1962.
       Upon returning to Europe for the first time since 1939,
S. finds the masses enthusiastically reading Frederic Mor-
ton's historical narrative of the Rothschild family, The
Rothschilds; A Family Portrait. Perhaps they seek conso-
lation in it and similar books though their world is threatened with ruin.

848   "Un Goncourt muy de nuestro tiempo, " 27 de noviem-
       bre, 1962.
       A favorable review of The Lost Shore (Les bagages de
sable), the 1962 Goncourt Prize-winning novel by the Polish
writer Ana Langfus (resident in Paris).

849   "Una mixtificación inspirada, " 24 de diciembre, 1962.
       A review of the just-published English version of Max
Aub's pseudo-critical biography of a painter, Jusep Torres

180 Works by Sender

Campalans. The book, well illustrated, "es una mixtificación inspirada. "

1963

850 "Los intrigantes etruscos," 7 de enero, 1963; Lectura,
154, 4 (15 de agosto, 1963), 122-26.
A discussion--in a light vein--of the Etruscans and of
the newly published French edition of D. H. Lawrence's
book, Promenades étrusques.

851 "Torquemada en los Estados Unidos," 23 de enero,
1963.
A favorable review of John E. Longhurst's book, The
Age of Torquemada, along with some observations on racial
problems in the United States.

852 "Las letras soviéticas de ahora," 7 de febrero, 1963.
Reflections on the present state of Soviet letters--in-
creasing signs of more freedom and changing attitudes.

853 "Una 'anti-historia' de España," 22 de febrero, 1963.
Criticism of A History of Spain, by Jean Descola, a
book which has "por lo menos un error en cada una de sus
quinientas páginas. En los nombres, en las fechas, en la
valoración comparativa de los hechos. "

854 "La verdad soviética y el escándalo," 9 de marzo,
1963; Lectura, 154, 2 (15 de julio, 1963), 60-64.
Discussion of A. Solzhenitsyn's book, One Day in the
Life of Ivan Denisovich, and comments on another Soviet
writer, Nekrasov.

855 "Rusia, los editores y los indios," 22 de marzo, 1963.
Observations on the book Those Americans by the Russian writers Mikhailov and Kossenko, problems caused by
Russia's not subscribing to international laws of copyright,
and on the falseness of Russian propagandistic claims that
the American Indians are "explotados y sometidos. "

856 "Simone y la sombra amada," 9 de abril, 1963.
Reflections suggested by the reading of the second
volume of Simone de Beauvoir's autobiography to be published in English, The Prime of Life.

857 "La risa es una cosa muy seria," 24 de abril, 1963.

An entertaining review of the novel, Before My Time, by the young American novelist Niccolo Tucci.

858   "Nuestro amigo Einstein," 8 de mayo, 1963.
Commentary suggested by the reading of a collection of Einstein's letters and moral and philosophical reflections in the book, Einstein on Peace, published in 1960 in England (with a preface by Bertrand Russell).

859   "Los rusos tampoco quieren la guerra," 22 de mayo, 1963.
If it were not for "las monstruosas estructuras estatales," which fear the simple truth, the Russian and the American citizen "se entenderían en veinticuatro horas, se cambiarían sus experiencias--incluídos los secretos nucleares--y se pondrían a trabajar cantando algo parecido a la canción pacifista de Yevtuchenko."

860   "Los gitanos inextinguibles," 9 de junio, 1963.
A review of Jean-Paul Clébert's book in its English translation, The Gypsies, and general observations on gypsies and literature on them.

861   "El 'retrato' de Paulo Prado," 21 de junio, 1963.
A review of the sixth edition of Paulo Prado's book, Retrato do Brasil--"uno de los documentos literarios más agudos y sutiles que han sido escritos en este continente."

862   "Quevedo en lengua inglesa," 1 de julio, 1963.
Observations on Quevedo upon the publication of two of his books in English translation--a reprinting of Visions (Sir Roger L'Estrange's version) and a new translation of El buscón (made by Hugh A. Harter).

863   "Los animales propicios," 17 de julio, 1963.
Comments on animals--their means of communication among themselves, the sensitivity of cats to "algunos estados psicológicos y temperamentales del hombre," etc. -- suggested by reading The Senses of Animals and Men by Lorus and Margery Milne.

864   "Montherlant, refugiado español," 3 de agosto, 1963.
A review of the famous French author's latest novel, Le chaos et la nuit.

865   "Poesía en el libro y en la escena," 20 de agosto, 1963.

A review of Robert Lima's book, The Theatre of García Lorca--"lo mejor que se ha hecho, hasta ahora al menos, en el nivel de la información seriamente, pero no estéril- mente académica"--and a discussion of lyricism on the stage.

866   "Mary McCarthy y sus amigas," 3 de septiembre, 1963.
A discussion of the novel, The Group, by Mary McCar- thy, and of the sexual liberty of college-age girls in the United States.

867   "El escándalo 'científico'," 20 de septiembre, 1963.
Velikovsky's sensational and once highly criticized theory about the comet Lucifer crashing into Earth 4000 years ago and going on to become the planet Venus, ex- pounded in his book Worlds in Collision, is now being veri- fied scientifically.   S. warns academicians never to scoff at works of imagination as antiscientific.*

868   "El dudoso gusto de mandar," 8 de octubre, 1963.
A discussion of the office of President of the United States inspired by Theodore C. Sorenson's book, Decision- Making in the White House.

869   "Baldwin, hijo de Harlem," 22 de octubre, 1963.
A discussion of James Baldwin and his career as an author.

870   "El falso pirata Frank Harris," 6 de noviembre, 1963.
A review of the reprint of My Life and Loves by the American writer, adventurer, and smuggler, Frank Harris, forty years after its first publication.   In it Harris "dice las mayores bellaquerías, poniendo a prueba la paciencia del lector."

871   "Wilson y la incomodidad angloamericana," 20 de no- viembre, 1963.
A review of Edmund Wilson's collection of short stories, Memoirs of Hecate County, and observations on American life.

872   "Otro Odiseo Moderno," 9 de diciembre, 1963; Lectura, 157, 1 (1 de enero, 1964), 28-32.
A discussion of the life and work of the Greek poet, George Seferis, winner of the Nobel Prize for Literature in 1963.

873   "La vida fabulosa de Diego Rivera," 18 de diciembre, 1963.
A discussion of Diego Rivera and his art upon the publication of Bertram Wolfe's book, The Fabulous Life of Diego Rivera.

1964

874   "El rey de las tres Catalinas," 7 de enero, 1964.
A discussion of Ford Maddox Ford's posthumously published trilogy, The Fifth Queen, Privy Seal, and Crowning of the Fifth Queen, and of Ford's career as a writer.

875   "Cervantes en Madison Avenue," 21 de enero, 1964.
A discussion of the newly published book, Interludes, a collection of English translations by Edwin Honig of Cervantes' entremeses.

876   "El novedoso Salinger," 5 de febrero, 1964.
A discussion of J. D. Salinger, his virtues and defects as a writer. The so-called novedades in Salinger's latest collection of stories were already old (for writers of Sender's age) in 1940.

877   "Frost, poeta nacional yankee," 17 de febrero, 1964.
A discussion of Robert Frost, the man and the poet, with special reference to a recently published book of the poet's letters to Louis Untermeyer.

878   "La leyenda de Fitzgerald," 3 de marzo, 1964.
A discussion of Francis Scott Fitzgerald. "Fitzgerald no me gusta.... Tenía un sentido falso--según creo--de los valores."

879   "Las noveletas de Miss Barker," 21 de marzo, 1964.
A discussion of Audrey Lillian Barker's fiction, especially of her three novelettes in one volume entitled, The Joy-Ride and After.

880   "Dino Buzzati en inglés," 6 de abril, 1964.
An enthusiastic review of The Love Affair by the Italian author Dino Buzzati (translated into English by Joseph Green).

881   "Sobre la caída de Alfonso XIII," 21 de abril, 1964.
Memories of and reflections on the Second Spanish

Republic, occasioned by the reading of Así cayó Alfonso XIII,
a book by Miguel Maura, a Minister in the first Republican
Government.

882   "El sexo en la novela de hoy," 5 de mayo, 1964.
    A review of The Wapshot Scandal by Cheever, together
with consideration of the growing treatment of sex in today's
novels.   "La cuestión está en determinar cuándo el talento
legitimiza el escándalo y cuándo no. "

883   "Las narraciones de Tennessee Williams," 23 de mayo,
        1964.
    S. , on reading the novels of Williams, finds in them
the same ostentatious decadence as in his plays--an adolescent sentimentality that lends a vulgar prestige to the frivolous sexual curiosity of the masses. *

884   "La máquina de los aplausos," 8 de junio, 1964.
    Though in the more developed nations the average per-
son lives "como un príncipe" (or even better than the princes
in the past), he has no subjects (to applaud him).   This situation may explain--in part--the high incidence of neurosis
and psychosis among the inhabitants of the so-called "developed" nations, while in the more primitive parts of the
world psychiatrists are scarcely needed.

885   "Pushkin, el paje asesinado," 22 de junio, 1964.
    On the publication of two English translations (by Wal-
ter Arndt and by Nabokov) of the verse novel, Eugene Onegin,
and the re-issue of Mirsky's critical biography of Pushkin,
S. recalls the circumstances of the mulatto aristocrat's life
and death and the effortless perfection of his work. *

886   "Somerset Maugham en sus noventa, " 4 de julio, 1964.
    Maugham has excelled in the contrasting genres of the
novel and the theater, and written penetrating essays.   A
model of professionalism in vivid expression and keen analysis, he will continue to be read by generations to come. *

887   "El ensayo como obra de arte, " 21 de julio, 1964;
        Lectura, 160, 4 (15 de agosto, 1964), 123-27.
    A critical discussion of the American writer George P.
Elliott, and of his first book of essays, A Piece of Lettuce,
recently published.

888   "Aquel extraño Mussolini, " 4 de agosto, 1964; Lectura,
        162, 4 (15 de diciembre, 1964), 123-27.

A review of two new books about Mussolini: The Day of the Lion, by Roy MacGregor-Hastie, and Mussolini; Study of a Demagogue, by Ivone Kirkpatrick.

889 "Cuatro libros sobre Lenín," 18 de agosto, 1964; Lectura, 161, 3 (1 de octubre, 1964), 92-96.
A synthesis of four books on Lenin, recently published in the United States: Life of Lenin (Louis Fischer), Impressions of Lenin (Angelica Balabanov), The Life and Death of Lenin (Robert Payne), and Lenin: The Impulsive Revolutionary (Stefan T. Possony).

890 "Las fronteras interiores," 1 de septiembre, 1964.
Keith Botsford's The March-Man analyzes in the third dimension the "border" conflict and synthesis between cultural-individualistic-decadent Europe and civilized-social-shallow America. *

891 "Ojos y oídos secretos," 16 de septiembre, 1964.
Vance Packard's The Naked Society warns U.S. citizens of the dangers of the institutional systems of information and investigation in their country. S., however, considers Packard's book unnecessarily alarming because there will always be an unbridgeable gap between the dead perfection of a mechanical system and the living imperfection (and imagination) of human beings. *

892 "Chaplin escribe sobre sí mismo," 5 de octubre, 1964; Lectura, 162, 1 (1 de noviembre, 1964), 28-32.
A discussion of Charles Chaplin on the occasion of the appearance of his autobiography, Chaplin.

893 "El otro Charles Chaplin," 19 de octubre, 1964; Lectura, 162, 2 (15 de noviembre, 1964), 61-64.
A continuation of the discussion of Chaplin's autobiography (892), with special attention on the actor's "socialismo humanitario."

894 "Las confesiones de Sartre," 3 de noviembre, 1964; Lectura, 162, 3 (1 de diciembre, 1964), 93-96.
Observations on Sartre on the occasion of the publication of the first volume of his autobiography, Words.

895 "Los caminos de la perfección," 19 de noviembre, 1964.
A discussion of Dag Hammarskjold and his posthumously published autobiography, Markings.

896   "Picasso y el homo ibericus," 3 de diciembre, 1964.
       Reflections on Picasso as the homo hispanicus vulgaris
suggested by a new book on the artist by one of his former
wives, Françoise Gilot.

897   "El misterioso universo," 21 de diciembre, 1964.
       Reflections on cosmology and man's basic ignorance,
based on a quick reading of The Mysterious Universe, by
James Jeans.

                              1965

898   "¿Son los yanquis hombres diferentes?," 5 de enero,
       1965; Lectura, 163, 4 (15 de febrero, 1965), 123-27.
       S. opines that the "Yanqui, aunque no es, como era a
principios del siglo pasado, superior al europeo ... sigue
siendo un tipo diferente del europeo y del latinoamericano."

899   "Verdad y riesgo de los vestiglios," 19 de enero,
       1965.
       Comments on Russian-American relations, based on
Laurens Van der Post's book, A View of All the Russias.

900   "La alegría religiosa," 4 de febrero, 1965.
       A discussion of Frederick Buechner's second novel,
The Final Beast. "El campo de la novela norteamericana
se dilata y enriquece con 'The Final Beast.' La bestia
apocalíptica es la tristeza."

901   "El arte de seleccionar hechos," 22 de febrero, 1965.
       A discussion of the art of writing history and a lauda-
tory review of René Sedillot's book, History of the World.

902   "Negros y 'niggers'," 5 de marzo, 1965; Lectura, 164,
       4 (15 de abril, 1965), 122-25.
       A review of the book, Nigger, by the American Black
author, Dick Gregory.

903   "La feria de los poetas," 19 de marzo, 1965.
       On the seventh centennial of Dante's birth (1265), S.
reflects on the condition (poetry prizes, ways of earning a
living, etc.) of poetry and poets in both Americas.

904   "Tesis polémicas de Dos Passos," 7 de abril, 1965.
       In Dos Passos' book of essays, Occasions and Pro-
tests, populism emerges as an active and positive faith. S.

agrees with Dos Passos on the whole, especially when he defends "el 'hombre natural' contra el producto artificial del industrialismo moderno."

905   "Sobre la muerte de Camus," 21 de abril, 1965; Lectura, 165, 2 (15 de mayo, 1965), 60-64.
A polemic in which S. refutes the idea that Camus had reached the limits of his "mundo expresable" at the time of his accidental death.

906   "Schweitzer, el santo natural," 11 de mayo, 1965; Lectura, 165, 4 (15 de junio, 1965), 121-24.
A review of Gerald McKnight's book, Verdict on Schweitzer.

907   "Sobre el libro de un Pontífice," 20 de mayo, 1965; Lectura, 165, 1 (1 de mayo, 1965), 20-23.
A discussion of Pope John XXIII, and of his book of memoirs, Journal of a Soul (tr. by D. White).

908   "En busca de Bisco, el negro," 6 de junio, 1965.
A review of Erskine Caldwell's book, In Search of Bisco (in which the author relates his experiences in trying to locate a Negro who was his inseparable friend fifty years earlier--when both Caldwell and Bisco were under five years of age).

909   "Una biografía de Gorki," 8 de junio, 1965; Lectura, 166, 1 (1 de julio, 1965), 29-32.
Reflections on the difficulties in discovering the true personality of Maxim Gorki on the occasion of the appearance of Dan Levin's book, Stormy Petrels; The Life and Works of Maxim Gorky.

910   "Una cuestión de veras candente," 23 de junio, 1965.
Literature and philosophy--having rejected established and universal values--have been in recent decades working in the void, trying to assimilate that emptiness (hence the antinovel). Can metaphysics or mysticism lead literature out of the void?

911   "Hemingway y otros excesos," 19 de julio, 1965; Lectura, 166, 4 (15 de agosto, 1965), 123-26.
A review of Nelson Algren's biography of Hemingway, Notes from a Sea Diary: Hemingway All the Way. S. insists that H. lacked originality in both style and substance.

188 Worksby Sender

912 "Un libro de opiniones infantiles," 20 de julio, 1965; Lectura, 167, 4 (15 de octubre, 1965), 123-27.
    Humorous examples of the writing of children from Art Linkletter's A Kindergarten of Errors.

913 "El catalán del revólver de oro," 5 de agosto, 1965.
    A review of Ian Fleming's posthumously published novel, The Man with the Gold Revolver (of which a Catalonian gangster is the protagonist, though the action occurs in Jamaica).

914 "Libros a la mar," 7 de septiembre, 1965; Lectura, 166, 2 (15 de julio, 1965), 61-64.
    Aboard an oceanliner S. becomes indignant when he observes a "camarero de aspecto civilizado" throwing books into the ocean because the books were used. Comments on the economic affluence and "incultura" that permit such a disrespectful waste.

915 "El arte de sobrevivir," 21 de septiembre, 1965; Lectura, 158, 2 (15 de noviembre 1965), 60-64.
    (Note: Apparently several volume numbers of Lectura were misprinted; volume 157 follows volume 166. The numbers as printed are given in this Bibliography.)
    A discussion of the book, The Art of Survival (1965), by Cord Christian Troebst.

916 "Quinientos filósofos," 4 de octubre, 1965; El Diario de Hoy (El Salvador), 24 de octubre, 1965; Lectura, 158, 1 (1 de noviembre, 1965), 28-32.
    Observations on Seneca on the occasion of the meeting in Córdoba of the International Congress of Philosophy.

917 "Sobre el Don desapacible," 19 de octubre, 1965; Lectura, 157, 2 (15 de septiembre, 1965), 61-64.
    (See note to 915.)
    Comments on the work of Michael Sholokhov, Nobel Prize winner for 1964 and author of the novel, The Silent Don.

918 "El 'Lazarillo' en Guatemala," 4 de noviembre, 1965; Lectura, 158 (see 915), 3 (1 de diciembre, 1965), 94-96.
    A discussion of the new book, Algunas observaciones sobre el Lazarillo de Tormes, by Salvador Aguado-Andrent, a professor at the University of Guatemala.

919   "Hace dos años que lo mataron," 16 de noviembre,
      1965; Diario de Barcelona, 23 de noviembre, 1965; El
      Mercurio (Valparaíso), 22 de noviembre, 1965; Lectura,
      158, 4 (15 de diciembre, 1965), 124-27.
      Praise and admiration for President John Kennedy upon
the second anniversary of his assassination.

920   "Zárate y la conquista del Perú," 2 de diciembre,
      1965; Lectura, 162, 2 (15 de julio, 1966), 61-64.
      A discussion of An Edition of Book V of Agustín Zá-
rate's "Historia del descubrimiento y conquista del Perú,"
edited by Dorothy McMahon, and published by the University
of Buenos Aires.

921   "Los italianos y la simpatía," 21 de diciembre, 1965;
      La Estrella de Panamá, 30 de diciembre, 1965.
      Comments on the Italians (their positive qualities and
their defects as people) inspired by the English translation of
Luigi Barzini's book, The Italians.

                              1966

922   "Maugham ha muerto," 6 de enero, 1966; Lectura,
      160, 4 (15 de abril, 1966), 125-27.
      An appreciative evaluation of the work of the English
author upon the occasion of his death.

923   "El centenario de Valle-Inclán," enero, 1966; La
      Crónica (Lima, Perú), 26 de enero, 1966; Diario de
      Yucatán (Mérida, México), 23 de enero, 1966; El Sur
      (Concepción, Chile), 30 de enero, 1966; Lectura, 160,
      3 (1 de abril, 1966), 92-96.
      S. points out some values in Valle-Inclán's life and
work on the occasion of the centennial of his birth.

924   "Gibraltar es una roca," ¿enero?, 1966; La Crónica
      (Lima, Perú), 31 de marzo, 1966; El Sur (Concepción,
      Chile), 13 de marzo, 1966; Lectura, 159, 2 (15 de
      enero, 1966), 60-64.
      A review of A Vision of Battlements by Anthony Bur-
gess, with general commentary on the meaning of Gibraltar
to the Spaniards.

925   "La narración y la magia," 7 de febrero, 1966; El
      Caribe (Santo Domingo) 2 de marzo, 1966.
      A review of the novel Silva by the French author

Vercors--in its English translation made two years earlier.

926   "El peligro de tener talento," 3 de marzo, 1966; El
      Universal (México), 17 de marzo, 1966; Lectura, 159,
      1 (1 de enero, 1966), 30-32.
      Comments on the sentencing of Andrei Sinyavsky,
"escritor de primer orden," to seven years of forced labor,
by a Soviet tribunal.

927   "Otro escritor ruso disconforme," 18 de marzo, 1966;
      El Caribe (Santo Domingo), 29 de marzo, 1966; Lectura,
      161, 1 (1 de mayo, 1966), 29-32.
      Comments on the Russian novelist Valery Tarsis and
the fact that Soviet authorities granted him permission to
leave Russia.

928   "La universidad de mañana," 4 de abril, 1966.
      S. discusses ideas inspired by Buckminster Fuller's
Education Automation. (The best professors should be freed
to pursue their investigations and give their findings in five
televised lectures each year while the rudiments of knowledge
would be taught by less able colleagues, writes S.)

929   "El pobre Papá Hemingway," 22 de abril, 1966; Diario
      de Barcelona, 14 de mayo, 1966; Lectura, 160, 2 (15
      de marzo, 1966), 60-64. (The March 15 issue of
      Lectura was perhaps delayed in its publication.)
      An adverse review of A. E. Hotchner's book, Pappa
Hemingway.

930   "Don Quijote en Broadway," 3 de mayo, 1966.
      Reflections on the values of Cervantes' masterpiece
upon the successful representation of Dale Wasserman's
adaptation, The Man from La Mancha, on Broadway. To
understand Don Quixote "es poner luz en nuestro laberinto
interior, el único que cuenta a la hora de la verdad."

931   "Carmen Laforet en inglés," 8 de mayo, 1966; Lectura,
      161, 3 (1 de junio, 1966), 94-96.
      Appreciative comments on Laforet upon the occasion of
the appearance of Andrea, an English translation of her
novel, Nada.

932   "Sobre personas y tendencias," 23 de mayo, 1966;
      Lectura, 161, 4 (15 de junio, 1966), 123-27.
      A review of The Modern Movement by Cyril Connolly.

933   "Un epitafio epigramático," 23 de junio, 1966; Lectura, 162, 1 (1 de julio, 1966), 30-32.
       Comments on the life of Somerset Maugham inspired by the reading of Somerset and All the Maughams, a biography by Robin Maugham, the illustrious writer's nephew.

934   "El whisky y los 'Beat' literarios," 6 de julio, 1966; Lectura, 162, 4 (15 de agosto, 1966), 123-27.
       Reflections upon reading the autobiography of the Irish novelist, Brendan Behan, Confessions of an Irish Rebel, which had just been published posthumously.

935   "Pues, señor, éste era un rey...," 19 de julio, 1966.
       With Frances Parkinson Keyes' The King as an example, S. reveals the formula for success in commercial bestseller-writing: to share the mentality and values of the not-too-cultured petit bourgeois, and to be foolish enough to believe in formulas.*

936   "Adios a Zinaida," 3 de agosto, 1966.
       On the death of Boris Pasternak's wife, S. looks back at the stubborn battle for freedom that the Pasternaks and other Russian poets waged in their homeland, choosing to risk their lives rather than run away or sacrifice art to politics. *

937   "Vejamen contra don Cristóbal," 17 de agosto, 1966.
       Professor Carl O. Sauer's book, The Early Spanish Main, alternates between passionate attacks on Columbus and attempts at documenting obvious and established historical facts, says S. "Sauer no nos dice nada nuevo, y algunas de sus afirmaciones nos hacen reír."*

938   "El drama de España: tres libros convergentes," 9 de septiembre, 1966.
       S. discusses three recent books on the Spanish Republic of the thirties and the Civil War: Revolución y contra-revolución en España (Joaquín de Maurín), León Blum, Humanist in Politics (by Joel Colton), and Bibliografía de la guerra civil española (Juan García Durán). "El libro de Maurín sería el número 6.249 de esa lista [Durán's Bibliografía], pero quedará entre la media docena que debieran haberse escrito."

939   "Dificultad de la tragedia," 20 de septiembre, 1966; Lectura, 163, 1 (1 de septiembre, 1966), 28-32. ("Dificultades..." in Lectura.)

The present epoch lacks the requisite elements for writing tragedy in the traditional sense.

940   "Esposas y amantes canceladas," 5 de octubre, 1966; Lectura, 163, 4 (15 de octubre, 1966), 123-27.
A review of My Life with Chaplin, a book written by the actor's ex-wife.

941   "Agentes dobles y terroristas," 22 de octubre, 1966; Lectura, 164, 1 (1 de noviembre, 1966), 28-32.
A review of Rebecca West's book, The Birds Fall Down (which reconstructs aspects of Russian terrorism at the end of the last century and the beginning of the present).

942   "¿La revolución en abundancia?," 9 de noviembre, 1966; Lectura, 165, 1 (1 de enero, 1967), 31-32 (As "La revolución de la abundancia").
Somber reflections on the possibility of an atomic conflict "entre dos tendencias que actúan en la misma dirección: la revolución por la abundancia [U. S. A.] y la revolución por la desesperación y la miseria" [China].

943   "Secretos de guerra," 19 de noviembre, 1966.
S. reviews The Secret Surrender, a book written by Allen Dulles, Director of the Central Intelligence Agency (CIA), in which there is told "la génesis secreta de la rendición de Alemania, en 1945."

944   "Donde mandan las mujeres," 8 de diciembre, 1966.
Investigation of the myth of female superiority in the U. S. A., as discussed in Charles Ferguson's The Male Attitude, leads S. to consider colonial conditions, parallels in the rest of the American continent, love as an "intelligent" operation, hombría, economic control, and woman as man's conscience. *

945   "Caminos de la novela de hoy," 21 de diciembre, 1966.
In discussing an anthology of recent European and American short stories, The World of Modern Fiction, S. comments on the expressionist and lyrical tendencies of today's novel, pointing out that traditional forms of realism and naturalism have become largely "extraliterary."*

1967

946   "Aquel joven llamado Stalin," 4 de enero, 1967.

A discussion based on Ellis Smith's recent book, El joven Stalin.

947   "La muerte de un presidente," 18 de enero, 1967.
Upon the publication of the first part of the proposed book, The Death of a President by William Manchester, S. defends the right of the individual to have a private life safe from the insatiable curiosity of the public.

948   "Aquel poeta agente de seguros," ¿enero?, 1967; Lectura, 165, 2 (15 de enero, 1967), 61-64.
A discussion of the poet Wallace Stevens, an insurance executive in Connecticut.

949   "Política, frivolidad y tragedia," ¿enero?, 1967; Lectura, 165, 4 (15 de febrero, 1967), 125-27.
A discussion of the book of photos of China by Marc Riboud, Tres banderas, and of the frivolous vanity of politicians who have their photos retouched.

950   "Divagación sobre las influencias," 20 de febrero, 1967.
A rambling discussion on cross-cultural influences between the "mundo iberoamericano (incluídas España y Portugal)" and the United States.

951   "Los papeles póstumos de Mark Twain," ¿febrero?, 1967; Lectura, 166, 1 (1 de marzo, 1967), 26-28.
Comments on the first six of a series of fourteen books which Yale University is publishing "con cartas personales, borradoras, proyectos frustrados y anotaciones más o menos brillantes del ciudadano Clemens que se hizo llamar en el mundo MARK TWAIN."

952   "Luces nuevas sobre el Quijote," 7 de marzo, 1967.
S. finds in Dominique Aubier's book, Don Quichotte prophète d'Israel, valuable information on the possible gestation of Cervantes' great novel and new light (which is of no real consequence) on the author's possible Jewish ancestry.

953   "La logoterapia y la angustia," 21 de marzo, 1967.
A sympathetic discussion of Dr. Viktor L. Frankl's logotherapy (for treatment of existential anguish) and of his book, Man's Search for Meaning.

954   "La virtud de decirlo todo," 19 de abril, 1967.

Comments on Bertrand Russell on the occasion of the publication of his latest book, The Autobiography of B. R.

955   "El dosel de los novios, " 4 de mayo, 1967.
Comments on The Bridal Canopy, a new novel by Nobel Prize-winning author S. Y. Agnon, and long quotations from an interview with Agnon by Emanuel Feldman (from the Saturday Review).

956   "Un tema siempre nuevo: la mujer, " 23 de mayo, 1967.
Reflections on women inspired by the reading of Casualties of Peace, the latest novel by the American Edna O'Brien.

957   "Turistas de ayer y de hoy, " 7 de junio, 1967.
Observations on traveling--in the past and in the present.

958   "El negro Ellison y los otros, " 22 de junio, 1967.
A discussion of Ralph Ellison's novel, The Invisible Man, and of the Black problem in the United States.

959   "Los mitos y los existencialistas, " 7 de julio, 1967.
Comments on Claude Lévi-Strauss's ideas on mythology and on Marcelino Peñuelas' book, Mito, literatura, y realidad.   Existential anguish is nothing new--man from the beginning has suffered it.

960   "Arabes, judíos y nazis, " 20 de julio, 1967.
Reflections on Treblinka, the book by Steiner which relates the extermination of 800,000 Jews (adults and children) in Poland during World War II, and on the difficult but necessary task of making that "fabulosa realidad verisimilar, " i. e. , assimilable to our minds.

961   "Arte y vida de Nabokov, " 15 de agosto, 1967.
Comments on Andrew Field's book, Nabokov, His Life and His Art, and on Field's polarization of sex and love (which the critic Field sees in Nabokov's work, at least in Lolita).

962   "Y de la guerra nuclear, ¿qué?, " 21 de agosto, 1967.
A discussion of William R. Kintner's Peace and the Problem of Strategy, a book on international politics which examines the reasons behind the armanent's "race" today.

963 "Humor negro y colonialismo," 5 de septiembre, 1967.
A discussion of black humor ("lo puso de moda en nuestros días, Valle-Inclán"), and of a tendency to look beyond our national borders (a "colonial" attitude) for literary excellence and innovations while ignoring what we have "en nuestra propia casa."

964 "El escándalo y el éxito," 18 de septiembre, 1967.
Although Frank Salas, the author of Tattoo the Wicked Cross, has "una gran devoción y algún talento natural" his novel is a deplorable example of scandal for scandal's sake, and it is not literature.

965 "El peligroso escándalo," 2 de octubre, 1967.
Comments on Stalin, inspired by the book Twenty Letters to a Friend by Svetlana Alliluyeva (the Soviet dictator's daughter). "Stalin fué el escándalo y la vergüenza de toda una época."

966 "El difícil humor 'fácil'," 19 de octubre, 1967.
A laudatory review of the Mexican humorist-writer Marco A. Almazán's book, Claroscuro, "una colección de crónicas ligeras y sabias a un tiempo."

967 "Una vez más Valle-Inclán," 9 de noviembre, 1967.
A review of two new books: Las estéticas de Valle-Inclán, by Guillermo Díaz-Plaja, and La estética de Valle-Inclán, by Antonio Risco.

968 "La 'ciencia-ficción'," 6 de diciembre, 1967; El Universo (Guayaquil), 24 de diciembre, 1967.
Comments on Los viajeros de las gafas azules, by Juan G. Atienza, and on science-fiction in general, in which S. finds "posibilidades poéticas y hasta metafísicas."

969 "Ogros, hadas y 'Poil de Carotte'," 21 de diciembre, 1967.
Discussion of the short novel for children, Poil de Carotte, by Jules Renard (originally published in French in 1894 but now published in English with its French title), and in general of literature for children.

1968

970 "La diferencia," 18 de enero, 1968.
Man essentially differs from animals not so much in

his ability to speak and to reason as in his power to create
or invent myths--which are then revered or worshipped by
man--opines S.

971   "La hija del héroe escribe," 6 de febrero, 1968;
Lectura, 173, 2 (15 de mayo, 1968), 55-58.
Reflections on the Jews inspired by two new books,
both by Yael Dayan, daughter of Moshe Dayan: Death Had
Two Sons: A Novel (1967) and A Soldier's Diary (1967).

972   "Aquella tribu de los Tolstoi," 22 de febrero, 1968.
Discussion of the Russian writer and a review of Henry
Troyat's book, Tolstoi.

973   "Los reyes y los estilos exóticos," 9 de marzo, 1968.
Reflections on the amorous style of certain monarchs,
inspired by Sanche de Gramont's book, Epitaph for Kings.

974   "Koestler y el gran problema," 22 de marzo, 1968.
Reflections on Arthur Koestler's book. The Ghost in
the Machine (1967). S. defends Koestler's right to philoso-
phize. "Filosofar no es más que vivir esencialmente."

975   "Seis millones de muertos," 6 de abril, 1968.
Comments inspired by Arthur D. Morse's documented
book, While Six Million Die (which relates the official apathy
of the United States and other nations towards the fate of
the Jews in Germany before and during World War II).

976   "América y la Atlántida," 22 de abril, 1968.
S. finds the book, Atlantis, by Ignatius Donnelly (and
published almost a century ago in New York) to be "un
escrupulso estudio antropológico, histórico, filológico" which
supports his theory of a common origin of World civilization in a continent which sank into the Atlantic Ocean, Atlantis.

977   "Más sobre lo mismo," 11 de mayo, 1968.
As a continuation of his immediately previous column
(976). S. recounts some facts which, in his opinion, link
the primitive American cultures with those of Europe and
thus support his theory of the former existence of the continent of Atlantis.

978   "Todavía la Atlántida," 22 de mayo, 1968.
More theorizing in support of S. 's belief that Atlantis
existed and that it was the "cradle" of American, European

and Asian civilizations.

979 "Las confidencias de Bertrand Russell," 20 de junio,
1968; Lectura, 173, 4 (15 de junio, 1968), 124-27.
    Reflections on Russell (including his Quixotic quality--
"su sentido absoluto del bien") inspired by the publication of
the second volume of the English author's memoirs.

980 "Orden del día: hippies," 4 de julio, 1968.
    Comments on "hippies" inspired by Joan Didion's book,
Slouching Towards Bethlehem. S. regards them as "gente
decadente. Su actitud budista, neocristiana o escéptica lleva
consigo una gran dosis de negación nihilista. Del orgullo de
la humillación, del placer de la pobreza. Con un asomo,
como se ve, de masoquismo."

981 "Los amores de Kafka," 25 de julio, 1968.
    Comments on Kafka and his tortured life and literature.
"En las novelas de Kafka--incluída 'Metamorfosis'--verán
los hombres del futuro la historia interior de nuestro siglo,
secreta pero determinante."

982 "Ases de la gran baraja," 7 de agosto, 1968.
    A discussion of William Hubben's book, Dostoyevski,
Kierkegaard, Nietzsche, and Kafka--with most attention devoted to the first of these figures.

983 "El diario de Che Guevara," 20 de agosto, 1968.
    The Complete Bolivian Diaries of Che Guevara and
Other Captured Documents, "carece de valor lírico, de ali-
ento épico y de otras cualidades que se podrían esperar."

984 "Aquella Nancy Cunard," 4 de septiembre, 1968.
    Comments on the English heiress Nancy Cunard (whom
S. knew and admired) upon the publication of the book,
Those Remarkable Cunards: Emerald and Nancy, by Daphne
Fielding.

985 "La jaula de los monos," 19 de septiembre, 1968.
    Comments on Kurt Vonnegut's book of short stories or
novelettes, Welcome to the Monkey Cage.

986 "Libros rusos clandestinos," 8 de octubre, 1968.
    Comments on Trip through the Whirlwind, the autobi-
ography of Eugenia Semyonovna Ginzburg, just published in
New York (after circulating clandestinely in Russia in typewritten or mimeographed copies), and on other clandestine
literature in the Soviet Union today.

987   "Más y más letras rusas," 22 de octubre, 1968.
A very favorable review of Solzhenitsyn's novel, The
First Circle.

988   "El atleta superviviente," 5 de noviembre, 1968.
A favorable review of Death Row, a book by the athlete
Patricio P. Escobal, in which the author's personal experi-
ences as a prisoner of the Nationalist forces during the
Spanish Civil War are related.

989   "Anticipación sobre Isak Dinesen," 21 de noviembre, 1968.
Having begun reading Parmenia Miguel's biography of
Isak Dinesen, S. reflects on the importance of really seeing
what one looks at, of not losing contact with the basic reality of our existence.

990   "La identidad y el nombre de pluma," 9 de diciembre,
1968.
A discussion of the difference between one's public or
professional identity and one's true self inspired by the appearance of the biography of the deceased Danish writer,
Isak Dinesen (Baroness Karen Blixen-Finecke), by Parmenia
Miguel.

991   "El 'escarabajismo' en el arte," 19 de diciembre, 1968.
Reflections on the Beatles and possible reasons for
their wide acceptance.   S. applauds the music of the Beatles
(though he personally prefers the Brazilian bossa nova).

1969

992   "En nuestro pequeño planeta," 8 de enero, 1969.
Upon reading Howard E. Evans' book, Life on a Small
Hardly Known Planet (La vida en un pequeño planeta apenas
conocido), S. reflects on what man might learn from in-
sects--cockroaches, ants, etc.

993   "Promesas y amenazas celestiales," 22 de enero, 1969.
Commenting on Arthur C. Clarke's book, Promises of
Space, S. expresses faith in science and technology "al margen de consideraciones morales." "La ciencia, como digo,
tiene la última palabra cuando las demás palabras no hacen
sino sumirnos en la perplejidad." It might even make war
so difficult as to be impossible.

994   "Malraux, Cohn-Bendit, etcetera," 10 de febrero,

1969.

S. sees the current polarization of French thought and action in André Malraux on one side and in the twenty-three-year-old Daniel Cohn-Bendit, leader of the uprising in the spring of 1968, on the other.

995   "Tiempo de nobles picardías," 20 de febrero, 1969.
A review of John Irving's first novel, Setting Free the Bears, and a general discussion of picaresque novels.

996   "La muerte al contado," 7 de marzo, 1969.
A review of the posthumously published memoirs of Louis-Ferdinand Celine, De castillo en castillo.

997   "Invitación a la náusea," 21 de marzo, 1969.
Reading Albertine Sarrazin's two novels, La fuga and El tobillo, Sender's reaction is first, "de piedad," and second, "de franca repugnancia." S. finds no redeeming grace in the filth of these novels.

998   "Los jóvenes airados," 7 de abril, 1969.
Inspired by reading Lewis S. Feuer's book, Conflict of Generations, S. reflects on the causes of the unrest and rebellious attitudes of the youth of today.

999   "Otra vez Hemingway," 21 de abril, 1969.
Reflections on Hemingway as a man (his publicity-seeking, his "inocencia casi infantil," etc.) upon the publication of Carlos Baker's biography of the American writer, "hasta ahora la más completa, aunque no la más inspirada."

1000   "¿Es peligroso vivir en California?," 5 de mayo, 1969.
Comments on Curt Gentry's book, The Last Days of the Late, Great State of California (1968, 1969), in which the author predicted that much of California would disappear into the Pacific Ocean in April of 1969.

1001   "Los tesoros de la luna," 19 de mayo, 1969.
Reflections on the upcoming first visit by man to the moon, and possible later "colonización" of the earth's satellite. "Los tesoros de la Luna consisten en los conocimientos que puede facilitarnos esta visita personal."

1002   "Glorias póstumas de Flannery," 6 de junio, 1969.
Upon the posthumous publication of Mystery and Habits by Flannery O'Connor, S. comments very favorably

on her life and short novels. Of her fiction S. says, "Yo
no he leído nada comparable [in twentieth-century American
novels]. "

1003   "Lecturas de verano, " 23 de junio, 1969.
        Comments on mystery and detective novels, especial-
ly the "Maigret" series by the French writer, Georges Sime-
non.

1004   "El príncipe Kropotkin, " 5 de julio, 1969.
        Upon the republication of Memories of a Revolutionary
by the Russian prince and anarchist, Peter Kropotkin,
seventy years after its original publication, S. finds that the
book is still alive and relevant to our aspirations today.

1005   "Nacimiento y riesgo del LSD, " 19 de julio, 1969.
        Comments based on John G. Fuller's book document-
ing the accidental taking of a kind of primitive LSD (lysergic
acid) by the inhabitants of the French village of Pont Saint-
Esprit (Provence) in 1951, The Day of St. Anthony's Fire
(1969).

1006   "Wells, el pequeño gran hombre, " 5 de agosto, 1969.
        Upon publication of a critical biography, The Turbu-
lent Life of Wells, by Lovat Dickson, S. reflects upon H.
G. Wells, the man and his vast literary work.

1007   "Muerte y resurrección de Kuznetsov, " 19 de agosto,
        1969.
        Comments on the persecution of honest Soviet writers
who disagree with the Government's viewpoints and, specifically, on Kuznetsov who had recently escaped from Russia
and who now wishes to write under the name of A. Anatol.

1008   "Del jardín de Epicuro, " 6 de septiembre, 1969.
        Inspired by Paul Nizán's book, Les Matérialistes de
l'antiquité (1965, 1968), S. marvels at the advanced physics
of Epicurus, "el primero, creo yo, que estableció la existencia del infinito en términos lógicos. "

1009   "Pájaros, bestias y parientes, " 23 de septiembre,
        1969.
        Observations on certain parallels between animals
and human beings inspired by the reading of Birds, Beasts
and Relatives (1969), a new book by the naturalist Gerald M.
Durrell.

1010 "El príncipe de Dinamarca," 7 de octubre, 1969.
Observations on the art of translation, English culture, Hamlet, and a new Spanish translation of Hamlet by
the director of stage and film, Alvaro Custodio (which S.
calls "la mejor traducción de Hamlet que conozco").

1011 "La cárcel silenciosa y el dragón," 21 de octubre,
1969.
Reflections on Stalin upon reading Svetlana Alliluyeva's
second book, Only One Year, written in the United States.
Her first was written "en la inmensa cárcel silenciosa que
es Rusia."

1012 "Lord Russell contesta el correo," 6 de noviembre,
1969.
Comments on Bertrand Russell based on a recently
published book of letters received and answered by the famous English writer from 1950 to 1968. Praises Lord Russell for his honesty and "falta de narcismo" (so rare among
intellectuals).

1013 "Pro y contra G.B.S.," 21 de noviembre, 1969.
Observations on Shaw inspired by two new books: a
collection of Shavian texts (published between 1856 and 1898)
edited by Stanley Weintraub and Bernard Shaw: A Reconsideration, by Colin Wilson. "Ellos [Shaw, Einstein, Freud,
etc.] eran la cultura y la civilización al mismo tiempo.
Ahora hay la tendencia (por incuria de los que deberían
continuar la tarea) a formas de anticultura y de anticivili-
zación."

1014 "Reflexiones sobre las ballenas," 6 de diciembre,
1969.
Imaginative parallels between men and whales inspired
by reading The Year of the Whale, a book by the biologist
Victor B. Scheffer. Sender's novel about whales (36) appeared shortly after this column.

1015 "Más sobre las ballenas," 23 de diciembre, 1969.
A continuation of the theme of 1014. More observations about whales and whaling based on Sender's reading of
two new books, Mapa ballenero, by Matthew Maury, and
Baleia! Baleia! Whale Hunters of the Azores (1969) by Bernard Venables, and a reprint of Charles Scammon's book,
The Marine Mammals of the North-Western Coast of North
America and the American Whale Fishery, originally published in 1874.

1970

1016   "El instinto de la libertad," 6 de enero, 1970;
        Comunidad Ibérica (México), núms. 44-45 (enero-
        abril, 1970), 9-10.
        S. sees in the "new left" nothing really new but ra-
ther "la revitalización en niveles actuales de nuestro más
viejo y poderoso instinto," the love of liberty.

1017   "El futuro comenzó ayer," 20 de enero, 1970.
        In the mythical sense the future began with man's
walking on the moon.   A kind of "desesperación positiva"
now marks the direction to the future.   The era of bourgeois
idealism seems about to end and will be replaced, so it appears to S., by "la fusión de la humanidad entera alrededor
del planeta en un sola familia, una sola nación, una sola
economía y una sola y misma cultura."

1018   "El mundo como un aeropuerto," 4 de febrero, 1970.
        Comments on Brigid Brophy's novel, In Transit (in
which the action occurs in an airport--with planes which go
nowhere), and on the inanities of today's world, especially
of most television programs.   "Uno de los inventos más
diabólicos que padecemos es el de la televisión gracias al
cual pueden entrar en nuestra casa ... esos individuos a
quienes jamás les abriríamos la puerta por las buenas."

1019   "Una revolución lírica," 19 de febrero, 1970.
        A discussion of the lyricism of the Beatles inspired
by the reading of the book The Beatles' Illustrated Lyrics,
edited by Alan Aldridge.   S. sees in the charm that the
Beatles have added to things formerly rejected, "las cosas
que decían y hacían los humildes," a lyrical revolution.

1020   "El ejemplo de César Chávez," 10 de marzo, 1970.
        A discussion highly laudatory of César Chávez, and
his fight for the improvement of working conditions among
the Mexican migrant agricultural workers in California.

1021   "¿A dónde van la novela y las artes?," 28 de marzo,
        1970.
        A discussion of Iris Murdoch's new novel, A Fairly
Honorable Defeat, and of the direction the novel takes today.
"La novela de hoy sigue, como decimos, a las demás artes."

1022   "Más testimonios rusos," 7 de abril, 1970; Comuni-
        dad Ibérica (México), núms. 47-48 (julio-octubre,

1970), 31-32.
A discussion of two recent books which testify to the
lack of freedom in the Soviet Union: The Demonstration in
Pushkin Square (1969), by Paul Litvinov, and My Testimony,
by the novelist, Anatoly Marchenko.

1023   "El amor, el odio y lo demás," 22 de abril, 1970.
A discussion of Karl Menninger's theories on love
and hate expressed in his book, Love Against Hate.   "Es un
libro brillante y ... utópico, también."

1024   "La poesía de Miss Moore," 5 de mayo, 1970.
Reflections on the poetry of Marianne Moore inspired
by George W. Nitchie's book, An Introduction to the Poetry
of..., and on poetry in general. For S., lyrical poetry is
"una manera de incorporar a nuestra conciencia elementos
nuevos sacados del rico e inexhausto e inagotable inconsciente de cada cual."

1025   "El instinto humano de agresión," 22 de mayo, 1970.
A discussion of human violence and a review of Kon-
rad Lorenz's book, On Aggression (1967).

1026   "La Unión Soviética en 1984," 11 de junio, 1970.
Comments on the possible collapse--which S. sees as
unlikely--of the Soviet Union and on the new book, Will the
Soviet Union Survive Until 1984?, by the Russian historian,
Andrei Amalrik.   "La oposición cultural rusa tiene en
Amalrik su expresión más aguda."

1027   "A propósito de Forster," 23 de junio, 1970.
Upon the death of E. M. Forster, S. reflects upon
the different ways in which novelists in different countries--
England, France, Russia, and Spain--are regarded by society at large, and praises the work of the deceased writer.

1028   "Todavía la vida es sueño," 7 de julio, 1970.
Upon the publication of a new English translation of
Calderón's La vida es sueño (which S. calls the best English translation that he has seen), S. states his conviction
that life is indeed a dream.   Reality "se basa en elementos
subjetivos que nosotros superponemos a los hechos."   An
important article for those wishing to understand S.'s view
of reality.

1029   "Negros y blancos," 20 de julio, 1970.
Having read Diary of a Harlem Schoolteacher (1969),

by James Haskins (for its testimonial, not literary, value),
S. reflects upon the racial problem in the U.S.A., and especially upon "el peor aspecto del problema"--the discrimi-
nation against whites by blacks.

1030   "La manía de las autobiografías," 5 de agosto, 1970.
        "Con los novelistas y los poetas la autobiografía no
es necesaria y resulta siempre inferior a su obra. ¿ Para
qué vamos a escribirla si la hemos escrito en nuestros
libros? ... En cuanto a Picasso, ¿qué mejor autobiografía que la de sus millares de dibujos, pinturas, grabados,
murales?"

1031   "Los peligros del esteticismo," 21 de agosto, 1970.
        S. comments on the dangers of estheticism (which
puts form before substance) inspired by his having read
Maurice Rowdon's book, The Silver Age of Venice (1970).

1032   "Los que no se enteraban," 11 de septiembre, 1970.
        Reflections on why Germany lost in World War II, in-
spired by the reading of the published memoirs of Albert
Speer, Hitler's Minister of Armaments, who claims to have
been unaware that thousands of Jews were being murdered
every day. "Lo que pasaba es que no querían [Speer and
other Nazi leaders] enterarse," writes S.

1033   "Un discípulo de Kafka," 22 de septiembre, 1970.
        A laudatory review of Isaac Bashevis Singer's book
of short stories, A Friend of Kafka and Other Stories (1970).
"Singer es un discípulo de Kafka, pero ve el mundo a su
manera y lo expresa sin imitar al maestro." S. stresses
the distinction between a "discípulo" and a mere "imitador."

1034   "Un libro de Lady Snow," 8 de octubre, 1970.
        S. discusses Pamela Hansford Johnson (wife of C. P.
Snow) and her latest novel, The Honours Board (1970).
"Los libros de Pamela ... como testimonios de un tiempo
que pronto será pasado no los hay ahora más fieles a la
realidad de fuera y a la de dentro."

1035   "Solzhenitsyn, Premio Nóbel," 23 de octubre, 1970.
        Praise for the Russian writer's talent and courage,
and a discussion of his novel, La Maison de Matriona,
which reveals Solzhenitsyn's great love for his native soil.

1036   "Sobre el mirar y el ver," 3 de noviembre, 1970.
        A discussion of the art of Maurits Escher and of his

newly reprinted book, The Graphic Work of M. C. Escher.
"Escher es el mejor dibujante de nuestro tiempo. "

1037 "Más señales de alarma, " 20 de noviembre, 1970.
Reflections on the possibility--predicted by some
sociologists--that man may destroy himself by 1980. "Si
esa catástrofe llega a producirse, ... la culpa la tendrá la
tendencia crecientemente individualista de nuestra sociedad
desde fines de la Edad Media. "

1038 "Un documento sensacional, " 8 de diciembre, 1970.
Commentary inspired by the reading of Khrushchev's
book of memoirs as it was being published in Life (before
the book appeared). Praises the Soviet leader for his
honesty and renunciation of violence in settling international
disputes.

1039 "El saber de los indios yaquis, " 22 de diciembre,
1970.
Commentary on Carlos Castañeda's book, The Yaqui
Way of Wisdom (English translation of a doctoral thesis in
anthropology at UCLA).

1971

1040 "En los tiempos del rey Eduardo, " 8 de enero, 1971.
Quotations (with brief commentary by S.) from the
writing of Bernard Shaw for whom S. has always had great
admiration and "simpatía humana. "

1041 "Elogio de la ciudad gris, " 21 de enero, 1971.
Upon the publication of the book, London, by Christo-
pher Hibbert, S. praises London and the English. The
Londoner is "el tipo de ciudadano más civilizado del mundo
occidental. Amable, impersonal, comunicativo, sin rígidez
alguna (somos más rígidos los hispanos), bien educado y
ante todo con una completa falta de afectación. "

1042 "Chesterton, el distraído, " 5 de febrero, 1971.
Quotations of G. K. Chesterton's aphorisms on various subjects with comments--entertaining also if not always
humorous--by S. Inspired by a book by J. B. Priestley on
the post-Victorian period in English letters.

1043 "Una novela póstuma de Hemingway, " 21 de febrero,
1971.

A review of the posthumous novel by Hemingway, Islands in the Stream (whose chief value is that of a self-
portrait), and discussion of the American author's search
for a metaphysical dimension in his work.

1044   "La novela 'pop' en los Estados Unidos," 7 de marzo,
       1971.
       Comments on Erich Segal's best-selling novel, Love
Story, which S. insists should not be called a "pop novel."
To call it that is to insult the intelligence of the pueblo, and
to attribute to the people its success "es injusto y ofensivo."
The novel is "una pequeña tontería. Ni siquiera grande
[tontería]...." And Segal's a good business man, S. says.

1045   "Cocteau en su hora difícil," 19 de marzo, 1971.
       Personal impressions of Jean Cocteau and a review
of Francis Steegmuller's biography of the French writer.
"Esta biografía no parece gran cosa," writes S., who considers an essay by Gómez de la Serna in the 1930's "la
mejor y la más justa apreciación del poeta francés."

1046   "Paladines de la mediocridad," 5 de abril, 1971.
       A review of Irving Stone's biography of Freud, The
Passions of the Mind, "la menos interesante de las biografías escritas sobre Freud, hasta ahora."

1047   "Figuras de un pasado reciente," 19 de abril, 1971.
       A discussion of Richard M. Ketchum's book of photo-
graphs and daguerrotypes of about forty figures in American
history accompanied by brief essays. For special discussion S. selects Dolly Madison, a chief of the Nez Percé
Indians, "Stonewall" Jackson, Booker T. Washington, Nor-
man Thomas, and Lizzie Borden.

1048   "El último año de Tolstoi," 5 de mayo, 1971.
       Reflections on Tolstoi's last year of life inspired by
a new book on the Russian count by Valentín Bulgakov, Tolstoi's secretary during the author's last months (in 1910).

1049   "Un libro curioso de Rilke," 17 de mayo, 1971.
       Comments on (and long translated quotations from) a
recent English edition of Rainer María Rilke's last book,
the novel Notebook of Malte Laurids Brigge. S. considers
the work semi-autobiographical.

1050   "¿En qué consiste ser judío?," 4 de junio, 1971.
       Reflections on "Jewishness," and the modern state of

Israel, inspired by the reading of The Israelis, a critical study by Amos Elon.

1051   "Los errores de Einstein, " 18 de junio, 1971.
        Comments inspired by Ronald Clark's book, Einstein: The Life and Times. "Einstein, y Freud, han cambiado el orden de nuestra civilización.

1052   "La campana de la asfixia, " 8 de julio, 1971.
        A review of the novel, Bell Jar, by Sylvia Plath, upon its publication in the United States (several years after its author committed suicide in London). It has "todo lo requerido para ser una obra de arte. "

1053   "A propósito de Frank Capra, " 22 de julio, 1971.
        Reflections on the possible place or importance of literature in the future in a world increasingly dominated by the audio and visual media. Inspired by the reading of the autobiography of Frank Capra--the Hollywood movie director.

1054   "El problema del arte visual, " 5 de agosto, 1971.
        In defense of his statement in his last column (1053) that a bad novel often gains when made into a movie, S. uses Henry Carrière's Papillón to illustrate how narration and description of external action can be represented on the screen better than in a novel. But good literature goes much beyond mere external action; it is reflective and meditative.

1055   "Un Séneca ocasional, " 14 de agosto, 1971.
        S. denies that Seneca was a saint or a great poet or a true philosopher. He knew, however, how to create an image or myth of himself which posterity has venerated, the "espléndido mito senequista. "

1056   "Un humorista mexicano, " 1 de septiembre, 1971.
        An appreciative discussion of Rediezcubrimiento de México, a book by the Mexican humorist, Marco Almazán, and of the pitfalls in writing humor.

1057   "Una novela de Vercors, " 20 de septiembre, 1971.
        A laudatory review of the English translation of Vercors' latest novel, The Raft of Medusa. "Vercors se mantiene en su nivel.... "

1058   "Un barco llamado 'Amistad', " 6 de octubre, 1971.
        Reflections on the racial problem in the U. S. A. upon

reading Mary Cable's historical chronicle, <u>Black Odyssey</u>
(which relates the uprising of Blacks on the slave ship,
"Friendship," in 1839).

1059   "El movimiento como enfermedad," 20 de octubre,
         1971.
         Reflections on the average American's need to affirm
himself through driving his automobile hither and yon, inspired by S.'s reading of John Burvey's informative book,
<u>La gran enfermedad americana del movimiento.</u>   "La ne-
cesidad del movimiento y la velocidad y el cambio revelan
antes que nada los engañosos placeres del individualismo.
Engañosos y de un peligro creciente."

1060   "Las multitudes inconformes," 5 de noviembre, 1971.
         Reflections on the rebellion of today's youth and the
possibility that their non-violent protest might eventually
produce revolutionary change.   'No hay duda de que estos
anarquistas sin bombas ni puñales están teniendo una importancia creciente en nuestras costumbres."

1061   "La paz y el cabello largo," 19 de noviembre, 1971.
         Intrigued by Henry Malcolm's book, <u>Generation of
Narcissus</u>, S. reflects on the "conflict of generations,"
which may--in the U.S.A. and other "países superdesarrolla-
dos"--replace the struggle between classes (and thus be revolutionary).   In so-called "revolutionary" Russia, however,
the conflict of generations is considered counter-revolutionary

1062   "Eleanor y Franklin," 14 de diciembre, 1971.
         A review of Joseph P. Lash's book, <u>Eleanor and
Franklin</u>, which S. calls "una obra monumental que refleja
la vida interior y, por decirlo así, confidencial de un brillante período de la vida norteamericana."   S. admires both
the President and his "hermosa (todo es según queramos
verlo) esposa Eleanor."

1063   "Más sobre Roosevelt," 27 de diciembre, 1971.
         More reflections on the significance of Franklin
Roosevelt's tenure as President of the United States, inspired by J. P. Lash's book, <u>Eleanor and Franklin</u>, discussed also in 1062.

                              1972

1064   "El pobre Verlaine," 13 de enero, 1972.

Reflections on the life and time of Paul Verlaine, inspired by Joanna Richardson's biographical study, Verlaine.

1065   "Del diario del conde Kessler," 25 de enero, 1972.
Comments on the book, In the Twenties, the English translation of the diary of Count Kessler (the Prussian diplomat and lover of art and literature), originally published in German in 1935.

1066   "Shiva, Vishnú y Gandhi," 8 de febrero, 1972.
A discussion of Gandhi inspired by George Woodcock's biography of the Indian leader, Ghandhi.

1067   "La hija del poeta," 18 de febrero, 1972.
A discussion of the life and work of Ezra Pound based on the autobiography of the poet's daughter, Mary de Rachewiltz, Discretions.   The book is in fact more of a biography of Pound than an autobiography.

1068   "El escándalo y la gracia," 7 de marzo, 1972.
A discussion of the fiction of the deceased (in 1964) American author, Flannery O'Connor.   Some of her short novels are "dignas de perpetua memoria."

1069   "La liberación de las mujeres," 21 de marzo, 1972.
"El destino preside la distribución y diferenciación de aptitudes y sabe lo que hace.   La mujer ... es amada física y metafísicamente por el hombre, adorada por los hijos, respetada en público.   ¿Qué buscan las liberadoras con su 'liberación'?"

1070   "Los gitanos y otros excesos," 6 de abril, 1972.
Upon reading George Borrow's book about Eastern European gypsies, The Zingali, S. comments on the gypsies and compares them with hippies.

1071   "La locura y el genio," 19 de abril, 1972.
Upon reading Celine's book, North, published posthumously, S. speculates upon the possible insanity of Celine as a result of a head injury in World War I.

1072   "No es todavía la hora," 9 de mayo, 1972.
The hour of "decadentismo en las letras" has not yet come despite two new novels, Not to Disturb, by Muriel Spark, and Don Juan's Bar, by Antonio Callado, which S. briefly reviews.   As a novel "es mucho mejor la de Callado que la de Muriel Spark."

1073   "Un poco de ciencia," 19 de mayo, 1972.
         Upon re-reading James Jeans' book, The Mysterious
Universe, S. reflects upon the metaphysical dimension of
that zone where the known ("hechos comprobados") encounters
the unknown--in pure science.

1074   "Esta luz que nos envuelve," 6 de junio, 1972.
         More speculations inspired by The Mysterious Uni-
verse by James Jeans (see 1073). Science and religion both
now point to light as "el supremo misterio que nos liga a la
divinidad. "

1075   "Luminosos enigmas," 22 de junio, 1972.
         A continuation of intuitive reflections begun in 1073
and 1074, based on The Mysterious Universe, by James
Jeans, in which S. discusses possible implications of the
discovery of negative protons. "Con el protón negativo
aparece la antimateria, sugeridora de la nada absoluta. "

1076   "La batalla contra la nada," 3 de julio, 1972.
         The fourth in a series of five columns (1073-1077)
devoted to The Mysterious Universe. The universe cease-
lessly transforms matter into energy in its struggle against
"la nada. " "En esa lucha somos sus aliados consciente o
inconscientemente. "

1077   "Hoyos negros y hoyos blancos," 20 de julio, 1972.
         The last of five columns (1073-1077) reflecting on
the ultimate nature of reality. A consumed star leaves "un
hoyo negro" in the universe but its energy may form "un
hoyo blanco" in a second universe, and vice versa, in sym-
metrical action. The "second universe" is different and
totally unknown to us. "¿Será ese el universo a donde vamos después de muertos? ¿Y por qué caminos? ¿Y para
qué?"

1078   "Kafka o el centro absoluto," 10 de agosto, 1972.
         Upon the publication in English of the complete works
of Kafka in a single volume, S. praises the writer for his
prophetic qualities and calls him, "como ha dicho alguien,
el centro absoluto de la realidad en el mundo de las letras
mundiales. " Others in that center: Dante, Shakespeare,
Cervantes, Goethe.

1079   "Quetzalcoatl, dios de dioses," 25 de agosto, 1972.
         S. defends his opinion that Quetzalcoatl was the name
the Mexican Indians gave to the comet which entered the

Earth's atmosphere (and which produced the Great Flood) about thirteen millenia ago. The Chinese dragon, the Japanese dragon, the Mexican dragon, and Quetzalcoatl (the Plumed Serpent) have their common origin in the appearance of the comet--now known as Venus, according to S.

1080   "Los escritores y la verdad," 8 de septiembre, 1972.
    Comments favorably on the published (but unspoken) speech of Solzhenitsyn upon accepting the Nobel Prize.

1081   "Los que se van," 22 de septiembre, 1972.
    Reminiscences and reflections upon the death of three of S.'s acquaintances: Jules Romains, John Dos Passos, and Américo Castro.

1082   "El suicidio de un escritor," 6 de octubre, 1972.
    Reflections upon the life and work of the French novelist and playwright Henry Montherlant (who committed suicide, September 21, 1972).

1083   "Ultima hora cristiana," 20 de octubre, 1972.
    A discussion of the life, work, and leading ideas of the recently deceased Protestant theologian, Reinhold Niebuhr.

1084   "Ezra Pound," 7 de noviembre, 1972.
    An understanding and sympathetic discussion of the recently deceased poet, Ezra Pound.

1085   "Cuando pasaba Lincoln," 21 de noviembre, 1972.
    Quoting from Walt Whitman's book, Specimen Days, in which the poet tells of seeing President Lincoln pass by his home frequently during one summer, S. compares the two men. In Lincoln there was genuine poetry and in Whitman's poetry a political dimension that was to grow "y abarcar las conciencias de todos los americanos que vinieron después."

1086   'Bernard Shaw, rara avis," 8 de diciembre, 1972.
    Comments on apparent contradictions in the personality of G.B.S., inspired by the publication of a collection of Shaw's letters, edited and prologued by Dan H. Laurence.

1087   "Sartre y Camus," 20 de diciembre, 1972; Presencia (La Paz, Bolivia), 30 de diciembre, 1972, p. 10.
    Commenting on Germaine Brée's book, Camus and Sartre, S. compares and contrasts the two French authors-- much to the advantage of Camus.

<u>1973</u>

1088   "El dragón por la cola," 5 de enero, 1973.
A laudatory discussion of the book, The Dragon by
the Tail, by John Paton Davies, Jr. , a former high official
in the U. S. State Department. Davies reveals much of the
diplomacy of the U. S. A. , England, and Russia with one another and with China during the Chinese Civil War which established the reign of Mao.

1089   "La mudable realidad," 20 de enero, 1973.
Commentary on a new preface by Edmund Wilson in
a recent (1972) reprint of his book, To the Finland Station,
originally published in 1940 (later in 1953). Reality "no
está nunca en un punto puerto sino que consiste en millones
de vibraciones magnéticas (digámoslo así) que son constantemente modificadas por hechos nuevos, fenómenos naturales
o artificiales, ideas y voluntades humanas en acción. "

1090   "Dos grandes observadores," 9 de febrero, 1973.
A discussion of Anna Freud and of her famous father.
"Freud y su hija Ana se detuvieron a observar lo aparente-
mente obvio en la conducta humana y hallaron, como suele
suceder, milagros que a todos nos afectan. "

1091   "Indios que sonríen," 23 de febrero, 1973.
Observations on American Indians inspired by the ap-
pearance of a collection of forty-six legends of the Zuni In-
dians (the only Indians S. has seen smile), translated by
Alvina Quam and published by the New Mexico University
Press.

1092   "El aprendiz de brujo," 9 de marzo, 1973.
Commentary on Carlos Castañeda's three best-selling
books: The Lessons of Don Juan; A Yaki Way of Knowledge,
A Separate Reality, and Journey to Ixtlan. Castañeda's books
"han añadido algo notable de veras a la lista de los que
tratan del mundo de nuestro inconsciente. "

1093   "¿Es la religión necesaria?," 23 de marzo, 1973.
A negative review of Andrew M. Greeley's book, The
Persistence of Religion, along with a brief discussion of
Michael Servet, whom S. calls the founder of the Unitarian
Church (and to whom S. is "probablemente pariente por el
lado materno").

1094   "La escalera y Samuel Beckett," 6 de abril, 1973.

A review of Beckett's short narrative, The Lost Ones, in which S. affirms that hope is always available to counter one's deepest despair or, at least, "el amor a la esperanza."

1095   "Cosas de Picasso," 20 de abril, 1973.
Anecdotes and comments about Picasso upon the occasion of his death.

1096   "Otro aspecto de la gran crisis," 8 de mayo, 1973.
Observations on the "crisis" (or polarization of viewpoints) within the Christian churches. "Las mismas dolencias que afectan a la sociedad civil y laica aquejan al mundo de la religión." Writers such as Teilhard de Chardin merely witness the transitional era we are in; they do not lead.

1097   "Picasso, padrino de bautizo," 22 de mayo, 1973.
An anecdotic account of Picasso's friendship with Parisian writers, especially with Max Jacob, the Jewish poet who was baptized a Catholic, and to whom Picasso was padrino.

1098   "Para una sicología del mal," 5 de junio, 1973.
Reflections on Adolph Hitler (whose historical image will remain as "un ejemplo elocuente para ilustrar una sicología del mal"), and on what the Jews may have learned from their experience in Nazi Germany. A short story with the same title (and essential ideological content) appeared later in El Urogallo (123).

1099   "Jugando a los dioses," 19 de junio, 1973.
Commenting on the book, Come, Let Us Play God, by the biologist Leroy Augenstein, S. considers the idea of sterilizing human beings who have defective genes. "Evitar la creación de monstruos parece que debe ser en sí mismo una virtud...."

1100   "Temas de verano," 7 de julio, 1973.
Reflecting on the possibilities science has or may have in the near future--to improve the human race through genetic control (and to give men pleasure through electrodes through activating pleasure centers in the brain) S. concludes that he is content to renounce those possibilities, "inclinándome un poco más por la selección natural que por las ciencias."

1101   "Para saber quienes somos," 24 de julio, 1973.

Half-serious, half-joking comments inspired by Paul
Shepard, a biologist, in his book, The Tender Carnivore
and the Sacred Game.   "Todo es para Shepard cuestión de
cinegética. " S. discusses the schizophrenia, "más o menos,"
of writers and quotes Scripture irresponsibly (out-of-context).

1102   "Confrontación con la doctora Deutsch, " 7 de agosto,
       1973.
Comments inspired by the autobiographical book,
Confrontations with Myself, by Helene Deutsch, the well-
known author of Psychology of Women, and the first director of the Institute of Psychoanalytical Training in Vienna,
founded by Freud.

1103   "Las profecías de Wells, " 23 de agosto, 1973; El
       Diario de Hoy (San Salvador, El Salvador), 9 de
       septiembre, 1973.
Reflections on H. G. Wells as the first to use "la
imaginación creadora" in science fiction and on the prophetic
nature of much of his work.   "Es cierto--como afirma Wells
--que el novelista es el verdadero creador y plasmador y
orientador de las sociedades futuras. "

1104   "Con motivo de Túpac Amaru, " 6 de septiembre,
       1973.
S. defends his novel, Túpac Amaru (39), from the
accusations of an irate reader, and expresses his belief that
within three generations most political boundaries will have
vanished while cultural "nations" or "zonas folklóricas de-
finidas por su historia y sus ciencias y artes" will have in-
creased.

1105   "Paréntesis seudorreligioso, " 20 de septiembre,
       1973; Lectura (México), 205, 1-4 (septiembre-octubre,
       1973), 29-32.
S. deplores "pop" religion (or "charlatanería teoló-
gica" or "seudoteología") represented by a proposed film to
be produced in Copenhagen on "la vida amorosa de Jesucris-
to, " a proposal which he calls "del todo disparatado, " and
again expresses his belief in the existence of Atlantis as the
origin of cultural factors common on both sides of the Atlantic in 1492.

1106   "Un poeta ha muerto, " 9 de octubre, 1973.
       Upon the death of W. H. Auden appreciative commen-
tary upon the poet's life and work.   In his poetry Baltasar
Gracián's description of lyrical emotion finds fulfillment:

"Una ponderación en el vacío que produce un helado deleite."

1107   "Aspirantes a la rehabilitación," 24 de octubre, 1973.
        S. recalls his friendship with two Soviet writers,
Antonof Ovseyenko and Mikhail Koltsov, who were executed
by Stalin (in 1938?) and who were posthumously "rehabilitated" by the Soviet regime in 1956. Russian writers today
who tell the truth may be "aspirantes a la rehabilitación,"
S. suggests.

1108   "El caracol como héroe literario," 9 de noviembre,
        1973; Lectura (México), núm. 206, 1-4 (noviembre-
        diciembre, 1973), 29-32.
        Comments on From the Diary of a Snail, a best-
selling book (in Germany) by the German author Günter
Grass, and memories of Sender's experiences with the Spanish dictator Primo de Rivera.

1109   "Otra vez Nancy Cunard," 22 de noviembre, 1973.
        Comments on the life and work of Nancy Cunard upon
the publication of a collection of writings about the deceased
English heiress by Hugh Ford.

1110   "Con motivo de una novela," 6 de diciembre, 1973.
        Comments on Susan Fromberg's first novel, Falling,
and on the collective moral madness that produced Hitler--
and could produce World War III. "La gran crisis sigue en
pie."

1111   "Riesgos del hablar y el escribir," 20 de diciembre,
        1973.
        S. recalls the secret killing of thousands of Polish
officers by Stalin's forces in Katyn (in the region of Smolen-
sk) in April of 1940, and reflects on the possibility that a
statement of his published in 1933 may have influenced the
Soviet dictator in his anti-Polish attitude.

                            1974

1112   "El terrible Kierkegaard," 10 de enero, 1974.
        Kierkegaard shows us the futility of all philosophy
and every form of metaphysics. "Terrible conclusión en un
alma como la suya, fundamentalmente religiosa," opines S.

1113   "Solzhenitsyn y el terror ruso," 24 de enero, 1974;
        España Libre (New York), 35, 1 (enero-febrero,

1974), 5.

Comments upon the publication in Paris of the Russian author's book, The Gulag Archipelago. Solzhenitsyn is "no solamente un hombre de genio literario, sino un héroe."

1114   "Beckett en un bar japonés," 8 de febrero, 1974.
In a California bar, S. borrows a copy of Beckett's play, Endgame. Later he reads it and finds it lacking the mystery and allegorical force found in Waiting for Godot.

1115   "Caminos nuevos," 22 de febrero, 1974.
Reflections on the new tendencies or directions of the novel in recent decades.

1116   "¿Yevtushenko también?," 7 de marzo, 1974.
S. sees hope in the fact that Yevgeny Yevtushenko, "poeta favorito del régimen," has dared to protest to Leonidas Brezhnev the Soviet Government's treatment of the recently exiled A. Solzhenitsyn.

1117   "La era de la desnudez," 21 de marzo, 1974.
Observations on nudity in today's society. Everybody seems to be interested "por alguna forma de desnudez física, moral, intelectual, política, etc." The Watergate scandals are a form of political nudity.

1118   "El culto de lo irracional," 5 de abril, 1974.
A great problem in today's art is that the artist does not make the effort to illuminate the dark zones of the unconscious but merely accepts the unconscious "como quiere manifestarse cuando y donde le parece bien."

1119   "Otra vez la Atlántida," 18 de abril, 1974.
The similarities in religion, customs, even language, etc., on both sides of the Atlantic are presented in support of Sender's insistent belief in the historical existence (and subsequent sinking into the Atlantic) of Atlantis.

1120   "Discrepancias sobre la Atlántida," 7 de mayo, 1974.
S. defends his thesis that the continent of Atlantis did in fact exist, that it was the focus of world culture, and that about 11,700 years ago it was sunk as a result of a comet's entering the earth's atmosphere. (According to S.,

following Velikovsky, the comet then fixed itself in space as what we know today as the planet Venus.)

1121   "El hombre, la nafta y el cometa, " 21 de mayo, 1974.
        Having read the Chilean writer Miguel Serrano's book, C. G. Jung y Hermann Hesse--Memoria de dos amistades, S. speculates on past catastrophes and the possible destruc- tion of the earth in the near future--perhaps by the cobalt bomb or perhaps by ignition of the earth's oxygen by Halley's comet (around 1986).

1122   "Hemingway por las nubes, " 11 de junio, 1974.
        A review of José Luis Castillo-Puche's book, Hem- ingway in Spain, along with S. 's own opinions of Hemingway, the man and the artist ("un niño grande, " his work lacked lyrical dimensions, he knew Spain only from the angle of a "sensacionalismo truculento, " etc.).

1123   "Las 'chakras' y Jung, " 25 de junio, 1974.
        Miguel Serrano's book, C. G. Jung y Hermann Hesse, is the point of departure for reflections on the possible achievement of human plenitude through the willful activation of one's chakras, psychic centers (or centers of conscious- ness) located along one's spinal cord.

1124   "Misterios del inconsciente, " 9 de julio, 1974.
        Two or three days after his return from Spain, S. dreamed that he talked with the noted histologist Santiago Ramón y Cajal and that Don Santiago had told him, in re- sponse to S. 's inquiry, that he was 121 years of age.   Upon awakening S. verified in the dictionary that Ramón y Cajal would indeed--were he to be living--be that age.   How does one explain this experience?

1125   "Chipre actual y prehistórica, " 23 de julio, 1974.
        Reflections on the importance of bulls in the history of Cyprus, and in the ancient and mythical continent of At- lantis.   "Las fiestas de toros de España ... parecen venir de esa remotísima lejanía [Atlantis]. "   The bull was wor- shipped in the center of Atlantis, in the city which was the capital "de los famosos Campos Eliseos. "

1126   "Bromas pesadas y ligeras, " 6 de agosto, 1974.
        In the journal Andalán, published in Zaragoza, a cri-

tic calls S. 's novel, La tesis de Nancy, "una tontería. "
"Espero que ese crítico áspero y malhumorado se de cuenta,
al final, de que la tontería tiene sus pretensiones de gravedad. Incluso de gravedad transcendente,," replies S.

1127   "Astronautas que escriben," 22 de agosto, 1974;
        Aragón Exprés (Zaragoza), 3 de septiembre, 1974, 3.
        Comments on Carrying the Fire, a book by the Ameri-
can astronaut Michael Collins. The experience of astronauts
"es para todo el mundo la más compleja posible y la más
trascendente," and has awakened in some American astronauts new philosophical and religious perceptions.

1128   "Un pequeño libro sobre un gran tema," 10 de septi-
        embre, 1974.
        Upon the publication of a book by Maxine Asher (no
title given), S. expounds upon one of his favorite theories
(that the mythical--to him historical--continent of Atlantis
[later a large island] "representó una cultura muy superior
a la que conocía el mundo hasta el siglo XIX de nuestra
era), and praises the Ancient Mediterranean Research Association for its continuing investigations concerning Atlantis.

1129   "Escándalos literarios," 19 de septiembre, 1974.
        Comments on Solzhenitsyn's recent demonstration that
the real author of And Quiet Flows the Don for which Sholo-
khov won the Nobel prize was a White Russian officer named
Fyodor Kryukov. Also discusses the deceits practiced by
the "false Tolstoi--Alexis Tolstoi, otro de los autores consa-
grados por Stalin. "

1130   "Un libro póstumo de Maurín," 8 de octubre, 1974.
        In a book published posthumously in Mexico, Joaquín
Maurín, founder and manager until his death of the American
Literary Agency, recalls his ten years in Spanish jails. The
book, whose title is not given here, contains "un excelente
prólogo de Germán Arciniegas. "

1131   "Del país del quetzal," 22 de octubre, 1974.
        Favorable comments on a book which seeks to relate
the Mayans with the Egyptians through the possible existence
of Atlantis, entitled Cuando se rompió el hilo (with the subtitle: La Atlántida y los mayas) and written by the Guate-
malan colonel, J. Enrique Ardón.

1132   "El caos viene de lejos, " 11 de noviembre, 1974.
        Chaos has always existed--even in the Middle Ages

(when in Spain Islamic mosques had "una sección dedicada
amistosamente al culto católico") but today chaotic conditions are--because of modern communications--almost uni-
versally known, and we now know that "si no nos ponemos
todos de acuerdo esta vez, el caos nos va a devorar. "

1133   "Ser o no ser, " 21 de noviembre, 1974.
        People everywhere--including, to S. 's surprise, many
young Spanish priests--are today enfadados, not because of
socio-political problems per se but because they are facing
the prospect of possible annihilation: the ancient problem
"de ser o no ser. "

1134   "Judíos y españoles, " 10 de diciembre, 1974.
        The best qualities of both Jews and Spaniards are
manifested in their individuality.   "El español es, tal vez,
el mejor individuo de Europa, pero como grupo social, y
sobre todo como nación es ya otro cantar. "   S. tells of his
recently having been named Honorary Citizen of Los Angeles
as one indication that a Spaniard "fuera de España y desli-
gado de su nación es alguien. "

1135   "La tontería en las artes, " 19 de diciembre, 1974.
        S. criticizes a new book, Stendhal, by Juana Richard-
son, in which she cites a letter from Stendhal in which he
wrote that he considered The Charterhouse of Parma "una
tontería. "   Such a statement by authors is an indication of
"modestia y de sentido crítico--más o menos humorístico--
que merece respeto e incluso admiración. "   To repeat it
"como un opinión propia representa impertinencia y también
carencia del sentido de los valores. "

Part 2

WORKS ABOUT SENDER

V. BOOKS
(including reviews of them)

1136   Rivas, Josefa, El escritor y su senda; Estudio crítico-
literario sobre Ramón J. Sender. Segunda edición.
México: Mexicanos Unidos, 1967, 340 p.
A revision of a doctoral thesis (1344) at the University of Valencia (June, 1964), directed by Francisco Sánchez-
Castañer; this first published version is, therefore, called
the second edition by Mexicanos Unidos. Critical analyses
of ten novels and two books of short stories. There are
errors in a biographical chapter ("Biografía de Ramón J.
Sender a través de su obra"). The chapter on S.'s style,
"Estilo de Sender," is an original and valuable study. Bibliographical references are few and sometimes faulty.

Marra-López, José R. Insula, núm. 253 (diciembre,
1967), p. 8.
Tovar, Antonio. La Gaceta Ilustrada (Madrid), enero,
1968, p. 9, 13.

Comunidad Ibérica (México), enero-febrero, 1968,
p. 52-53 (By S.G.).

King, Charles L. Hispania, 51, 4 (December, 1968),
p. 925-26.

1137   Carrasquer, Francisco. "Imán" y la novela histórica
de Ramón J. Sender. (Primera incursión en el
"realismo mágico" senderiano). Amsterdam: University of Amsterdam, 1968, 294 p.; "Prólogo de
Sender," "Imán" y la novela histórica de Sender.
London: Tamesis Books, 1970, 302 p.
A detailed stylistic study of Imán in one long chapter

221

and critical analyses of all historical novels published by
mid-1968: Mr. Witt en el cantón, Bizancio, Los Tontos de
Concepción, Carolus Rex, La aventura equinoccial de Lope
de Aguirre, Tres novelas teresianas, and Las criaturas saturnianas. In the Prologue to the second edition S. expresses
his concept of the historical novel, and discusses "magic
realism" (97).

Mainer, José-Carlos. Insula, núm. 277 (diciembre,
1969), p. 19.
Rivas, Josefa. Hispania, 56, 2 (May, 1973), p. 504.

King, Charles L. Hispania, 53, 1 (March, 1970), p. 151.
(March, 1973), p. 491-95.
Rivas, Josefa. Hispania, 56, 2 (May, 1973), p. 504.

1138   Peñuelas, Marcelino C. Conversaciones con R. J.
Sender. Madrid: Magisterio Español, 1970, 291 p.
(Col. Novelas y Cuentos; Sección Cultura; Serie Entre-
vistas).
Tape-recorded conversations that Professor Peñuelas
(of the University of Washington) had with S. concerning his
own literary work as well as the literary world in general
are here reproduced in print. Illuminating insights into S.
and his work by both the novelist and his interrogator, Professor Peñuelas. An invaluable book for incipient Senderian
scholars.

Mainer, José-Carlos. Insula, núm. 281 (abril, 1970),
p. 8-9.
Montón Puerto, Pedro. Amanecer (Zaragoza), 6 de
abril, 1972, p. 13.

King, Charles L. Hispania, 54, 3 (September, 1971),
p. 601.

1139   Peñuelas, Marcelino C. La obra narrativa de Ramón
J. Sender. Carta Prólogo de Ramón J. Sender.
Madrid: Gredos, 1971, 294 p. (Biblioteca Románica
Hispánica. II. Estudios y Ensayos, 153).
In addition to penetrating analyses of Imán, El verdu-
go afable, Réquiem por un campesino español, and La
esfera, this book provides a solid understanding of S. as a
man and as a literary artist. Prologue (98).

King, Charles L. Hispania, 56, 2 (May, 1973),
p. 504-05.

1140   King, Charles L. Ramón J. Sender. New York:
        Twayne, 1974, 196 p. (Twayne's World Authors
        Series, 307).
        An analytical-critical study of S. 's literary work with
special attention (one chapter each) given to two novels, The
Sphere and The King and the Queen, with an emphasis on
their philosophical-religious dimensions.   Includes a biographical chapter, and brief critical examinations of all S. 's
novels published through 1971, a chapter entitled, "Other
Genres, " in which brief sketches of S. 's non-narrative books
are given, and a Selective Bibliography.

        Mendicutt, Eduardo. La Estafeta Literaria, núm.
        557 (1 de febrero, 1976), p. 1991-92.

        Olstad, Charles F. Books Abroad, 49, 2 (Spring
        1975), p. 295.
        Kurfehs Navarro, Judith. Modern Fiction Studies, 21,
        2 (Summer 1975), p. 316-22.
        Peñuelas, Marcelino C. The Modern Language Jour-
        nal, 59, 5-6 (Sept. -Oct. , 1975), p. 308.

        Choice, 11, 12 (February 1975), p. 17.

(Part 2, cont.)

VI. SPECIAL ISSUE OF A JOURNAL

1141   Norte (Amsterdam), año XIV, núms. 2-4, marzo-
agosto, 1973.
Entire issue devoted to S. A drawing of S. on the
cover. Index: "Presentación" by Francisco Carrasquer,
"En un futuro próximo" by S. , "El gitano como entidad
frénetica, " by S. (first chapter of Nancy, doctora en gitanería, 41), "Sobre la narrativa del primer Sender, " by
Víctor Fuentes (1292), "La crítica a rajatabla de Víctor
Fuentes, " by Francisco Carrasquer (1293) (a reaction-article
to the one by Fuentes in this issue), "Vuelta a La Esfera de
Sender, " by Julian Palley (1295), a Spanish version of Palley's article in English by the same title (1285), "La parábola de La Esfera y la vocación de intelectual de Sender, "
by Francisco Carrasquer (1294), and a 'Nota bibliográfica. "

(Part 2, cont.)

VII. CONTRIBUTIONS IN BOOKS

1142 Valle-Inclán, Ramón del. "Prólogo" to Ramón J.
Sender, El problema religioso en Méjico, 1928 (57).
Introduction of S. as a young journalist with special
knowledge of the subject matter of his first book.

1143 Enciclopedia universal ilustrada. Madrid: Espasa-
Calpe, 1933. "Sender," Apéndice 9, 1230-31.
Bio-bibliographical data. Cites a review of Imán by
Luis Bello.

1144 Castán Palomar, F. , ed. Aragoneses contemporáneos.
Diccionario biográfico. Zaragoza: Herreim, 1934,
496-98.

1145 Mitchell, Peter Chalmers. "Translator's Introductory
Note," in Ramón J. Sender, Seven Red Sundays, 1936,
9 (4).
Brief comments on S. as a man and as a novelist.

1146 Hall, Florence. "Introduction" to textbook ed. of
S. 's Crónica del alba. New York: Appleton-Century-
Crofts, 1946, v-viii (11).
A laudatory introduction to S. (with quotations from
other critics), designed for college students, written by the
author's wife, Florence Hall Sender.

1147 Kunitz, Stanley J. , and Howard Haycraft, eds.
Twentieth Century Authors; A Biographical Dictionary
of Modern Literature. New York: H. W. Wilson,
1942, 1262-63. First Supplement, edited by Stanley
J. Kunitz, 1955, 892-93.
Bio-bibliographical information. The 1955 edition up-

225

dates and corrects information from the 1942 edition.

1148   Mann, Klaus, and Hermann Kesten, eds. Heart of
        Europe. New York: L. B. Fischer, 1943, 958.
        The Best in Modern European Literature, Philadelphia:
        Blakiston, 1945, 958.
        Brief bio-critical material.

1149   Adams, Nicholson B. The Heritage of Spain. New
        York: Holt and Co., 1943, 281-82. Rev. ed., 1959,
        297-98.
        Bio-bibliographical-critical material. For Spanish
translation see 1152.

1150   Aub, Max. Discurso de la novela española contempo-
        ránea. México: Colegio de México, 1945, 103-04.
        (Jornadas, 50.)
        Half a page of adverse judgment of Sender's work.

1151   Hall, Florence. "Preface" (p. v-vii) and "Introduc-
        tion" to schooltext ed. of Sender's Crónica del alba.
        New York: Appleton-Century-Crofts, 1946, 11-21 (11).
        Bio-bibliographical material (English text).

1152   Adams, Nicholson B. España: Introducción a su
        civilización. New York: Holt and Co., 1947, 314-
        15.
        Attributes to S. a poetic sense united with an acute
sense of reality, and a vigorous and direct style. Spanish
translation of 1149.

1153   Fichter, William L. "Ramón José Sender" in Colum-
        bia Dictionary of Modern European Literature, ed. by
        Horatio Smith. New York: Columbia University
        Press, 1947, 738-39.
        Bio-critical-bibliographical information (some errone-
ous).

1154   Barea, Arturo. Introduction to Ramón J. Sender,
        Dark Wedding, 1948 (see 10, London edition).

1155   Del Río, Angel. Historia de la literatura española,
        tomo II. New York: Dryden Press, 1948, 265.
        A brief critical review of Sender's work.

1156   Amo, Julián, y Shelby, Charmion. La obra impresa
        de los intelectuales españoles en América, 1936-1945.

Stanford, Calif.: Stanford Univ. Press, 1950, 114-15.
A biographical note and a list of S.'s books published in America, 1936-1945.

1157   Chabás, Juan. Literatura española contemporánea, 1898-1950. La Habana: Cultural, 1952, 576-77.
Although attributing important values to S.'s novels, Chabás finds in them a lack of "íntima autenticidad."

1158   Pérez Minik, D. Novelistas españoles de los siglos XIX y XX. Madrid: Guadarrama, 1957, 302-06.
S. is "el novelista más importante de España situado entre las generaciones de la Dictadura y la actual." Includes a study of El rey y la reina which P.M. sees as having "un valor extraordinario, por su misterio, su calidad y su personal concepción." Notable as the first book in Spain to give serious attention to S. since the Civil War.

1159   Sainz de Robles, Federico Carlos. La novela española en el siglo XX. Madrid: Pegaso, 1957, 204-05.
A bio-critical review.

1160   Palacín Iglesias, Gregorio B. Historia de la literatura española, 2a ed., corregida y aumentada.
Mexico: "La Impresora Azteca," 1958, 502.
A bio-bibliographical note.

1161   Martínez, Carlos. Crónica de una emigración (la de los republicanos españoles en 1939). México: Libro Mex, 1959, 211-14 y 283-84.
Brief reviews of Hipogrifo violento and Mosén Millán. Some attention to El rey y la reina, Epitalamio del prieto Trinidad, Mexicayotl, and Unamuno, Baroja, Valle-Inclán y Santayana.

1162   Benardete, Mair José. "Ramón Sender, Chronicler and Dreamer of a New Spain," in Ramón J. Sender, Réquiem por un campesino español, bilingual ed. of 1960, VI-XXIX (15).
Sees S. as an excellent chronicler more than a novelist; the term "chronicler," as he explains, is not to be understood as being less than a novelist but as one who has lived and chronicled our epoch. Bio-bibliographical-critical material, followed by a discussion of (a) the iberismo vital of S., (b) "Spain and the Interpretation of Catholicism and Death in Sender," and (c) the work, Réquiem itself (9 p.).

For Spanish version see 1163.

1163   Benardete, Mair José.   "Ramón Sender, crónista y
       soñador de una España nueva"; tr. from English by
       Ida Martínez; in Réquiem por un campesino español,
       Argentine ed., 1961, 1966, 1969, 1973 (15), 79-109
       (in the ed. of 1969, the 4th ed. by Proyección).
       Also in Réquiem para un campesino español (México:
       Mexicanos Unidos, 1968, 1970, 1972, 1974), 97-122
       (15).
       Spanish text of "Ramón Sender, Chronicler and
Dreamer of a New Spain." See 1162.

1164   Chandler, R. E., and Kessel Schwartz.   A New His-
       tory of Spanish Literature.   Baton Rouge: Louisiana
       State University Press, 1961, 251-55.
       Bio-bibliographical and critical material.

1165   Eoff, Sherman H.   The Modern Spanish Novel.   New
       York: New York University Press, 1961, 213-54.
       A superb analysis of the philosophical implications of
The Sphere (12) and A Man's Place (8).

1166   Alborg, Juan Luis.   Hora actual de la novela española,
       tomo II.   Madrid: Taurus, 1962, 26-73.
       After a brief discussion of S.'s "irreductible indivi-
dualismo," and his status as an "escritor comprometido,"
Alborg reviews the following books: Imán, La noche de las
cien cabezas, Viaje a la aldea del crimen, Mr. Witt en el
cantón, El verdugo afable, Los cinco libros de Ariadna, El
rey y la reina, Mosén Millán, El lugar de un hombre, Epitalamio del prieto Trinidad, La esfera, Los laureles de
Anselmo, Crónica del alba (I), Bizancio, and La llave.

1167   García López, José.   Historia de la literatura espa-
       ñola, 7a ed., ampliada.   Barcelona: Vicens-Vives,
       1962, 670-71.
       Succinct criticism in which S. is considered "sin
disputa como el más importante de los novelistas españoles
que residen en el extranjero y aun tal vez la figura cumbre
de nuestra novela actual."

1168   Nora, Eugenio G. de.   La novela española contempo-
       ránea, tomo II, partes 1 y 2.   Madrid: Editorial
       Gredos, 1962; parte 1, 282-85; parte 2, 35-48 (Bibli-
       oteca Románica Hispánica, II. Estudios y Ensayos,
       41).

In part 1 S. is placed at the head of Spanish novelists "de tendencia social de la preguerra." In part 2 Nora finds S.'s esthetic route to be in "el análisis psicológico-moral del 'hombre-eterno' a través de circunstancias sociales o anécdotas conretas, perfiladas con un arte matizadamente realista." Brief reviews of Imán, Siete domingos rojos, Mr. Witt, Epitalamio, El rey y la reina, and Volume I of Crónica del alba.

1169   Marra-López, José R. Narrativa española fuera de España--1939-1961. Madrid: Guadarrama, 1963, 341-409.
        This book and those by Nora (1168), Pérez Minik (1158) and Alborg (1166) were most important in awakening interest in S. after decades of almost total silence (in Spain) about the exiled novelist. Marra-López devotes four chapters to S.: "Aparición de un escritor," "El exilio," "El narrador en el exilio," and "Colofón." He finds S. difficult to classify; his advance has been "en rápidos y cambiantes zigzags" jumping from one genre to another, from one theme to its opposite.

1170   West, Paul. The Modern Novel. London: Hutchinson, 1963, 416-17 and passim.
        Briefly traces Sender's evolution as a novelist from Imán (1930) to Crónica del alba (1942).

1171   Diccionario de literatura española, dirigida por Germán Bleiberg y Julián Marías, 3a ed., corregida y aumentada. Madrid: Revista de Occidente, 1964, 733-34; 4a ed., corregida y aumentada, 1972, 837. (The 1964 ed. has 1036 pages; the 1972 ed., 1280.)
        The first and second editions do not list S. at all. The brief bio-bibliographical information in the third edition was updated for the 1972 edition. Contains factual errors-- year and place of birth, for example, are wrong as well as the statement that "casi todos sus libros están traducidos al inglés."

1172   Duncan, Robert M. "Introducción" in textbook ed. of Sender's short novel, Mosén Millán. Boston: D. C. Heath, 1964, 5-7. (See 15.)
        In a brief introduction containing bio-bibliographical information on S., Duncan seeks to root the Aragonese author firmly in the Spanish literary soil.

1173   Hall, Florence. "Preface" to Ramón J. Sender,

textbook ed. of Jubileo en el Zócalo. New York:
Appleton-Century-Crofts, 1964, v-vi (54).
  Advice to the student as to how to use the book, its
purpose, explanation of its structure and of its subtitle ("retablo conmemorativo"), and brief comments on S. as a writer.

1174   Torrente Ballester, Gonzalo. Panorama de la litera-
        tura española contemporánea, 3a ed. Madrid:
        Guadarrama, 1965, 428-29 (Col. "Panoramas").
        A brief bio-critical review--some biographical errors.

1175   Marín, Diego and Angel Del Río. Breve Historia de
        la literatura española. New York: Holt, Rinehart
        and Winston, 1966, 320-22.
        A critical analysis of Sender's novelistic production.
"En general, la opinión crítica le considera hoy como el
novelista más importante de los que viven fuera de España,
por su capacidad inventiva, dotes de observactión minuciosa,
habilidad narrativa y hondo interés en el destino del hombre"
(p. 320).

1176   Devlin, John. Spanish Anticlericalism: A Study in
        Modern Alienation. New York: Las Americas, 1966,
        168-83.
        Discusses Sender's anticlericalism, defined strictly
as such, as well as his deeper rebellion against institution-
alized religion, a struggle, in Devlin's opinion, with the God
whom the Aragonese author cannot escape.

1177   Laforet, Carmen. "Presentación," in Ramón J.
        Sender, La aventura equinoccial de Lope de Aguirre,
        1967, 1968, 1970 (29), 7-16.
        Calls S. "Posiblemente el más grande, original, sin-
cero y potente creador de nuestra literatura española actual.... Su riqueza abruma." Includes a discussion (4 pages)
of the novel being introduced, "una novela extraordinaria."

1178   Benedetti, Mario. Sobre artes y oficios (ensayo).
        Montevideo: Alfa, 1968, 161-68.
        In a short chapter, "Una imagen y tres relatos de
Ramón Sender," Benedetti relates the "imagen" he received
of S. during a short visit with him in Albuquerque, New
Mexico, followed by an appreciative critical-analysis of the
three stories in the collection of short stories, La llave,
as published in Montevideo in 1960 (see 46). Benedetti's
"imagen" of S. as a professor is quite humorous. "Al parecer, cuando algún alumno de Sender osaba balbucear una

opinión que no coincidía con el planteo enunciado por el profesor, éste pasaba directamente de la literatura al frenesí, y siempre cabía la posibilidad de que el incidente terminara con la expulsión del muchacho o la muy audible emisión de un castizo improperio" (p. 161).

1179   Schwartz, Kessel. "Animal Symbolism in the Fiction of Ramón Sender," in The Meaning of Existence in Contemporary Hispanic Literature, ed. by Kessel Schwartz. Coral Gables: University of Miami Press, 1969, 99-111.
    A reprinting of an article by the same title (Hispania, 46, 3 [September, 1963], 496-505). (See 1233.)

1180   Bosch, Rafael. La novela española del siglo XX, tomo I. New York: Las Américas, 1970, 41, 42. Passing references to S. on pages 41 and 42.

1181   Bosch, Rafael. La novela española del siglo XX, tomo II. New York: Las Americas, 1970.
    Numerous references to S. (p. 41 to 332) with five chapters devoted exclusively to S.: "El lugar de 'Imán' en la novela contemporánea" (p. 251-57), "La 'species poética en 'Imán,' de Sender" (p. 259-66, reprinted from Hispanófila, núm. 14, enero de 1962. See 1230), " 'El viaje a la aldea del crimen,' de Sender" (p. 267-74), " 'El lugar de un hombre' y la novela filosófica" (p. 291-98), and "El planteamiento de 'El verdugo afable' " (p. 299-307). Bosch calls Viaje "la crucial contribución de S. a la fundación de la novela-reportaje española" (p. 269), and finds that it marks "el punto de giro de S. hacia una prosa más sencilla y directa, y sobre todo de emoción más reprimida y menos llena de comentarios del autor que sus obras anteriores. "

1182   Iglesias Laguna, Antonio. Treinta años de novela española, 1938-1968, Vol. I, 2a ed. Madrid: Prensa Española, 1970.
    Makes passing references intermittently to S. throughout the book (37 times, pages 12 to 348), but never focuses discussion on the Aragonese novelist.

1183   Naval, Eduardo. "Prólogo" in Ramón J. Sender, El verdugo afable. México: Aguilar, 1970, 9-12 (14).
    A concise, appreciative introductory analysis of El verdugo afable. "Para construir la vida de Ramiro [el verdugo] acude [S.], por una parte a la fantasía, y, por otra, a su autobiografía, uniéndolas de tal forma que cobran un nuevo valor, puramente literario. "

1184   Sobejano, Gonzalo. Novela española de nuestro
        tiempo. Madrid: Prensa Española, 1970, 479 p.

1185   Díaz-Plaja, Guillermo. Cien libros españoles (Poesía
        y novela, 1968-1970). Salamanca: Anaya, 1971, 351-
        55.
            An intelligent discussion of En la vida de Ignacio
Morel. Díaz-Plaja finds "una constante bastante habitual en
la prosa narrativa de S., que oscila constantemente, como
un sismógrafo, entre puntas de elevación poética y descensos
a una realidad absolutamente vulgar. En este sentido, S.
es un escritor de sorprendente irregularidad, o si queréis,
de una voluntaria oscilación temática. "

1186   Elliott, George P. "Two Good Novels and an Over-
        sized God, " Conversions. New York: Dutton, 1971,
        28-36.
            Elliott praises S. 's novel, A Man's Place, and Jean
Giono's The Horseman on the Roof as "minor masterpieces,
in the range with such esteemed works as Fitzgerald's The
Great Gatsby, Gide's Strait is the Gate, Mann's Felix Krull,
or Greene's The Labyrinthine Ways, " and attributes their
relative obscurity to the fact that both S. and Giono are
honest authors who "did not do homage to the great god
Zeitgeist. Not only did they neglect honoring him; they did
not even set out to flout him--flouting, after all, is an ad-
mission of importence. " A provocative and important essay.

1187   King, Charles L. "Ramón J. Sender, " in Encyclo-
        pedia of World Literature in the Twentieth Century,
        Vol. III (O-Z). Wolfgang B. Fleischmann, General
        Editor. New York: Frederick Ungar, 1971, 257-58.
        Biobibliographical material, with some critical com-
ments. Sender's birthdate is inaccurately reported.

1188   Naval, Eduardo. "Prólogo" in Ramón J. Sender,
        Examen de ingenios; los noventayochos (ensayos
        críticos). México: Aguilar, 1971, 9-14 (65).
            Praises the book as a valuable contribution to the
study of the Generation of 1898--despite certain shortcomings
or defects which are freely recognized by Naval.

1189   Ponce de Leon, José Luis S. La novela española de
        la guerra civil (1936-1939). Madrid: Insula, 1971,
        62-68 and passim on 31 other pages.
            An enlarged and revised edition of Ponce de León's
doctoral thesis (1345). Gives most attention to Los cinco

libros de Ariadna with some references to Contraataque en España, Crónica del alba, and Réquiem por un campesino español.

1190 Iglesias Laguna, Antonio. Literatura de España día a día (1970-1971). Madrid: Editora Nacional, 1972, 12, 13, 54, 69, 73-78, 145-50, 169-73, 406, 407.
Much attention is given to S., especially to En la vida de Ignacio Morel (p. 73-78), Carolus Rex (p. 145-50), and Zu (p. 169-73), the first and third of these being reprints of review-articles in La Estafeta Literaria (March 1, 1970 and March 15, 1971, respectively), and the second a reprint from an article in ABC of Madrid (August 19, 1971).

1191 Peñuelas, Marcelino C. "Al lector" in Páginas escogidas. Madrid: Gredos, 1972, 7-8. (See 73.)
Peñuelas explains that he chose the selections in the book from those which had made the greatest impact upon his memory and sensibility.

1192 Sanz Villanueva, Santos. Tendencias de la novela española actual (1950-1970). Madrid: Cuadernos para el Diálogo, 1972, 25, 38, 40, 46, 55, 103-108, 118, 241.
Tries to show that S. "y el gallego Alvaro Cunqueiro son los más representativos de esta tendencia [realismo mágico]." Divides S.'s work into two main groups: those with "ambientación histórica," and those with an intellectual orientation, "obras intelectuales."

1193 Tovar, Antonio. Novela española e hispanoamericana. Madrid-Barcelona: Alfaguara, 1972, 11-27.
In a chapter, "La vuelta de Sender," Tovar reprints reviews of Las criaturas saturnianas, Tres novelas teresianas, En la vida de Ignacio Morel, Crónica del alba, and Nocturno de los 14, with the dates of their appearances in La Gaceta Ilustrada. An important contribution to Senderian criticism.

1194 Domingo, José. La novela española del siglo XX, tomo 2. Barcelona: Labor, 1973, 71-73, 75, 77, 104, 113, 149, 155.
A critical paragraph or two on each of the following: Contraataque, Epitalamio del prieto Trinidad, El rey y la reina, Réquiem por un campesino español (Mosén Millán), Los cinco libros de Ariadna, and Crónica del alba, with bibliographical notes on several other novels. Incorrectly

reports that S. was born in 1902.

1195   Martínez Cachero, J. M.   La novela española entre
       1939 y 1969.   Madrid: Castalia, 1973, 11, 17, 18,
       28, 61, 225, 229, 248, 258.
       Passing references to S. on the pages indicated above.
On p. 18 mistakenly reports that S. was awarded the National Prize for Literature in 1937 for Contraataque.

1196   Gogorza Fletcher, Madeleine de.   The Spanish His-
       torical Novel 1870-1970 (A Study of Ten Spanish
       Novelists, and Their Treatment of the "Episodios
       Nacionales").   London: Tamesis Books, 1974, p.
       107-28 and 169-72 (Col. Támesis.   Serie A--Mono-
       grafías, 32).
       Most of this book was formerly an unpublished doc-
toral thesis at Harvard University.   The author devotes a
chapter each to Galdós, Baroja, Unamuno, Valle-Inclán, and
Sender.   Her treatment of S. (p. 107-28) is divided into
three sections: "Novels Written Prior to the Civil War" (in
which she deals primarily with Mr. Witt en el cantón),
"Post-Civil-War Novels" (Bizancio, Los cinco libros de
Ariadna), and "Novels of the Distant Past" (Carolus Rex,
Los Tontos de la Concepción, La aventura equinoccial de
Lope de Aguirre, and Tres novelas teresianas).   A short
bibliography and "Background Material on Specific Works"
(Bizancio, Carolus Rex, La aventura equinoccial de Lope de
Aguirre, and Los Tontos de la Concepción) are included on
pages 169-72.

(Part 2, cont.)

VIII.   CONTRIBUTIONS IN PERIODICALS

A.   BIBLIOGRAPHIES

1197   Domenicali, Dena.   "A Bibliography of the Works by
        and about Ramón José Sender in the English Language, "
        Bulletin of Bibliography, 20, 3 (September-December,
        1950), 60-63; and 20, 4 (January-April, 1951), 93.
        Quite complete through 1949.   Has helpful annotations.
The bibliography was limited to English at S. 's suggestion.

1198   King, Charles L.   "Una bibliografía senderiana
        española (1928-1967), " Hispania, 50, membership
        issue (October, 1967), 629-45.
        Annotated.   Includes only material (including reviews)
published in Spanish.   Incomplete but a good beginning.

1199   King, Charles L.   "A Senderian Bibliography in Eng-
        lish, 1950-1968, with an Addendum, " The American
        Book Collector, 20, 6 (March-April, 1970), 23-29.
        Continues annotated bibliography where Domenicali
(1197) stopped.   Addendum lists reviews in English of books
in Spanish.

1200   Espadas, Elizabeth.   "Ensayo de una bibliografía
        sobre la obra de Ramón J. Sender, " Parte I en
        Papeles de Son Armadans, año 19, tomo 74, núm.
        220 (julio, 1974), 89-104; y Parte II en año 19, tomo
        74, núms. 221-222 (agosto-septiembre, 1974), 231-
        62.
        Part I consists of "Estudios sobre su obra en gene-
ral" listed in alphabetical order, with brief annotations in
some cases.   Part II, "Estudios sobre obras individuales, "
lists criticism (reviews for the most part but some articles
and material in books are included) of most of S. 's books.

Building on the bibliographies of Domenicali (1197) and King
(1198, 1199) Espadas has occasionally included reviews in
German, French, and Italian. Bibliography includes only
secondary sources, i. e. , works about S.

B. CRITICAL ARTICLES, ESSAYS, AND ABSTRACTS

1201   Prats y Beltrán, Alardo. "Actualidad literaria,"
        La Libertad, núm. 3223 (17 de julio, 1930), 4 (s. n.
        impresa).
        Includes interesting comments on Imán (1).

1202   Cansinos Assens, R. "Crítica literaria," La Liber-
        tad, núm. 3583 (13 de septiembre, 1931), 9.
        A four-column article in which S. , among others, is
discussed. Esteems S. highly.

1203   Cansinos Assens, R. "Ramón J. Sender y la novela
        social, I," La Libertad, núm. 3992 (4 de enero,
        1933), 8.
        The first of a series of six articles in La Libertad
on S. --the first two serving as a general introduction to the
young Aragonese author and the last four as a laudatory review of Siete domingos rojos. Bio-bibliographical information. "Ramón J. Sender es el nuevo gran escritor que ha
venido a animar nuestra Literatura. De la postguerra acá
... él ha sido la única revelación. "

1204   Cansinos Assens, R. "Ramón J. Sender y la novela
        social, II," La Libertad, núm. 3996 (8 de enero,
        1933), 9.
        Part II of a series of six articles on S. and the so-
cial novel. Discusses briefly other writers of social novels
of the time: Joaquín Arderíus (Los campesinos, 1931),
César Arconada (La turbina), and Rosa Arciniegas, the
Spanish-American author of Dinamos, followed by a brief
consideration of Imán and O. P. by S.

1205   Cansinos Assens, R. "Ramón J. Sender y la novela
        social--'Siete domingos rojos' (1932). --Figuras repre-
        sentativas, Star García y Lucas Samar, III," La
        Libertad, núm. 4005 (19 de enero, 1933), 9.
        Discusses Star García and Lucas Samar, who with
Amparo García, are representative characters in Siete

domingos rojos. Each one "marca un aspecto del complejo
social." Third article in a series of six on S. and the social novel.

1206   Cansinos Assens, R.   "Ramón J. Sender y la novela
       social. --'Siete domingos rojos' (1932). --La dulce y
       brava figura de Amparo, IV," La Libertad, núm.
       4010 (25 de enero, 1933), 8.
       An analysis of Amparo in whom the conflict between
her bourgeois upbringing and her love for Samar, a revolutionary, eventually leads to her suicide.

1207   Cansinos Assens, R.   "Ramón J. Sender y la novela
       social. --'Siete domingos rojos' (1932). --Inducción de
       una filosofía," La Libertad, núm. 4015 (31 de enero,
       1933), 8.
       Siete domingos rojos is "tan sólo--y en ello estriban
su fuerza y su interés--un trozo de vida contemporánea. "
The rebellion of the masses requires new forms of artistic
expression; the norms of yesterday will not serve.   "La
novelística moderna ha nacido del periodismo, así como la
antigua había nacido de la Mitología.   La novela de S. es
un reportaje elevado a la categoría épica. "

1208   Cansinos Assens, R.   "Ramón J. Sender y la novela
       social. --'Siete domingos rojos' (1932). --Apreciación
       literaria," La Libertad, núm. 4023 (9 de febrero,
       1933), 10.
       The last in a series of six articles on S.   They--or
at least five of them--were reprinted together in a pamphlet
no longer accessible or existent.
       The well-known critic finds in S. 's novel a masterly
expression of the new art, totally in tune with the times.
"Gran novela, que difícilmente encontrará su igual en las
que este año se publiquen. "

1209   "Where We Stand," International Literature, No. 5
       (1934).
       The editors of IL ask three questions, which are
answered by S. , Arconada, Serrano Plaja, and others:
(1) What influence has the October Revolution had upon your
work?, (2) What is your opinion of Soviet literature?, and
(3) What problems interest you most at this time?

1210   Kelyin, W.   "Literary Spain," tr. from the Russian
       by S. D. Kogan, International Literature, No. 6
       (December, 1934), 93.

Condemns "reactionary" writers such as Unamuno,
Ortega y Gasset, Gómez de la Serna, and praises revolu-
tionaries such as S. , Rafael Alberti, and others. Calls S.
"an apostate from the bourgeoisie. "

1211   Time, vol. 32 (November 7, 1938), 59-60.
        In a review of André Malraux's book about the Spanish
Civil War, L'Espoir (Man's Hope) S. is said to be the inspiration for Manuel in the book. In a personal letter to the
bibliographer, S. denies the resemblance between him and
Manuel. Portrait of S.

1212   Lord, David. "This Man Sender," Books Abroad, 14,
        4 (Autumn 1940), 352-54.
        Perceptive and appreciative insights into S. as a man.

1213   Scholastic, 43 (December 6, 1943), 20.
        A biographical note.

1214   News Letter of Phi Sigma Iota Romance Language
        Honor Society, 20 (November 15, 1948), 1 +.
        Bio-bibliographical-critical material.

1215   News Letter of Phi Sigma Iota Romance Language
        Honor Society, 21, 2 (April 15, 1950), 7.
        Brief survey of S. 's literary work.

1216   Penn, Dorothy, "Ramón J. Sender," Hispania, 34,
        1 (February, 1951), 79-84.
        Critical evaluation of five novels: Orden Público,
El lugar del hombre, Crónica del alba, El rey y la reina,
and Epitalamio del prieto Trinidad.

1217   Ornstein, Jacob. "The Literary Evolution of Ramón
        Sender," The Modern Language Forum, 36, 1-2
        (March-June, 1951), 33-40.
        Finds a shift in emphasis from the socio-political in
S. 's pre-war novels to a more philosophical-symbolical-
lyrical approach in his post-Civil War works.

1218   King, Charles L. "Sender: Aragonese in New
        Mexico," The Modern Language Journal, 36, 5 (May,
        1952), 242-44.
        Discusses S. as a man and as a teacher. Biographic,
bibliographic, and critical material.

1219   King, Charles L. Abstract of Ph. D. thesis, "An

Exposition of the Synthetic Philosophy of Ramón J.
Sender," Abstracts of Dissertations, 1953. Los
Angeles: University of Southern California Press,
1953, 57-60. Thesis dated June, 1953.
See thesis (1340).

1220   King, Charles L. "Sender's 'Spherical' Philosophy,"
        Publications of the Modern Language Association, 69,
        5 (December, 1954), 993-99.
        A discussion of the philosophical and religious content
of The Sphere (12).

1221   "Between Reality and Dream," The Times Literary
        Supplement (London), April 3, 1959, 185-86. (Anony-
        mous author.)
        Though primarily a review of Before Noon (the Eng-
lish translation of Volume I of the Crónica del alba series)
this article relates the book to Sender's other works, and
seeks to give a total evaluation of S. as an author, calling
him "the most interesting and--in the true, unhackneyed
sense--most important Spanish prose writer alive."

1222   Rodríguez Monegal, Emir.   "Sender," Marcha (Monte-
        video), 30 de abril, 1959.

1223   Fasel, Oscar A.   "Reminiscence and Interpretation;
        An Evaluation of Ramón J. Sender's Essay: 'Unamuno,
        Sombra Fingida'," Hispania, 42, 2 (May, 1959), 161-
        69.
        Attacks the views on Unamuno expressed by S. in his
book of Essays: Unamuno, Valle-Inclán, Baroja y Santayana
(64).

1224   Milla, Benito.   "Ramón J. Sender; un novelista
        español en el destierro," Deslinde (Montevideo), 12
        (septiembre, 1959), 8-9. (Deslinde suspended publi-
        cation with its number 16, June, 1961.)
        Bio-bibliographical data and a rather long criticism
of Los cinco libros de Ariadna, which Milla calls a "crónica
emocional" of the Spanish Civil War.

1225   Milla, Benito.   "Ramón J. Sender," España Libre
        (New York), 22, 6 (18 de marzo, 1960), 1.
        A well-informed bio-bibliographical sketch. S. "tal
vez fue el escritor más comprometido y militante de su pro-
moción." The first commentator to state (correctly) that S.
was born in Chalamera del Cinca, not in Alcolea de Cinca,

and to give his full baptismal name: Ramón José Blas Antonio.

1226   Adam, Carole. "The Re-Use of Identical Plot Material in Some of the Novels of Ramón José Sender,"
       Hispania, 43, 3 (September, 1960), 347-52.
       A critical analysis of the re-use of material in S.'s
novels, especially in El verdugo afable (14).

1227   Olstad, Charles. Abstract of Ph. D. thesis, "The
       Novels of Ramón Sender: Moral Concepts in Development," Dissertation Abstracts, 21, 6 (Wisconsin,
       1960), 1570.
       See thesis (1341).

1228   Maslow, Vera. "Baroja's Realism According to
       Ramón Sender," La Voz (New York), 5, 5 (February,
       1961), 4-5.

1229   Palley, Julian, "Existentialist Trends in the Modern
       Spanish Novel," Hispania, 44, 1 (March, 1961), 21-
       26.
       Existentialist themes in S.'s novels are discussed on
pages 23-24.

1230   Bosch, Rafael. "La 'Species Poetica' en 'Imán,' de
       Sender," Hispanófila, núm. 14 (enero, 1962), 33-39.
       A valuable study of the poetic dimensions in S.'s
first novel.   Reprinted in Volume II of Bosch's La novela
española del siglo XX, tomo II (1181).

1231   Jassey, William. Abstract of Ed. D. thesis, "A
       Handbook for Teaching Spanish Civilization Through
       Ramón Sender's Réquiem por un campesino español
       as Selected Literature in the First Term of Fourth-
       Year Spanish in High School," Dissertation Abstracts,
       23, 5 (November, 1962), (Columbia), 1703.
       See thesis (1342).

1232   Bosch, Rafael. " 'The Migratory Images' of Ramón
       Sender," Books Abroad, 37, 2 (Spring 1963), 132-37.
       An appreciative and valuable study of Sender's first
book of poetry, Las imágenes migratorias (71).

1233   Schwartz, Kessel. "Animal Symbolism in the Fiction
       of Ramón Sender," Hispania, 46, 3 (September, 1963),
       496-505.

A catalog of animals in S. 's fiction with little, if any, demonstration of their symbolic functions. Republished as a chapter in the book, The Meaning of Existence in Contemporary Hispanic Literature (1179).

1234   Lluis, J. "Los sentimientos edípicos en la novelística de Ramón Sender," Boletín Informativo del Instituto de Medicina Psicológica (Barcelona), 5, 49 (diciembre, 1963), 9-10, 12-17, 19-20, 22-23.
An effort to establish the roots of S. 's anti-authoritarian and pro-revolutionary attitudes in adult life in his early conflict with and dislike of his father, a stern disciplinarian.

1235   Olstad, Charles. "The Rebel in Sender's 'El lugar del hombre'," Hispania, 47, 1 (March, 1964), 95-99.
(8).   An examination of the theme of rebellion in El lugar
(See 1249.)

1236   Marra-López, José R. "Ramón J. Sender, novelista español," Insula, núm. 209 (abril, 1964), 5.
A discussion of Crónica del alba, I and II, which M-L calls "una de las mejores obras de nuestra literatura contemporánea," and opines that since the death of Pío Baroja, S. is "el mejor novelista español vivo."

1237   Losada Jávega, Rosario. Abstract of doctoral thesis, "Algunos aspectos de la novela española en la emigración," University of Barcelona, June 23, 1964, 24 p. (Available at the Library of the University of Barcelona.)
See thesis (1343).

1238   Marra-López, José R. "La nueva generación," Estudios y documentos, 16 (enero, 1965), 70.
Calls S. "la mayor figura novelística no sólo del exilio sino, muerto Pío Baroja, de todo el ámbito español."

1239   Vilanova, Antonio. "La novela de Ramón J. Sender," Destino, 19 de febrero, 1966.
A bio-bibliographical introduction to S. with several errors in biography.

1240   Mainer, José-Carlos. "Actualidad de Sender," Insula, núm. 231 (febrero, 1966), 1, 12.
A discussion of Novelas ejemplares de Cíbola, El bandido adolescente, and Volume I of Crónica del alba.

Calls "el retorno de Sender" to Spain in the form of his books as an important event.

1241   Ullán, José-Miguel.   "Sender entre nosotros," El Adelanto (Salamanca), 13 de marzo, 1966.
       Commentary on the author's "literary return" to
Spain.

1242   Tovar, Antonio.   "Dos capítulos para un retrato lite-rario de Sender," Cuadernos del Idioma (Buenos Aires), 1, 4 (abril, 1966), 17-35.
       The former President of the University of Salamanca
reviews Hernán Cortés, Epitalamio del prieto Trinidad, El rey y la reina, La "Quinta" Julieta, Bizancio, La llave, Los Tontos de la Concepción, La esfera, and Unamuno, Baroja, Valle-Inclán, y Santayana.   Of special interest are his observations on the last named book.

1243   Rivas, Josefa.   "Carolus Rex, una novela histórica de Sender," Norte, año 7, núm. 5 (septiembre-octu-bre, 1966), 113-19.
       An examination of the historical background of Caro-
lus Rex.

1244   Aranda, J.   "Pequeña introducción a la obra de Ramón J. Sender," Heraldo de Aragón (Zaragoza), 12 de octubre, 1966.

1245   Marco, Joaquim.   "Ramón J. Sender y la novelística española," Destino, 5 de noviembre, 1966.
       A brief review of Sender's early career in Spain and
brief commentaries on many of his post-Civil War books.
Photograph of Sender at about age thirty-five.

1246   Ponce de León, L. S.   Abstract of Ph.D. thesis, "Cuatro novelistas de la guerra civil de España (1936-1939)," Dissertation Abstracts, 27 (1966), 3467-A (Stanford).
       See thesis (1345).

1247   Masoliver, Juan Ramón.   "De un Ramón que vuelve a su sendero," La Vanguardia Española (Barcelona), 21 de enero, 1967.

1248   Milián Mestre, Manuel.   "Redescubrir, o el ser de otros españoles," El Noticiero Universal (Barcelona), 17 de febrero, 1967.

Laments the ignorance of S. among Spanish youth for almost three decades, but applauds the recent "rediscovery" of S. in Spain. Hopes that Spaniards (in Spain) can now "volver a iniciar la convivencia, al menos espiritual, con los demás españoles tanto tiempo inconexos de nuestra realidad viva."

1249 King, Charles L. "The Role of Sabino in Sender's El lugar de un hombre," Hispania, 50, 1 (March, 1967), 95-98.
    An interpretation of Sabino's role in El lugar contrary to that expounded by Olstad (1235).

1250 Castillo, Othón. "Ramón Sender, el poeta, el escritor y el hombre," Norte, 8, 5 (septiembre-octubre, 1967), 109-12.
    A general bio-bibliographical sketch with emphasis on the author's poetic talent. "Ramón Sender es sobre todas las cosas un poeta" (p. 109).

1251 Morelli, Diana Lee. Abstract of Ph. D. thesis, "The Sense of Time in the Fiction of Ramón Sender," Dissertation Abstracts, 29, 1 (1968-1969), 234-A (University of Washington). Thesis dated October, 1967.
    See thesis (1346).

1252 Rodríguez Monegal, Emir. "Tres testigos españoles de la guerra civil," Revista Nacional de Cultura (Caracas), núm. 182 (1967), 3-22.
    A discussion of the books of S., Arturo Barea, and Max Aub which most directly portray the Spanish Civil War. In a subsection entitled "Ramón J. Sender: el culpable y el inocente" (p. 6-12), formerly published in a version "a la vez más larga y dispersa" in Marcha (Montevideo, April 30, 1959), Contraataque and Los cinco libros de Ariadna are compared and contrasted--the first praises the Communists, the second (two decades later) damns them.

1253 Conte, Rafael. "En torno a 'Crónica del alba'," Cuadernos Hispanoamericanos, núm. 217 (enero, 1968), 119-24.
    Some interesting observations on S.'s career, the effects of exile, his "reappearance" in Spain, etc., in addition to an evaluation of Crónica--"la serie novelesca más interesante y dramática publicada en España en los últimos lustros" (p. 124).

1254   Peñuelas, Marcelino C.   "Diálogos con Ramón J.
       Sender," La Estafeta Literaria, núm. 394 (20 de
       abril, 1968), 10-12.
       Selected dialogues republished later in Conversaciones
con R. J. Sender (1138).   Photographs of S. and of the
campus of the University of Washington where the novelist
was a visiting professor in the summer of 1967.

1255   Peñuelas, Marcelino C.   "Diálogos con Ramón Sender,
       el novelista 'social'," Insula, núm. 257 (abril, 1968),
       1, 4-6.
       Professor Peñuelas recorded his conversations with
S. during the summer of 1967 at the University of Washington.   Dialogues having to do with S. 's social views are reproduced here; they later form part of Peñuelas' book, Conversaciones con R. J. Sender (1138).

1256   Rivas, Josefa.   "Carta a Sender," Revista Científico-
       Literaria (Madrid), abril, 1968, 26-27.
       Nine questions of a literary nature made by Rivas,
and S. 's short responses to them.

1257   Peñuelas, Marcelino C.   "La novela del futuro; diá-
       logo con Ramón Sender," Asomante, 24, 2 (abril -
       junio, 1968), 24-28.
       A conversation by S. and Peñuelas tape-recorded and
reproduced here, "palabra por palabra."   Published later in
Conversaciones con R. J. Sender (1138).

1258   King, Charles L.   "Surrealism in Two Novels by
       Sender," Hispania, 51, 2 (May, 1968), 244-52.
       An attempt to show S. 's close affinity to the French
Surrealist movement by an exposition of Surrealist themes in
La esfera and El rey y la reina.

1259   Marino, Rose Marie.   Abstract of Ph. D. thesis,
       "Death in the Works of Ramón J. Sender," Disserta-
       tion Abstracts, 30, 4 (1969), 1569-A (St. Louis Uni-
       versity).   Thesis dated June, 1968.
       See thesis (1347).

1260   Giacomán, Helmy.   "En torno a 'La Esfera' de
       Ramón Sender," Symposium, 22, 2 (Summer 1968),
       172-75.
       An interpretation of S. 's ontology as expressed in La
esfera.   "En la ontología de Saila (Sender) la multiplicidad
se reduce a la unidad omnipresente en él; el pluriverso a

universo esferoidal" (p. 174).

1261   Tovar, Antonio. "La vuelta de Sender," La Gaceta
       Ilustrada, 15 de septiembre, 1968.
       Comments on S. 's literary, but not yet personal, re-
turn to his homeland.

1262   Molera, Juan Carlos. "La novela histórica de Ramón
       J. Sender," Madrid, 9 de noviembre, 1968, 13.
       Commentary on La aventura equinoccial de Lope de
Aguirre ("quizá uno de los mejores libros de los últimos
tiempos y una de las obras máximas de Sender") and Jubileo
en el Zócalo, "una novela-retablo magnífico. "

1263   Rivas, Josefa. "Luz y color en las novelas de
       Ramón J. Sender," Cuadernos del Idioma (Buenos
       Aires), año 3, núm. 10 (1968), 89-104.
       Republication of a chapter from Rivas' book, El escri-
tor y su senda (1136).

1264   Pérez Sandoval, Rafael. Abstract of Ph. D. thesis,
       "El pensamiento religioso de Ramón J. Sender,"
       Dissertation Abstracts, 29 (1968), 2273-A (Southern
       California).
       Abstract in English of thesis in Spanish which pre-
sents S. 's principal religious concepts. "Sender thinks of
Christianity as a product of man's essential nature which
yearns for liberty, love, and God. " See thesis (1348).

1265   Rivas, Josefa. "El ingenioso novelista Ramón J.
       Sender," Comunidad Ibérica (México), año 7, núm.
       38 (enero-febrero, 1969), 23-32.
       A critical discussion of the four short stories in
S. 's book, Las gallinas de Cervantes y otras narraciones
parabólicas (49). (These same stories appeared later also
in Novelas del otro jueves [51]--along with three new
stories.)

1266   Wey, Valquiria. "Otra vez Sender," Revista de la
       Universidad de México, núms. 5-6 (enero-febrero,
       1969).

1267   Peñuelas, Marcelino C. "Sobre el estilo de Sender
       en 'Imán'," Insula, núm. 269 (abril, 1969), 1, 12.
       A valuable stylistic study of Imán which Peñuelas
calls "una obra madura, densa y acabada, una de las mejores de la narrativa española de los últimos cincuenta años. "

1268   Mainer, José-Carlos. "La culpa y su expiación:
        dos imágenes en las novelas de Ramón Sender,"
        Papeles de Son Armadans, año 14, 54, 161 (agosto,
        1969), 116-32.
        An exceptionally illuminating exposition of guilt and
its expiation in several works. Also includes valuable insights into S. 's interest in the relation individual-society,
and the expression of that interest in his narratives.

1269   Santos, Dámaso. "Sender en sus libros y entre sus
        compañeros de generación," Pueblo (Literario) (Ma-
        drid), 22 de octubre, 1969, 32.
        A valuable discussion of S. and an effort to relate
him to the so-called Generation of 1927. "El aragonés del
Cinca, revolucionario y después exiliado, no ha tenido una
verdadera crítica ni valoración justa. "

1270   Cerezales, Manuel. "Sender," ABC (Madrid), 20 de
        noviembre, 1969.
        A one-page discussion (for Spanish readers) of S. as
a man and as a writer. "Sender es uno de los novelistas
españoles actuales más leídos. Tal vez hoy el más leído. "

1271   Iglesias, Ignacio. "Acercamiento a Ramón J. Sender,"
        Mundo Nuevo, 39-40 (septiembre-octubre, 1969), 97-
        116.
        A perceptive essay on S. the man and the artist with
special attention to his "realism," style, interest in man,
and the following books: El lugar de un hombre, Mexicayotl, Epitalamio del prieto Trinidad, Mosén Millán, El
verdugo afable, El rey y la reina, Los cinco libros de
Ariadna, Crónica del alba, and Tres novelas teresianas.

1272   Mainer, José-Carlos. "Sender, una vida agitada, "
        Indice de Artes y Letras (Madrid), núm. 256 (1969),
        22-23.

1273   Schneider, Marshall J. Abstract of Ph. D. thesis,
        "Man, Society and Transcendence: A Study of the
        Thematic Structure of Selected Novels of Ramón José
        Sender," Dissertation Abstracts International, 30
        (1969), 3475A-76A (Connecticut).
        See thesis (1349).

1274   Fuentes, Víctor. "La novela española (1928-1931), "
        Insula, núm. 278 (enero, 1970), 1, 12-13.
        A discussion of the social dimensions in the novels

of Joaquín Arderius, José Díaz Fernández, Julián Zugaza-
goitia, and in S.'s Imán.

1275   Uceda, Julia. "Realismo y esencias en Ramón
        Sender," Revista de Occidente, 28, 82 (enero, 1970),
        39-53.
        A study of S.'s concept of "essential reality," the
kind of "reality" which S. seeks to interpret and express in
his work, largely through poetic elements. Tries to link
"essential reality" to the modern existentialist concept of the
individual in liberty creating his own "essence" through his
own actions. "Desde lo elemental humano, su obra es un
trabajo que busca lo esencial metafísico en una integración
hacia dimensiones últimas."

1276   Busette, Cedric. "Religious Symbolism in Sender's
        Mosén Millán," Romance Notes, 11, 2 (Spring 1970),
        482-86.
        Evidence is shown to support the position that Paco
in Mosén Millán is a Christ figure, a fact which "enhances
the poignancy of his misunderstood and unappreciated plea
and his final assassination" (p. 482).

1277   Morelli, Diana. "A Sense of Time Through Imagery,"
        Romance Notes, 12, 1 (Autumn 1970), 36-40.
        A sensitive analysis of the role of the three images
in the short story, "El buitre": wind, shadow, and sun.
Though presented in a realistic manner they ultimately "become symbols of something more universal than themselves"
(p. 40). The plot--the flight of the vulture--creates the illusion of temporal reality within the present while the
imagery suggests the eternal, a time beyond time. See
Morelli's thesis (1346).

1278   Peñuelas, Marcelino C. "En torno a 'La vida de
        Ignacio Morel,' de Sender," Papeles de Son Arma-
        dans, año 15, 59, 177 (diciembre, 1970), 250-60.
        A masterly exposition of the internal thematic unity
of Sender's En la vida de Ignacio Morel. Though there are
different levels and modes of expression in the work they
are all dynamically related in an "internal structure";
Peñuelas demonstrates that they all enrich the development
of a common theme: the relationship or opposition between
life and literature.

1279   Amor y Vázquez, José. "Presencia de México en
        tres escritores españoles: Jarnés, Moreno Villa,

Sender," Actas del Tercer Congreso Internacional de Hispanistas, México, D. F. : El Colegio de México, 1970, 77-88.

A discussion of the reflection of Mexico in the works of three Spaniards who emigrated to Mexico between 1937 and 1939: S. , Benjamín Jarnés, and José Moreno Villa. Briefly reviews the following works by S. : El problema religioso en Méjico, Proverbio de la muerte, El lugar de un hombre, Hernán Cortés, Epitalamio del prieto Trinidad, Mexicayotl, and Novelas ejemplares de Cíbola--all with reference to their reflection of Mexican life. All but the first (1928) and the last (1961) were published in Mexico during Sender's residence there (1939-1942). Suggests that a continued study of the literary relations between Spain and America offers many possibilities.

1280   Béjar Hurtado, Manuel.   Abstract of Ph. D. thesis, "La personalidad en la novela de Ramón J. Sender," Dissertation Abstracts International, 31 (1970), 4150A (Utah).
        See thesis (1350).

1281   O'Brien, Mary M. E.   Abstract of Ph. D. thesis, "Fantasy in the Fiction of Ramón J. Sender," Dissertation Abstracts International, 31 (1970), 2931A (Colorado).
        See thesis (1351).

1282   Artiles, Jenaro.   "Telón de fondo de una generación literaria: un testimonio," Revista de Estudios Hispánicos, 5, 1 (enero, 1971), 19-29.
        Artiles recalls his service on the staff of El Sol during which time S. , his fellow worker, read to him passages from a manuscript he was preparing--the novel, Imán (p. 26).   Brief mention of several other members of the so-called "Generation of 1936. "

1283   Godoy Gallardo, Eduardo.   "Problemática y sentido de Réquiem por un campesino español, de Ramón Sender," Letras de Deusto (Bilbao), 1, 1 (enero-junio, 1971), 63-74.
        A critical-analytical study of perhaps S. 's best short novel.

1284   Castillo, Othón.   "Ramón Sender," Letras de Ecuador, 149 (abril, 1971), 23.
        A journalistic, biographical sketch of "este Ramón

Sender, uno de los mejores escritores del mundo. Complejo hombre es Sender. No solamente en su producción, sino en sus pensamientos que tienen un norte bien definido. "

1285   Palley, Julian. "The Sphere Revisited," Symposium,
        25, 2 (Summer 1971), 171-79.
        A penetrating and appreciative evaluation of S. 's
most ambitious poetic-philosophical-religious work. Palley concludes that La esfera "is a successful work of art, because it creates for us a meaningful myth of man's responsibility and guilt in the twentieth century. " (See 1295.)

1286   Alvarez, Elsa D.   Abstract of Ph. D. thesis, "La
        obra de Ramón Sender (Estudio de los personajes
        femeninos)," Dissertation Abstracts International, 32
        (1971), 5216A-17A (Michigan State).
        See thesis (1352).

1287   Mellado de Hunter, Helena.   "Estudio comparativo de
        dos novelistas españoles actuales: Francisco Ayala y
        Ramón Sender," Asomante (Puerto Rico), 26, 1 (1972),
        24-33.
        An analysis of Muertes de perro and El fondo de vaso
by Ayala and S. 's Epitalamio del prieto Trinidad, and a comparison of the first two novels with the last. Concludes that all three novels "son magníficas por la riqueza expresiva, el uso adecuado del lenguaje, la sutil ironía que cubre los relatos, la caracterización de personajes y el desarrollo del tema del hombre y su quehacer. " The critic Keith Ellis is consistently referred to as Ellis Keith.

1288   Alvarez, Elsa.   "Sender de nuevo," Sagitario (Western
        Michigan University), 1, 2 (February, 1971), 28-29.
        Author expresses disapproval of an unfavorable re-
view of S. 's novel, Carolus Rex, by C. Murciano in La Estafeta Literaria, and approval of a favorable review by A. Iglesias Laguna of another S. novel, Zu, el ángel anfibio (also in La Estafeta)--without in either case adequately (convincingly, logically) supporting her view.

1289   Seale, Mary L.   Abstract of Ph. D. thesis, "The
        Problem of the Individual in Sender: A Formal and
        Thematic Approach," Dissertation Abstracts Interna-
        tional, 33, 1 (July, 1972), 328-A (Washington).
        See thesis (1354).

1290   Barber, Janet.   Abstract of Ph. D. thesis, "Mexican

Machismo in Novels by Lawrence, Sender, and Fuentes, " Dissertation Abstracts International, 33, 7
(January, 1973), 3630-A (Southern California). (See 1353).

1291   Marti Gómez, José.   "Ramón J. Sender, su 'Verdugo
        afable' y la 'Vida de Pedro Saputo', " El Correo Cata-
        lán (Barcelona), 27 de febrero, 1973.
        Discussion of and quotations from a thesis for the
licentiate degree by Juan Egea Pont at the University of
Barcelona (directed by José Manuel Blecua), "Crónica del
alba, estudio sobre la frustración, " in which Egea seeks to
demonstrate that parts of the first edition of El verdugo
afable and of the first novel in the series, Crónica del alba,
were inspired by Vida de Pedro Saputo, a novel published in
Zaragoza during the first half of the nineteenth century.
(See 1328.)

1292   Fuentes, Víctor.   "Sobre la narrativa del primer
        Sender, " Norte, año 14, núms. 2-4 (marzo-agosto,
        1973), 35-42.
        Argues that all of S. 's pre-exile novels show a dual-
ism: crude realism reflecting an historical-social dimension and an imagist-allegorical style reflecting an ontologi-
cal dimension.   Although identifying himself with the prole-
tariats on the realistic level, S. novelizes the struggles of
the workers "desde una perspectiva derrotista, " imbuing
their cause with "un pesimismo pequeño burgués, " although
on the symbolic-allegorical level this pessimism appears at-
tenuated--or overcome--through "la afirmación cósmico-
vitalista. "   In a companion article Carrasquer demolishes
Fuentes' main points (1293).   (See also 1141.)

1293   Carrasquer, Francisco.   "La crítica a rajatabla de
        Víctor Fuentes, " Norte, año 14, núms. 2-4 (marzo-
        agosto, 1973), 43-55.
        A persuasive and vigorous refutation of the thesis ad-
vanced by Víctor Fuentes in his article (1292) in the same
issue of Norte: that S. "ha sido siempre un pequeño burgués, pero en sus primeras obras era un pequeñoburgués
con ideales obreristas sobre un fondo pesimista, y en las
siguientes ya no le queda más que ese fondo. "   Using a
Marxist criterion in judging S. 's works, Fuentes has over-
looked the fact that S. is an artist, and not a political prop-
agandist. (See 1141.)

1294   Carrasquer, Francisco.   "La parábola de La Esfera
        y la vocación de intelectual de Sender, " Norte, año

14, núms. 2-4 (marzo-agosto, 1973), 67-93.

A perceptive essay divided into three parts: (I) "¿ Por qué La Esfera?," (II) "La metafísica de Sender en La Esfera," and (III) "Las anticipaciones de La Esfera." Sees certain elements in La Esfera which are found in Pythagoras, the Gnostics, Descartes, Parmenides, Spinoza, Schopenhauer, Nietzsche, Rudolph Otto, Kierkegaard, Bergson, A. Machado, Merleau-Ponty, and Camus. Carrasquer calls the novel "el resumen filosófico-poético de toda su obra." (See 1141.)

1295   Palley, Julian. "Vuelta a La Esfera de Sender," Norte, año 14, núms. 2-4 (marzo-agosto, 1973), 56-66.

A Spanish translation of "The Sphere Revisited" (1285). (See also 1141.)

1296   Béjar, Manuel. "Las adiciones a Proverbio de la muerte de Sender: La esfera," Papeles de Son Armadans, año 18, 69, 205 (abril, 1973), 19-41.

A comparative study of Proverbio de la muerte and La esfera in which Béjar, with great perception, demonstrates how the modifications and additions incorporated into La esfera (especially of the white ship, the Jebusite, and Christel) round out and improve the earlier novel. "Con las innovaciones señaladas, Sender ha novelado en La esfera elementos que se hallaban reducidos en Proverbio a una existencia casi exclusivamente teórica" (p. 40).

1297   Porcel, Baltasar. "Encuentro con Ramón J. Sender," Destino, núm. 1857 (5 de mayo, 1973), 25-26.

Porcel visits S. in California. The exiled author's current views on contemporary Spanish theater, exile, style, oneiric and surrealist elements in much of today's literature, Catalan literature, etc., are recorded verbatim, along with Porcel's comments on S.'s views and his personal impressions of S. Two large photographs: one of S. and the other of his home in San Diego.

1298   Béjar, Manuel. "Estructura y temática de 'La noche de las cien cabezas' de Sender," Cuadernos Hispanoamericanos, núms. 277-78 (julio-agosto, 1973), 161-86.

An able exposition of S.'s concepts of "persona" and "hombre" (or "hombría") as expressed structurally and thematically in La noche de las cien cabezas (further developed in La esfera). Originally a chapter in Béjar's doctoral thesis (1350).

1299   Kirsner, Robert. "La tesis de Nancy: Una lección
       para los exilados," Papeles de Son Armadans, año
       18, 121, 211 (octubre, 1973), 13-20.
       A penetrating analysis of La tesis de Nancy which
sees in the novel "una expresión literaria de la tragedia humana del exilado que abarca dos mundos sin vivir ni siquiera en uno. ... Nancy, los españoles, los ingleses, todos
son víctimas del rencor senderiano."

1300   Palley, Julian. " 'El epitalamio,' de Sender: mito
       y responsabilidad," Insula, núm. 326 (enero, 1974),
       3, 5.
       A superbly written examination of the mythical struc-
ture of Epitalamio del prieto Trinidad which Palley regards
as a parable "de inocencia, culpa, elección y responsabilidad." Includes a brief comparison of the work with Tirano
Banderas by Valle-Inclán.

1301   Salinero, Fernando G. "Sender, la picaresca y 'La
       tesis de Nancy'," Letras de Deusto, 4, 7 (enero-
       junio, 1974), 193-98.
       Seeks to relate La tesis de Nancy to the Spanish
picaresque novel: "... creo que La tesis de Nancy se puede
colocar en la misma línea estructural de El Lazarillo en el
sentido de que uno y otro son dos libros de burlas, a pesar
de las naturales distancias. ... [La tesis] es un libro de
burlas, un registro de la broma, un escenario de buen humor."

1302   Pérez Montaner, Jaime. "Novela e historia en 'Mr.
       Witt en el cantón'," Cuadernos Hispanoamericanos,
       núm. 285 (marzo, 1974), 635-645.
       Argues that Mr. Witt is essentially a historical novel
of the popular uprising in Cartagena in 1873 more than a
psychological study of the Englishman, Mr. Witt--"lo esencial no es el personaje inglés, sino el pueblo de Cartagena"
(p. 635). Attributes the second position to Corrales Egea
("Entrando en liza. Cinco apostillas a una replica," Insula,
núms. 152-53 [1959], p. 26) and to Marcelino Peñuelas.

1303   King, Charles L. "Ramón J. Sender: Una reseña
       biográfica," Destino, núm. 1911 (18 de mayo, 1974),
       48-49.
       A condensation and publication (in Spanish) of part of
the biographical chapter in King's book in English on S.
(1140).

1304   Bertrand de Muñoz, Maryse. "Los símbolos en 'El
        rey y la reina' de Ramón J. Sender," Papeles de Son
        Armadans, año 19, 74, 220 (julio, 1974), 37-55.
        An intelligent attempt to "ahondar en la complejidad
temática de este maravilloso relato que es El rey y la
reina" by means of an examination of its use of symbols:
the tower, water, childhood, the tapestries on different
levels of the tower, the Duchess, the dwarf in the basement,
etc. The palace is seen as a microcosmos of the human
condition.

1305   Henn, David. "The Priest in Sender's Réquiem por
        un campesino español," The International Fiction Re-
        view, 1, 2 (July, 1074), 106-11.
        Examines S. 's treatment of the priest Mosén Millán
in Réquiem in an attempt to demonstrate that the author's
principal objective in the novel is to reveal the deficiency
of the Spanish Church (especially its lack of a social conscience).

1306   Amargo, Antón. "El rincón del confesor," Insula,
        núms. 332-33 (julio-agosto, 1974), 37-38.
        Anecdotes about S. 's visit to Spain--his lecture in
Zaragoza, in the Ateneo in Madrid attending the "despedida"
of Miguel Angel Asturias, etc.

1307   Cano, José Luis. "Un texto de Ramón J. Sender
        sobre su ideología," Insula, núms. 332-333 (julio-
        agosto, 1974), 31.
        Publication of a letter S. sent to Insula, dated De-
cember 30, 1955, in which he protested the fact that Ateneo
had recently stated that he was a Communist, and brief commentary by J. L. Cano in which he compares the accusations leveled against Pío Baroja as an anarchist with those
against S. as a Communist. S. 's letter now appears for
the first time in print. (Insula was suspended during much of
1956 by the Spanish Government--as punishment for its
liberalism.) "De ningún modo," wrote S. in 1955, "soy un
comunista y si en mi juventud simpaticé con esa secta ha
pasado mucho tiempo desde entonces."

1308   O'Brien, Mary Eide. "Fantasy in 'El Fugitivo',"
        Journal of Spanish Studies: Twentieth Century, 2, 2
        (Fall 1974), 95-108.
        Vital themes are lyrically blended with fantastic re-
ality in a particularly effective manner in the novel, El fugitivo. The fugitive, Joaquín, first flees death, then life,

and finally death--thus giving a circular structure to the
novel.

1309   Guillén, Sid.   Abstract of Ph. D. Thesis, "La obra
        americana de Ramón J. Sender," Dissertation Ab-
        stracts International, 35, 6 (1974), 3740A-3741A
        (Purdue University).
        See thesis (1355).

1310   Day, William Franklin, III.   Abstract of Ph. D. thesis,
        "A Profile of the Senderian Protagonist," Dissertation
        Abstracts International, 35, 7 (1974), 4510A (Florida
        State University).
        See thesis (1356).

1311   Nonoyama, Michiko.   Abstract of Ph. D. thesis, "El
        anarquismo en las obras de Ramón J. Sender," Dis-
        sertation Abstracts International, 35, 12 (1975), 7917A
        (University of Illinois at Urbana-Champaign).
        See thesis (1357).

C. NEWS ARTICLES

1312   "Dos obras de Ramón J. Sender traducidas al inglés,"
        La Libertad (Madrid), núm. 4632 (3 de febrero, 1935),
        7.
        Announces the translation of Imán and Siete domingos
rojos into English.

1313   "Concurso nacional de literatura," La Libertad (Ma-
        drid), núm. 4916 (2 de enero, 1936), 5.
        Announces S. 's winning the National Prize for Litera-
ture (Novel Section) for 1935 for Mr. Witt en el cantón.
Photo of S.

1314   The Albuquerque Tribune, 26, 36 (May 15, 1948), 4.
        Reports S. 's having been named "Author of the week"
by the Associated Press for his novel, The King and the
Queen (13).

1315   Mayo, W. K.   "Sender vuelve a España," El Mer-
        curio (Valparaíso, Chile), 27 de mayo, 1966.

1316   Paredes, Rogelio.   "Ramón J. Sender de nuevo edi-
        tado en España," La Voz de Galicia (La Coruña), 28

de octubre, 1966.
Comments on the author's literary "reappearance" in Spain.

1317   "Ramón J. Sender, reconocido en España," Pueblo
        (Madrid), 18 de febrero, 1967.
        Reports and comments on S.'s receiving of the City
of Barcelona Prize for Crónica del alba.   "Hay que subrayar
el acontecimiento."

1318   "Ramón J. Sender, Premio Planeta," ABC (Sevilla),
        16 de octubre, 1969, 45.
        A report on the selection of S.'s En la vida de Igna-
cio Morel for the Planeta prize for 1969 on the seventh vote
of the judges (José Manuel Lara, Martín de Riquer, Baltasar Porcel, R. Fernández de la Reguera, and Sebastián Juan
Arbó), three to two.   (The two votes were for Redoble por
Rancas by the Peruvian writer, Estorza, who was declared
the finalist.)

1319   "Sender: esperanza de volver pronto a España,"
        ABC (Madrid), 17 de octubre, 1969 (ed. de la ma-
        ñana), 61.
        Quotations by S. upon being interviewed in Los Ange-
les by telephone from Washington, D.C. by the news agency
"Efe" upon the occasion of Sender's winning the Planeta
Prize for 1969.   (See 1322.)

1320   Carrascal, José María.   "Sender habla para Pueblo,"
        Pueblo (Madrid), 22 de octubre, 1969, 31 y 3 del
        Suplemento.
        Nadal winner Carrascal interviews S. in Los Angeles:
the effects of exile, the novel La tesis de Nancy (called
"una broma" by S.), S.'s possible intentions of returning to
Spain, S.'s current success in Spain, etc.

1321   Iglesias Laguna, Antonio.   "El XVIII Premio Planeta,"
        La Estafeta Literaria, núm. 431 (1 de noviembre,
        1969), 15-16.
        Journalistic report--step by step--of the meeting in
Barcelona for the final voting on the Premio Planeta.   S.
finally won three to two.

1322   "Sender no piensa regresar por ahora a España,"
        ABC (Sevilla), 22 de octubre, 1970, 55.
        The news agency in Washington, D.C., Efe, inter-
viewed Sender by telephone regarding rumors that he was

planning to return to Spain soon. (See 1319.)

1323   Medina, Tico. "Ramón J. Sender tal vez mañana...,"
        ABC (Madrid), 18 de febrero, 1973, 18-24.
        Tico Medina, sent to San Diego by ABC to interview
the Aragonese author, relates in a masterly manner "una
tarde inolvidable y única con Ramón J. Sender." The article is accompanied by four recent photographs of S. and a
photograph of a painting by Picasso of S. as a child.

1324   Fuembuena, Eduardo. "Ramón J. Sender: nostalgia
        de Aragón," El Aragón Exprés (Zaragoza), 19 de
        mayo, 1973.
        An interview of S. with emphasis on Aragón, Arago-
nese friends especially remembered by S., and the Aragonese
character in general.

1325   "Ramón J. Sender en España," España Cultural (Ma-
        drid), núm. 9 (1 de julio, 1974), 1.
        Reports on S.'s first visit to Spain since he left that
country late in 1938. "Ya no es aquel denunciador airado
de otro tiempo. El tiempo y la lejanía, el dolor y la madurez, si no han cambiado sus juicios, sí han cambiado sus
actitudes."

1326   Castillo-Puche, J. L. "Ramón J. Sender: Un largo
        exilio que ha durado treinta y seis años," Destino,
        núm. 1920 (20 de julio, 1974), 24-27.
        The leading article in this issue of Destino. Beauti-
fully written by the well-known novelist and journalist, Castillo-Puche, the article relates the warm reception accorded
S. upon his visit to Spain during a two-week period in June
of 1974. It includes several large photos in color--of S.
and many leading literary figures of Spain, e.g., Buero
Vallejo, Carmen Laforet, Miguel Delibes, García Pavón,
Fernández Santos, Torrente Ballester, Castillo-Puche,
Francisco Umbral, José Vergés, Baltasar Porcel, etc.

1327   "Ramón J. Sender en España," Mundo Hispánico (Ma-
        drid), núm. 316 (julio, 1974), 68-69.
        Includes an interview with S. upon his arrival in
Barcelona; commentary by Néstor Luján, one of the editors
of Destino; and a press interview in the Ateneo of Madrid
by the Madrilian press as reported by the newspaper, Ya.
S. reveals that he accepted the invitation of the Fundación
Mediterránea to return to Spain only when the Spanish government removed its prohibition of the publication and circulation of some of his works in Spain.

(Part 2, cont.)

IX. THESES

A. LICENTIATE

1328   Egea Pont, Juan.   "Crónica del alba, estudio sobre
la frustración," thesis for the Licentiate degree,
Facultad de Filosofía y Letras, Universidad de Barcelona, ¿ 1972?, ¿hojas? (director: José Manuel Blecua).
    Seeks to demonstrate that a nineteenth-century novel,
Vida de Pedro Saputo, published in Zaragoza, has certain
parallels with passages from El verdugo afable and the first
part of the series, Crónica del alba.   See 1291.   (The compiler has been able to read only the article [1291] about this
thesis, not the thesis itself.)

B. MASTER'S

1329   Trevarrow, Vivian R.   "The Spanish Revolution and
Civil War as seen in Some of the Modern Novels of
Spain," University of Southern California, February,
1940, 127 ℓ.
    Three of S. 's novels (Pro Patria [Imán], Seven Red
Sundays, and Counter-Attack in Spain) are reviewed for their
ideas on revolution and the Spanish Civil War.

1330   Kranz, Margaret L.   "Ramón José Sender y El lugar
del hombre," Florida State University, December,
1949, 49 ℓ. (director: D. Lincoln Canfield).

1331   Lo Ré, Anthony G.   "Social Conflict in the Early
Works of Ramón José Sender," Louisiana State University, August, 1949, 63 ℓ.
    Examination of the nature of S. 's protest against the

Spanish socio-political status quo, as reflected in five pre-exile works: Pro Patria, Orden público, Seven Red Sundays, Viaje a la aldea del crimen, and Counter-Attack in Spain.

1332   King, Charles L. "The Philosophical and Social Atti-
        tudes of Ramón J. Sender as Revealed in His Repre-
        sentative Novels," University of Southern California,
        June, 1950, 97 ℓ.
        Studies of social protest in eight novels: Pro Patria,
Seven Red Sundays, Counter-Attack in Spain, Mr. Witt
Among the Rebels, A Man's Place, Chronicle of Dawn, Dark
Wedding, and The Sphere.   Bibliography.

1333   Rosenbaum, Rosalia. "The Philosophical Outlook of
        Ramón Sender," Washington University, June 1955,
        71 ℓ.
        Traces S.'s outlook through the pre-War period, the
War years, and exile until 1954.

1334   Adam, Carole Anne. "The Novels of Ramón J. Send-
        er (1952-59)," University of Tennessee (Knoxville),
        1959.   (Available on Kentucky Microcards, Series A.
        Modern Language Series 41, sponsored by the South
        Atlantic Modern Language Association.)

1335   Borsi, Emilia E. "Symbolism in the Post-War
        Novels of R. J. Sender," Columbia University, June
        1967, 137 ℓ.
        An exposition of S.'s use of symbolism in several
post-war novels with special attention to the interpretation
of Los cinco libros de Ariadna (The Five Books of Ariadne),
preceded by an introductory chapter, "Symbolism in Spanish
Literature."

1336   Gordon, Robert A. "Sender's Spain in Crónica del
        Alba," University of Colorado, June, 1967, 90 ℓ.
        (director: Charles L. King).
        A study of Spanish society as interpreted by S. in
his semi-autobiographical work, Crónica del alba, vols. I
and II.   A third volume has since completed the series.

1337   Gutiérrez, Walter Padilla. "La ideología de Sender
        vista a través de sus ensayos," Southern Illinois Uni-
        versity (Carbondale), August, 1971, 110 ℓ. (director:
        Hensley C. Woodbridge).
        A consideration of S.'s views--literary, socio-politi-
cal, economic, and religious--as expressed in selected

articles (most of them in <u>Lectura</u> and <u>Ibérica</u>).

1338   Smith, Abe Benavides. "Religion and Fantasy in Se-
        lected Novels of Ramón J. Sender," North Texas
        State University, May, 1974, 108 ℓ. (director: J. L.
        Gerding).
        I.   Introduction, II. Religion (<u>Crónica del alba</u>,
<u>Hipogrifo violento</u>, <u>Mosén Millán</u>, <u>Los Tontos de la Concepci-
ón</u>, "<u>La hija del doctor Velasco</u>"), III. Fantasy (<u>Crónica del
alba</u>, <u>Tres novelas teresianas</u>, <u>Emen hetan</u>), IV. Conclusion.
Smith concludes that S. is "liberal, humanistic, and occasionally attracted to the fantastic." Contains a short bibliography of works consulted.

1339   Stone, Barbara Leigh. "Commitment Regarding the
        Spanish Civil War as Seen in Selected Novels of
        Ramón J. Sender," The University of Texas at Austin,
        August, 1974, 56 ℓ. (director: Rudolph Cardona).
        In chapter 1 an attempt (not too successful) to define
"commitment" is made. <u>Réquiem por un campesino español</u>,
<u>Crónica del alba</u> (part 1 of the series), and <u>Contraataque</u>
are discussed in chapters 2, 3, and 4, respectively. In the
last chapter, chapter 5, Ms. Stone examines certain charac-
teristics which the three books have in common. All chapters are untitled. The one-page "Bibliography" contains
twelve items, four of which are books by S.

C.   DOCTOR'S

1340   King, Charles L. "An Exposition of the Synthetic
        Philosophy of Ramón J. Sender," University of
        Southern California, June, 1953, 473 ℓ. (director:
        Dorothy McMahon).
        A short biography followed by a critical examination
of all of S.'s works until 1952 with special analyses of <u>The
Sphere</u> and <u>The King and the Queen</u> for philosophical content,
a general discussion of S.'s world view, and "Conclusions."
The first Ph. D. thesis to be written on S. Abstract (1219).

1341   Olstad, Charles F. "The Novels of Ramón Sender:
        Moral Concepts in Development," University of Wis-
        consin, August, 1960, 274 ℓ.
        "The study identifies Sender's view of man in society
and traces its development from the first novel to the pre-

sent. "   Abstract (1227).

1342   Jassey, William.   "A Handbook for Teaching Spanish
        Civilization Through Ramón Sender's Réquiem por un
        campesino español as Selected Literature in the First
        Term of Fourth-Year Spanish in High School," Colum-
        bia University, 1962, 270 ℓ. (project sponsor: Daniel
        Girard).
        A reworking of Réquiem into cultural and literary
units for achievement of maximum pedagogical effectiveness
at the fourth-year high school level, with supplementary material on each unit.   (This thesis is in fulfillment of require-
ments for the Ed. D. degree, not the Ph. D. degree.) Abstract (1231).

1343   Losada Jávega, Rosario.   "Algunos aspectos de la
        novela española en la emigración," Facultad de Filo-
        sofía y Letras, Universidad de Barcelona, junio,
        1964, 582 hojas escritas a máquina (director: José
        Manuel Blecua).
        Contains five chapters: "Vida y obras," "Característi-
cas: lo que aparece en sus obras," "Ideología," "El lenguaje," and "El estilo de Sender."   The last chapter is probably the most useful part of the thesis.   Abstract (1237).

1344   Rivas, Josefa.   "La senda de Sender," Facultad de
        Filosofía y Letras, Universidad de Valencia, junio,
        1964, 399 hojas escritas a máquina (director: Fran-
        cisco Sánchez-Castañer).
        For published version see 1136.

1345   Ponce de León, Luis Sierra.   "Cuatro novelistas de
        la guerra civil de España (1936-1939)," Stanford Uni-
        versity (Stanford, California), 1966, 135 hojas escri-
        tas a máquina (director: I. M. Schevill).
        The Civil War in the novels of Francisco Ayala, Max
Aub, Arturo Barea, and Ramón Sender.   Text is in Spanish.
Speaks of the "diáspora republicana."   Abstract (1246).
(See also 1189.)

1346   Morelli, Diana Lee.   "The Sense of Time in the
        Fiction of Ramón Sender," University of Washington,
        October, 1967, 267 ℓ. (director: Marcelino C.
        Peñuelas).
        "Undertakes to show that the meaning of time and
space in the most important novels of Sender follows the
same lines as those expressed by the author in his philo-

sophical novel, The Sphere. That is to say, that the philosophical concept which Sender has of time and space finds
expression, perhaps unconsciously, in his narrative art."
Abstract (1277).

1347 Marino, Rose Marie. "Death in the Works of Ramón
      J. Sender," St. Louis University, June, 1968, 178 ℓ.
      (director: R. R. Mazza).
      A biographical chapter and a discussion of S.'s
"spherical philosophy" which regards "death" as the hidden
hemisphere of the "life-death" sphere. Abstract (1259).

1348 Pérez Sandoval, Rafael. "El pensamiento religioso
      de Ramón J. Sender," University of Southern Cali-
      fornia, June, 1968, 285 ℓ. (director: Everett W.
      Hesse).
      A discussion of S.'s highly subjective religious inter-
pretation of ultimate reality. Man is "an integral part of
the infinite intellect of God." Abstract (1264).

1349 Schneider, Marshall J. "Man, Society and Trans-
      cendence: A Study of the Thematic Structure of Se-
      lected Novels of Ramón J. Sender," University of
      Connecticut, 1969, 244 ℓ. (director: Josefina Romo-
      Arregui).
      S.'s concerns for man's struggles to find a satisfying
place in society and transcendental meaning in the cosmos
provide his novels with their basic motivation, and determine their thematic structure. The last chapter (Chapter V)
deals with the Crónica del alba series which Schneider sees
as "particularly valuable for seeing the genesis of Sender's
attitudes." Abstract (1273).

1350 Béjar Hurtado, Manuel. "La personalidad en la
      novela de Ramón J. Sender," University of Utah,
      August, 1970, 383 ℓ. (director: Luis Lorenzo-
      Rivero).
      A highly competent discussion of S.'s concept of per-
sonality as revealed in the structure and context of Imán,
La noche de las cien cabezas, Siete domingos rojos, and
more explicitly developed in Proverbio de la muerte and La
esfera. The chapter on La noche was later published as an
article--see 1298. Abstract (1280).

1351 O'Brien, Mary M. E. "Fantasy in the Fiction of
      Ramón J. Sender," University of Colorado, June,
      1970, 420 ℓ. (director: Charles L. King).

Advances the thesis that in S.'s narrative work "Fantasy and reality are blended and fused harmoniously to yield an all-encompassing or total reality." Covers S.'s prose fiction published through 1968, discussing twenty-seven specific works in which fantasy is a prominent feature. Fantasy is divided into the following three categories (to facilitate discussion): dreams and day-dreams, magic and the supernatural, incongruity and allegory. Abstract (1281).

1352   Alvarez, Elsa D. "La obra de Ramón Sender (Estudio de los personajes femeninos)," Michigan State University, 1971, 353 ℓ. (director: Julia Uceda Palacios).
Attempts to expound S.'s feminine ideal by focusing upon leading Senderian feminine characters (Milagritos, the Duchess [in El rey y la reina]; Valentina, Ariadna, Santa Teresa, Elvira, Lucha, the Princess María [in Bizancio]; and Lizaveta [in Las criaturas saturnianas]), with a final chapter (the sixth) devoted to a few secondary feminine characters in S.'s works, which, according to Alvarez serve to "acentuar o destacar alguna idea del autor." Abstract (1286).

1353   Barber, Janet. "Mexican machismo in Novels by Lawrence, Sender and Fuentes," University of Southern California, 1972, 415 ℓ. (director: Dorothy McMahon).
Discusses machismo as Barber sees it in The Plumed Serpent, Epitalamio del prieto Trinidad, and La muerte de Artemio Cruz, by Lawrence, S., and Fuentes, respectively. Abstract (1290).

1354   Seale, Mary L. "The Problem of the Individual in Sender: A Formal and Thematic Approach," University of Washington, 1972, 254 ℓ. (director: Marcelino C. Peñuelas).
After an introductory chapter, "The Changing View of Individual Man," Seale deals in three separate chapters with S.'s treatment of the individual in the novels Hipogrifo violento, El verdugo afable, and Imán, followed by Chapter V, "Conclusion." Abstract (1289).

1355   Guillén, Sid. "La obra americana de Ramón J. Sender," Purdue University, May, 1974, 381 ℓ. (director: Juan Luis Alborg).
According to Guillén, more than a third of S.'s total literary production portrays life in the New World. "Sender wrote first about themes which he could personally investi-

gate, as he did in the stories of Mexicayotl. " His attitude
towards Mexico and the U.S.A. "is for the most part positive, " and Guillén regards S. 's portrayal of these two countries as "an excellent and rather accurate interpretation of
the past and present American scene. " Abstract (1309).

1356   Day, William F. , III.   "A Profile of the Senderian
        Protagonist, " Florida State University, June 8, 1974,
        164 ℓ. (director: José Angeles).
        Chapter I considers atavism, Chapters II-IV the Sen-
derian dichotomy of hombría-persona and its correlative,
"essential action"; Chapters V and VI deal with the anguish,
solitude and isolation suffered by the author's protagonists.
The concluding chapter (VII) provides "a profile of the Senderian protagonist" as a kind of recapitulation of the previous
chapters.   Abstract (1310).

1357   Nonoyama, Michiko.   "El anarquismo en las obras de
        Ramón J. Sender, " University of Illinois (Urbana),
        June, 1974, 321 ℓ. (director: Anthony M. Pasqua-
        riello).
        An analysis of newspaper articles and books published
by S. during the period 1928-1936 reveals that S. started by
defending anarchist ideals, "gradually adopted the more practical line of syndicalism" (see Abstract, 1311), and then
became a Communist sympathizer.   In exile, however, S. 's
works exhibit a bitter deception with Russian Communism
and a return to anarchistic ideals, though now "in a metaphysical plane rather than in a political plane" (Abstract,
1311).

INDEXES

[All references in the several following indexes
are to page numbers, not entry numbers]

AUTHOR INDEX

Authors, editors, and translators of books and articles about Sender and reviewers of books by and about Sender.

265

PERIODICAL AND NEWSPAPER INDEX

PERSONS-AS-SUBJECTS INDEX

People discussed by Sender

INDEX OF BOOKS BY SENDER